BIKERS'
THE TOURS

BIKERS' BRITAIN
THE TOURS

Simon Weir

Published by AA Publishing (a trading name of AA Media Limited, whose registered office is Fanum House, Basing View, Basingstoke RG21 4EA; registered number 06112600).

© AA Media Ltd 2016.

Tours 2–5, 10–13, 15, 17–21, 24–26, 28, 30–34, 36–38, 44 and selected images (see page 207) © Bauer Consumer Media (Publishers of *RiDE* magazine)

Contains Ordnance Survey data © Crown copyright and database right 2016.

A CIP catalogue record for this book is available from the British Library.

The contents of this book are believed correct at the time of printing. Nevertheless, the publishers cannot be held responsible for any errors or omissions or for changes in the details given in this book or for the consequences of any reliance on the information provided by the same. This does not affect your statutory rights.

The maps in this book should be easy to follow. If you're unsure where you are at any point, find a safe place to stop and check – don't take your eyes off the road to study a map while you're moving. Never attempt to read the route descriptions while riding.

Cartography provided by the Mapping Services Department of AA Publishing.

Design by Austin Taylor

Printed and bound in China by 1010 Printing International.

Visit AA Publishing at **theAA.com/shop**

978-0-7495-7736-0
978-0-7495-7797-1 (SS)

A05334

Right: Applecross to Shieldaig (Tour 44, Day 5)

Page 1: The A487 between Dolgellau and Machynlleth (Tour 25)

Previous page: Between Garth and Brecon (Tours 23 and 29)

CONTENTS

Introduction

I was delighted to be asked for a sequel to *Bikers' Britain* – and daunted too. Delighted the first book was so popular. Daunted because, let's face it, there hasn't been a flurry of road building recently. I'd already crammed most of the good biking roads – and definitely all the best ones – into the original volume. How could I make a second book out of, essentially, the same ingredients?

As I sat in the kitchen, thinking a second book about Britain's best biking roads was impossible, I spotted my wife's copy of *A Bird In The Hand* – a cookery book that's just about chicken. One bird, served in many ways, with different combinations of key ingredients producing different dishes. I realised it was possible to look at Britain the same way – using different combinations of key roads to produce very different rides.

If the first *Bikers' Britain* was a smorgasbord of British roads – with everything from individual roads and half-day rides to one-day and regional routes – then *Bikers' Britain: The Tours* is the á la carte menu serving up the best riding the country has to offer as carefully planned touring routes.

About half the routes were developed for *RiDE* magazine and about half were created specifically for this book. There are one-day tours, three-day regional tours, five-day trips and more challenging seven-day tours. Like the best recipes, everything has been thoroughly tested to make sure there's nothing half-baked – and to ensure that there are tours to suit every taste.

The process of compiling these routes also allowed me to answer that age-old question: why did the chicken cross the road? To get to a better road – one recommended here. Enjoy *Bikers' Britain: The Tours* and enjoy your riding.

Simon Weir DEPUTY EDITOR, *RiDE*

RiDE Each month, *RiDE* magazine is filled with touring stories, bike and products tests and practical tips to help you get the most out of your bike. *See* **www.greatmagazines.co.uk/ride**

TOURING BRITAIN

Selecting the right route is the start of a great tour – but there's more to having a brilliant riding holiday than not getting lost.

THIS BOOK is all about touring mainland Britain by motorcycle. It's a fabulous and varied island with beautiful countryside and charming towns and villages, all linked by some amazing roads, but it's also well-populated, with some large cities and areas with a lot of traffic or restrictive speed limits on the roads. That's where this book comes in: its routes are designed to keep your tour on track, taking you to the best destinations along the best biking roads in Britain.

The routes

This book contains 31 day-trip routes, any of which could form the core of a short tour. They're based around pleasant towns with good facilities for the visiting motorcyclist. Take a day to ride to the base town, spend the next day riding our route, then ride home the day after that – a perfect long-weekend biking break.

There are also 13 full tours, from two to eight days in length. The pillion-friendly 'Relaxed' tours are designed to allow for later starts, longer lunches or a spot of sightseeing along the way. The 'High-Mile' tours aim to pack the maximum amount of riding satisfaction into each day in the saddle. Several of the tours link towns where day-trip routes are based, so they can be easily extended with another riding day.

The routes here avoid multi-lane roads as much as possible, focusing on the twistier, 'biking' roads. The 'High-Mile'

tours may include some narrower or more challenging roads than the 'Relaxed' tours. All of the routes come with specified mileages and the regional tours are broken into morning and afternoon legs, though we don't specify stops on the day trips.

Each route also includes a riding time estimate but this does not account for time off the bike. Every stop – whether for lunch, coffee, petrol or picture taking – will extend the day and the longer the stops, the later you'll get to that night's hotel. Generally, if you start a High Mile tour at 9am, you should finish the day's ride by 6pm. A 9:30 start on a Relaxed tour should still see you at your hotel by 5pm, even with a good lunch.

Visiting Britain

If you're visiting Britain from Europe, we have four tours based around crossing points: two from Dover/Folkestone (Channel Tunnel and ferries) and two from Hull (Rotterdam or Zeebrugge ferries). Of course, these tours also work well for UK residents.

A sense of adventure and a full tank of petrol can deliver a superb trip. But you never know if you're on the best road or visiting the best places – and you never know where you'll sleep until you find somewhere. In remote areas, that's not always so easy.

Our tours remove that uncertainty. With fixed destinations at the end of each great ride, you can book your accommodation in advance (usually getting the best rates by booking early). If travelling in a group, early booking ensures that everyone stays in the same place. You can find rated accommodation at www.theaa.com/bed-and-breakfast-and-hotel or at specialist motorcycle-travel website www.motogoloco.com.

The key touring decision is whether to include a rest day (or two) when you don't do much or any riding, but relax and see the sights. This can be a very good thing, especially when touring two-up. With your itinerary worked out in advance, you can also plan your sightseeing stops. For some attractions, it may be possible to pre-book tickets to avoid queuing.

Using the directions

This spiral-bound volume is designed to slip into a tankbag, so you can easily see the clear AA map of each route. Each tour is also accompanied by turn-by-turn directions. It's best to read these before setting off to get a feel for the route. If unsure when riding, stop and check the directions – but don't attempt to read them while going along. Always keep your eyes on the road when riding and find somewhere safe to stop if you need to check the map or directions.

Planning your tour

Spontaneous touring – just jumping on the bike and riding off – can be great fun.

Mileages and stops

Always check the mileage and riding time for each route to make sure it's in line with the kind of touring you want to do. Keen solo riders can happily cover 250–300 miles in a day; pillions often find the fun wears a bit thin if they're on the bike for much more than 200 miles in one sitting.

It's important to allow time for rest stops when touring – sustained high-mile riding can be deceptively tiring. We'd recommend at least one tea stop (or coffee break if you're not a tea drinker) in the morning and one in the afternoon, as well as a lunch stop. When travelling two-up, two stops in the morning and afternoon may be in order.

Be sure to drink plenty of fluids when riding – especially in hot weather. A glass of water at each stop should help avoid dehydration, which can lead to headaches and diminished concentration: very bad when riding. However, it is important to manage how long you spend at each stop: the longer you spend off the bike during the day, the later you will get to your destination.

Packing

If you're setting off for your first motorcycle tour, it's important to get to grips with the number-one rule: travel light. Don't forget your waterproofs, though – wet British summers aren't unknown. Likewise, using luggage that doesn't leak is important: if in doubt, pack clothes in plastic bags.

As long as your bike is mechanically sound, you shouldn't need to carry large quantities of spares. A small can of chain lube under the seat is a good idea (for chain-driven bikes) and, if there's space, a puncture repair kit. However, it's more important to have enough clothes for the trip than to have a spare head gasket…

We would recommend packing a disc lock for the bike. If possible, a security

chain is even better – especially when travelling in a group, as one chain can lock several bikes securely together. However, the best security measure is still finding accommodation with secure parking.

Bike prep

If your bike is roadworthy and well serviced, it should be fine. If in doubt, get it properly serviced before you set off. The roads in Britain are generally of a good standard and our routes avoid unpaved roads (if you find yourself on one, you've gone off the route). If travelling two-up, you should adjust the suspension accordingly. Consider increasing the preload if travelling solo with a lot of luggage.

The most important area of bike prep is always the tyres. Check the mileage for your chosen tour, including the riding needed to reach the start point and get home from the end point. If there's any doubt about whether your tyres will last, replace them before setting off (you can always save a part-worn set to refit later). Going through a tyre and needing to find a replacement while on tour won't ruin your holiday, but it will ruin at least one day of it. Setting off with fresh rubber will spare you the hassle and the heartache.

Breakdown insurance

We'd strongly recommend breakdown insurance for any tour. You don't want to pay for mechanical assistance or a recovery truck if something does go wrong. Getting the correct breakdown cover gives peace of mind. Always make sure you have the policy details with you when travelling. See www.theaa.com/insurance/motorbike-insurance.html for more details.

Group tours

A bike trip is great. A riding holiday with a pillion is better. And a tour with a group of friends can be the best thing you do with a bike. A little preparation will make sure it runs smoothly and everyone enjoys it.

Booking accommodation is the first step, and if you're going to be doing a long riding day reserving a table for the evening meal when you book the rooms can make a big difference – just arrive, shower and go to dinner without fuss. On shorter days, the flexibility of being able to explore a town and find a restaurant is generally better.

Always make sure every rider has a copy of the route and is familiar with where they're going. However, if one rider is leading, those following should go with them… even if they think he's missed a turn. It's better to stay as a group and get back on track together than to have the group split up because following riders have spotted a navigational error. Even so, make sure everyone has the mobile phone numbers of each member of the group in case you do get split up.

Synchronise your petrol stops. Even if one bike has a superior range, still top up the tank at the same time as the bikes with smaller ranges. With other stops, agree when you'll be setting off again: it's easy for coffee stops and sightseeing stops to become very drawn out with a group, but this can lead to very long days. Try to limit each stop to half an hour, with perhaps an hour for lunch. Shorter stops are always better if you can manage it.

RIDING IN GROUPS

➤ **Leave plenty of space** between yourself and the rider in front – and never ride directly behind them. Always ride in an offset pattern. For corners, where everyone will want the same line, drop back a bit to give yourself space.

➤ **Ride for yourself.** Don't go faster than you normally would. Go at a speed you're comfortable with and assess each bend to make sure you can get round it safely. Don't push yourself to keep up with faster riders, as this is not safe – especially not over the longer distances involved in touring.

➤ **Make your own overtakes.** Just because the rider in front can get past a car, it doesn't mean it's safe for you to follow them. Assess each overtake for yourself and only pass when it's safe for you to do so.

➤ **Don't leave the least experienced rider** at the back of the group. The rider at the back tends to have to work harder to keep up. Let the least experienced rider follow the leader, while the more experienced riders bring up the rear.

➤ **Don't leave your wingman.** Make sure you know who is riding behind you and check they're with you at each turning or junction. If they're not, wait for them before you turn.

➤ **If someone does drop off** the back of the group, the first step is to stop and call their mobile phone. If the rest of the group is on the correct route, find somewhere safe to wait while one person backtracks to find the straggler – don't scatter the group.

➤ **If you're the person who drops off** the group, stop and try calling one of the other riders. If there's no answer, retrace your steps to a point you know was on the route and call him or her again.

Right: On the Pass of the Cattle (see Tour 34)

TOP 25 ATTRACTIONS

You could spend a lifetime exploring Britain and still discover something new and surprising each day.

Out of this wonderful choice of places to visit we've selected a top 25 with a few city locations added for extra interest. For each of the sites, we've added tour numbers so you'll be able to place them in the context of the tours in this book. You'll also find further recommended places to visit, as well as viewpoints and recommended cafés, on most of the day tour maps (shown by ✪).

If you're hungry for more, then there are thousands of places to visit for every conceivable interest listed on the AA website at **www.theaa.com/event-and-days-out** You can also check the route ahead for traffic and potential parking locations using the AA Route planner at **www.theaa.com/route-planner**

Southwest England

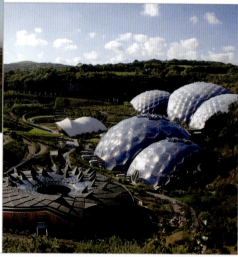

▾ Eden Project

TOURS 11 & 14 • Created in the mid-1990s from an exhausted quarry, the Eden Project is a modern marvel; an eco-tourism site that aims to educate and entertain. Everything about it is good – even the obligatory gift shop, which is packed to the rafters with eco-friendly and ethical goodies.

Stonehenge & Avebury ▴

TOURS 6, 8 & 40 • Stonehenge is Britain's greatest prehistoric monument and a World Heritage Site too. It contains the substantial remains of the last in a series of monuments erected between around 3000 and 1600 BC. Avebury, to the north, is comprised of three neolithic henge monuments.

Southwest & Southeast England

Cheddar Gorge ▶

TOURS 9 & 14 • This limestone gorge in the Mendip Hills is one of Britain's most iconic landscapes. It's a spectacular natural sight – especially to ride through – and at 3 miles in length and almost 400ft deep is England's largest gorge. There are plenty of viewpoints and the area is well served by cafés and pubs.

▼ Roman Baths & Pump House

TOURS 9 & 14 • Built next to Britain's only hot spring more than 2,000 years ago, the baths once served the sick, and the pilgrims visiting the adjacent Temple of Sulis Minerva. The site still flows with natural hot water and no visit is complete without a taste of the famous hot spa water.

LONDON

■ **Tower of London** A must-see for any London visit – be dazzled by the Crown Jewels and learn the legend of the ravens.

■ **British Museum** 'Of the world and for the world' – this museum brings together astounding examples of universal heritage, for free.

■ **London Eye** Moving on a gradual 30 minute, 360-degree rotation, experience views of London from a height of 135m/443ft.

Blenheim Place ▶

TOURS 5, 8, 41 & 42 • Home of the Dukes of Marlborough and birthplace of Sir Winston Churchill, Blenheim Palace is an English Baroque masterpiece. Fine furniture, sculpture, paintings and tapestries are set in magnificent gilded staterooms that overlook sweeping lawns and formal gardens. 'Capability' Brown landscaped the 2,100-acre park, which is open to visitors and offers four pleasant walks around the gardens – all offering beautiful views.

TOP ㉕ ATTRACTIONS
Southwest & Southeast England

Warwick Castle

TOURS 5 & 42 • From the days of William the Conqueror to the reign of Queen Victoria, Warwick Castle has provided a backdrop for turbulent times. Attractions include the world's largest siege engine, thrilling jousting tournaments, birds of prey, daredevil knights, and an entire castle full of colourful characters.

National Motorcycle Museum

CLOSE TO TOUR 42, DAY 4 • Located in Birmingham, this is largest motorcycle museum in the world and a great tribute to the British industry that dominated world markets for some 60 years. With more than 1,000 machines and 170-plus marques across five huge halls, the museum is a must-visit for all motorcyclists.

▲ Imperial War Museum, Duxford

TOUR 41 • Duxford is Britain's best-preserved World War II fighter station and has seven hangars filled with an extraordinary collection of aircraft and vehicles. See around 200 aircraft, naval vessels and military vehicles, plus areas dedicated to the Parachute Regiment and the Royal Anglian Regiment.

◀ Holkham Hall and Estate

TOURS 1, 8 & 42 • Explore the interior splendour of Holkham Hall and discover the beautiful grounds, which include a walled garden and a great obelisk. You'll need a whole day to see everything and that's not including the estate's nature reserve and the beautiful and vast beaches of the nearby coast.

Battle Abbey

TOUR 40 • Completed in 1094 on part of the site of the Battle of Hastings, this partially ruined collection of buildings offers visitors the chance to see the abbey church (its altar is reputedly where King Harold died) and wander across the battle site listening to an audio description of one of Britain's most famous scenes.

Leeds Castle ▶

TOURS 40 & 41 • Set in 500 acres of beautiful parkland, with more than 900 years of fascinating history, Leeds Castle has been a Norman stronghold, a royal residence for six medieval queens of England, a favourite palace of Henry VIII and a grand country house. Special events run all year round.

Northern England

Housesteads Roman Fort

TOUR 43 ● The most visited fort on Hadrian's Wall, it's worth going for the site alone, but the remains of the ancient fort are in surprisingly good shape, considering they're almost 2,000 years old. Visit the museum first to get the big picture and admire archaeological treasures, then climb to the remains of town buildings by the South Gate.

▲ Bamburgh Castle

TOUR 41 ● Rising dramatically from a rocky outcrop, Bamburgh Castle is a huge, square Norman castle. Last restored in the 19th century, it has an impressive hall and an armoury with a large collection of armour from the Tower of London. Experience the sights, stories and atmosphere of the centuries.

York Minster

TOURS 19, 20 & 22 ● Dating from 1220–1472, York Minster is dedicated to St Peter, and its twin western towers and dominant central square tower can be seen for miles around. Visit for the superb east window of c.1250 – an amazing site and the world's largest area of medieval stained glass.

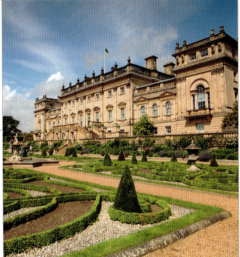

▲ Harewood House

TOUR 19 ● One of the treasure houses of England, this historic Georgian property sits within a landscape designed by 'Capability' Brown. Inside you'll find Chippendale furniture, and exquisite state rooms. Outside, the bird garden is home to penguins, flamingoes, parrots, cranes and many more species.

▲ Lincoln Castle

TOURS: 16, 21 & 22 ● Built in 1068 by William the Conqueror, the castle dominates the Bailgate area alongside the great Cathedral. The beautiful surroundings are ideal for picnics and feature many special events including jousting, Roman re-enactments, and vintage vehicle rallies. The castle is the home of the Magna Carta.

Donington Grand Prix Exhibition

TOUR: 44 ● This museum of motor-racing cars, based at the Donington Park Motor Racing Circuit in Leicestershire contains more than 130 exhibits. An entire hall is devoted to McLaren Formula One cars and you can also see Stirling Moss's Lotus 18 from the 1961 Monaco Grand Prix. A must-see for lovers of historic racing cars.

TOP ㉕ ATTRACTIONS
Wales

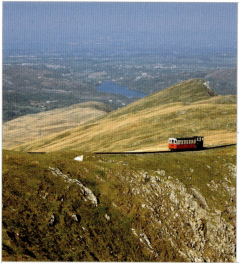

Caernarfon Castle

TOURS 26, 28 & 40 • Incredibly rich in history, Caernarfon was built in the 12th century and has been a site of royal investitures since 1301 (Prince Charles was invested here in 1969). The great walls with stones in banded colours were inspired by the walls of Constantinople, which Edward I admired while on a crusade.

◄ Snowdon Mountain Railway

TOUR 26 • The journey of just over 4½ miles takes passengers more than 3,000ft up to the summit of Snowdon; breathtaking views include, on a clear day, the Isle of Man and the Wicklow Mountains in Ireland. The round trip to the summit and back takes 2.5 hours including a half hour at the summit.

National Showcaves Centre for Wales

TOURS 23 & 28 • This award-winning attraction includes three separate caves – Dan yr Ogof Cave with more than 10 miles of passageways to explore, Cathedral Cave with its delicate straw-like stalactites, and Bone Cave, where 42 Bronze-Age skeletons were discovered.

■ **Cardiff Castle** Located in the heart of the city, learn about the castle's 2,000-year history from the Romans to the Victorians.

■ **Wales Millennium Centre** A centre for performing arts including opera, musicals, ballet, circus and contemporary dance.

■ **St Fagans Natural History Museum** An open-air museum detailing how Welsh people have lived and worked since Celtic times.

CARDIFF

▶ Portmeirion

TOUR 26 • Welsh architect Sir Clough Williams-Ellis built his fairy-tale, Italianate village on a rocky, tree-clad peninsula on the shores of Cardigan Bay. A bell-tower, castle and lighthouse mingle with a watch-tower, grottoes and cobbled squares among pastel-shaded picturesque cottages let as holiday accommodation. The 60-acre Gwyllt Gardens include miles of dense woodland paths. Best known as the location for 1960s cult TV show, *The Prisoner*.

Eilean Donan ▶

TOURS 35, 39, 42 & 44 • Standing picturesquely on its rocky island, at the point where three great sea lochs meet, the first fortress was built here in 1220 by Alexander II to protect against Vikings raids. Pounded to pieces by the guns of an English man-of-war, it remained a ruin until it was restored and rebuilt in the 20th century.

Burrell Collection

TOURS: 39, 41 & 44 • Set in Pollok Country Park, an award-winning building makes the priceless works of art on display seem almost part of the woodland setting. There is a good collection of Chinese and other Oriental ceramics. Paintings on display include works by Rembrandt and the Impressionists.

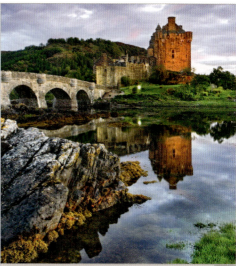

■ **Edinburgh Castle** Standing high above the city, the castle features the Crown Room and the Scottish National War Memorial.
■ **Real Mary King's Close** A fascinating warren of 'closes' or streets hidden deep beneath the Royal Mile.
■ **The Scotch Whisky Experience** Learn the story of whisky and gain an insight into how the drink is made.

EDINBURGH

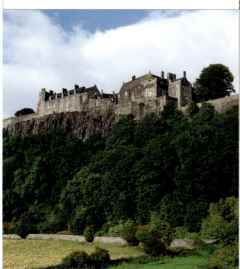

▼ **Urquhart Castle**

TOURS 35, 38 & 39 • The castle was once Scotland's biggest and overlooks Loch Ness. It dates mainly from the 14th century, when it was built on the site of an earlier fort, and was destroyed before the 1715 Jacobite rebellion. Displays tell the stories of the Durward, MacDonald and Grant families.

▲ Stirling Castle

TOURS 32 & 39 • Built upon a 250ft rock, Stirling Castle has witnessed many events in Scotland's history. James II was born at the castle in 1430. Mary, Queen of Scots spent time there, and it was James IV's childhood home. Among its finest features are James V's splendid Renaissance palace, and the Chapel Royal, rebuilt by James VI.

Southeast England

From Royal Berkshire and the Home Counties to the Garden of England, the south is England at its most traditionally English, the countryside dotted with stately homes and quaint towns. However, our routes concentrate on the countryside and weave their way between the most interesting destinations on the best biking roads.

1. **Cromer Loop** 22
2. **Southwold Loop** 24
3. **Brentwood Loop** 26
4. **Bedford Loop** 28
5. **Woodstock Loop** 30
6. **Salisbury Loop** 32
7. **Brighton Loop** 34
8. **Central and Southeast Tour** 36

TOUR ① Cromer Loop

WITH ITS Victorian pier, broad beaches and famous fresh crabs, Cromer is a classic English seaside resort, nestled on the coast of England's driest county. It's also surrounded by some fantastic riding.

Our day-long route heads out on the A149 – the classic North Norfolk coast road. It takes in some of the most beautiful coastline in the county – though be warned that there are regular speed limits and, at weekends, there can be a bit of tourist traffic. But this isn't a road for high-speed hooning, more relaxed cruising, taking in the windswept vistas and the fresh sea air. Cutting inland, skirting the back of the

Cromer Pier

Queen's Sandringham estate, the route heads to Norwich, but only fleetingly. Leaving the city behind we go across the beautiful Norfolk Broads, before heading to the wildest shores of the east coast and then back to Cromer.

TOUR ① Cromer Loop

| ROUTE TYPE Loop | DISTANCE 145 miles |

START/FINISH Cromer
VIA Blakeney, Docking, Wroxham and Sea Palling
DISTANCE 145 miles
RIDING TIME 4.5 hours

Route Description

➤ **Leave Cromer on A149** towards Sheringham. This is a long and scenic road, but does have plenty of speed limits and can be busy in tourist season.

➤ **After 40 miles,** on the outskirts of Heacham, turn left on B1454 towards Fakenham.

➤ **In Docking,** turn right on B1153 towards King's Lynn. When it meets A148, turn right then after half a mile, turn left to continue on B1153 to Gayton.

➤ **In Gayton turn left** on B1145 to Litcham. Go straight over the staggered x-roads with A1065, staying on B1145 all the way to Bawdeswell.

➤ **Turn right on A1067,** then after half a mile, turn left to rejoin B1145 to Reepham.

➤ **Look out:** in Reepham, turn left towards Cawston to stay on B1145. If you reach the market place, you've missed the turn.

➤ **At roundabout with B1149,** turn right towards Norwich. At the next roundabout, join A140 to Norwich.

➤ **Go left around Norwich** ring road, following signs for Great Yarmouth. At the second roundabout turn left on A1151 towards Wroxham and the Norfolk Broads.

➤ **At double rbt in Hoveton,** turn right on A1062 to Potter Heigham.

➤ **At A149,** turn right to Great Yarmouth.

➤ **After nearly 2 miles,** turn left on the minor road to Winterton-on-Sea. At the T-junction go left (effectively carrying on straight) to Sea Palling. Follow the road round to Stalham and through the town centre.

➤ **At A149,** turn right to return to Cromer and the coast, where this route finishes.

WHAT TO VISIT

Holkham Hall One of the finest examples of Palladian revival architecture in England, with room after room of glittering splendour, Holkham was transformed from heathland in the early 17th century. Today, enjoy the lawns or wander through the landscaped parklands.
www.holkham.co.uk

TOUR ② Southwold Loop

SOUTHWOLD'S A bustling seaside town, home to the Adnams brewery and some magnificent beaches. It's a sharp contrast with sleepy Orford and Aldeburgh (the town that inspired Benjamin Britten). This ride takes in all three and, away from the coast, a maze of minor roads that offer some of the best riding in the east of England.

One of the shorter routes in this book, it still takes a full day to complete as you'll want to take time to look around not only the coastal gems, but also Halesworth and Framlingham – once the town named the best place to live in Britain. Will you prefer the sweeping rural roads or open coastal ones? Only you can say, but they're all inspiring.

START/FINISH Southwold
VIA Aldeburgh, Orford, Framlingham and Halesworth
DISTANCE 110 miles
RIDING TIME 3.5 hours

Route Description

➤ **Leave Southwold** on A1095, then turn left on A12.
➤ **In Blythburgh,** turn left after the pub. After about 2 miles take the easily missed left turn to Dunwich.
➤ **Follow road round,** to Westleton. At T-junction, turn left on the main road (B1125).
➤ **At B1122,** turn left to Aldeburgh.
➤ **In Aldringham, turn left** on B1353 to Thorpeness, then follow the coast road to Aldeburgh.

➤ **Aldeburgh,** turn right by war memorial. Leave on A1094.
➤ **After about 5 miles** turn left on B1069 to Snape Maltings.
➤ **In Tunstall, turn left** on B1078 to Orford, turning left when it meets B1084.
➤ **After visiting Orford,** backrack along B1084, staying on it all the way to Melton.
➤ **Follow A12 signs.** Join dual carriageway to first roundabout. Right on B1079 to Grundisburgh.
➤ **In Helmingham,** turn right on B1077 to Debenham.
➤ **A1120 jctn,** right to Yoxford.
➤ **At Saxtead Green,** turn right onto B1116 to Framlingham.
➤ **In Framlingham turn left** on the B1116 to Dennington.
➤ **Dennington,** turn right then left. Stay on B1116 to Harleston.

➤ **Look out:** don't miss the right-hand turn to stay on B1116 4 miles outside Dennington, just after a tight left-hander.
➤ **7 miles later,** take sharp right turn for B1123 to Halesworth.
➤ **In Halesworth,** follow signs for Southwold. You'll go under a railway bridge and about half a mile later carry on straight when road turns sharply to the right, taking B1124 to Beccles.
➤ **A145 jctn,** turn left to Beccles.
➤ **In Beccles,** turn right at the lights, then right again opposite the park, following the signs for Lowestoft. Then turn right at the rbt on B1127 to Wrentham.
➤ **Look out:** don't miss the right turn, 3 miles after the roundabout, to stay on B1127.
➤ **In Wrentham,** cross A12 to return to Southwold on B1127.

WHAT TO VISIT

Framlingham Castle
Walk right around the 13 connected towers of the late 12th-century battlemented walls. There are beautiful views over the mere and exhibitions on the castle's colourful history, from local stronghold to 16th-century prison and subsequent poorhouse.
www.english-heritage.org.uk

TOUR ③ Brentwood Loop

WHEN VISITING LONDON, or riding past it on the way to a Channel crossing, you could be forgiven for thinking that there's nothing but traffic jams in the Southeast. The reality is different, but finding the best riding takes a local guide and some patience. Most of the surfaces are immaculately lovely to

ride – perfect for both pillions and solo riders. You can start the route from the Essex town of Brentwood. It's easily found by jumping off the M25 at J28 for the A12. There are a few speed limits and there'll be some traffic as the route heads out of Brentwood and through Chipping Ongar.

START/FINISH Brentwood
VIA Finchingfield, West Mersea, Burnham-on-Crouch
DISTANCE 150 miles
RIDING TIME 5 hours

Route Description

➤ **From Brentford** take A128 to Chipping Ongar before getting on B184 through Fyfield.
➤ **At A1060,** hang a left and go to Hatfield Heath.
➤ **At Hatfield,** on huge village green, take first right for Hatfield Broad Oak on B183.
➤ **At traffic lights** in Takerley, turn right on B1256 to Great Dunmow.
➤ **Go through** Great Dunmow, following signs for Thaxted, until you pick up B1057 to Finchingfield (where you can stop for coffee at Bosworth's). Beware: this popular biking road is often well policed.
➤ **From Finchingfield** take B1053, the minor road to Sible Hedingham and follow signs to Castle Hedingham.
➤ **Stay on this road** until A131, then turn left to Sudbury.
➤ **Follow Sudbury** one-way system and pick up B1508 to Bures. This road leads to Colchester – follow signs to train station when you're near.
➤ **Colchester:** at roundabout by station, take B1025 to West

Mersea for lunch at the Art Café. Retrace your steps off Mersea Island to rejoin the route.
➤ **On the Shellgripped** turn by The Peldon Rose inn, take left-hand fork towards Tolleshunt d'Arcy.
➤ **Take B1026,** which leads you to Maldon.
➤ **Take A414** round Maldon, then go straight over Morrisons rbt on B1018 towards Burnham-on-Crouch. Road becomes B1010.
➤ **At isolated mini-roundabout,** turn left to Latchingdon and leave B1018 on minor road to Bradwell.
➤ **Look out:** Don't miss the right turn, four miles after Steeple, for B1021 into Burnham-on-Crouch. Go into town and get a coffee by the quay.
➤ **Leaving Burnham** the way you came in, but take B1010 towards Chelmsford.
➤ **Stay on B1010** as it becomes B1012 to South Woodham Ferrers.
➤ **Turn right** at first rbt to Wickford, then at the next roundabout turn right on B1418 to Bicknacre.
➤ **Skirting Bicknacre,** take the left turn to East Hanningfield, where you go right at the mini-roundabout.
➤ **Take A12** to Brentwood or, for one last hit of good

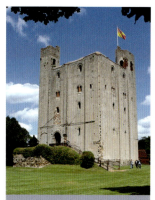

WHAT TO VISIT

Hedingham Castle
Well-preserved, fascinating Norman castle set in 160 manicured acres. Experience medieval jousts and sieges with authentic living-history displays and encampments. There's a cafe on site as well.
www.hedinghamcastle.co.uk

riding, take the minor roads via Ingatestone:
➤ **Leave A12** at junction 15 on B1002 to Ingatestone.
➤ **On Ingatestone** High Street, take small right turn on Fryerning Lane. Follow to T-junction and turn left to Blackmore.
➤ **Return to Brentwood** through Wyatts Green and Doddinghurst.

TOUR ③ Brentwood Loop

ROUTE TYPE Loop	DISTANCE 150 miles

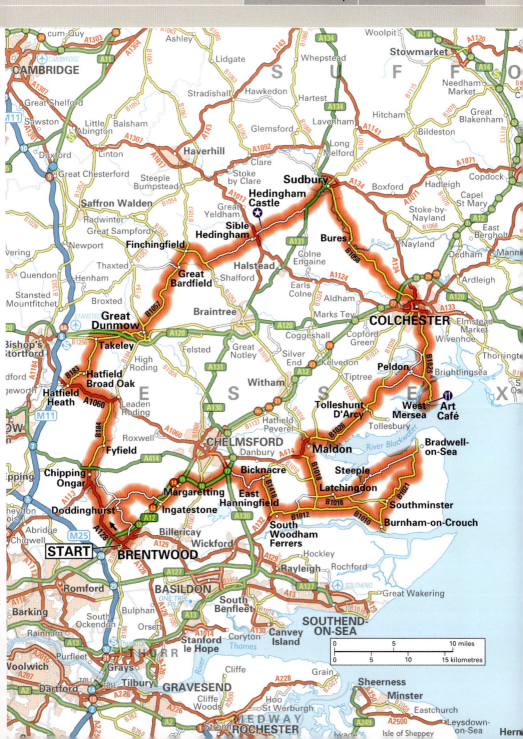

TOUR ④ Bedford Loop

IT'S THE combination of great bends and a classic, photo-friendly English-country background that make these roads perfect. The route has every kind of corner from fast turns and tight turns to S-bends and even a hairpin – all found in quiet, relatively traffic-free countryside. The route runs from Bedford, which is a great place for touring riders. It's accessible and has a charming centre – all the capacity of a city with a small-town feel.

START/FINISH Bedford
VIA Huntingdon, Uppingham, Earls Barton and Cranfield
DISTANCE 150 miles
RIDING TIME 4 hours

Route Description

➤ **From Bedford, take A603** to Sandy. Go straight across A1 roundabout and turn right at the next rbt, on B1042 to Potton.

➤ **Leaving Wrestlingworth,** turn left to stay on B1042 to Tadlow.

➤ **At the roundabout,** turn left on A1198 to Huntingdon.

Visit historic towns on this tour

➤ **At Godmanchester,** join A14 towards Kettering for one junction.

➤ **Take A141** around Huntingdon, crossing two roundabouts. At the third, turn left to Abbots Ripton.

➤ **Look out:** 1½ miles after Abbots Ripton, turn right to stay on B1090 to Wood Walton.

➤ **At the rbt,** turn right on the old A1, running parallel to A1(M). Stay on it for 3 miles, crossing three roundabouts, following signs for Glatton.

➤ **Look out:** don't miss right-turn off for B660. At T-junction, turn left towards Glatton.

➤ **After 8 miles,** turn right at T-junction on B662 to Oundle.

➤ **At roundabout,** turn right on A605. After 1½ miles, take slip road on the left into Oundle.

➤ **Turn left at the church** on A427 to Corby.

➤ **In Weldon,** turn right then, at the rbt, turn right on A43 to Stamford.

➤ **After 9 miles,** turn left at rbt on A47 to Leicester.

➤ **At next roundabout,** turn left into Uppingham. At traffic lights, turn right and follow signs for B664 to Market Harborough.

➤ **At T-junction,** turn right on A427 then take the first exit at the rbt: A6 to Kettering.

➤ **Cross the A14** and take the second exit at the rbt on the minor road to Lamport.

➤ **In Lamport,** turn left on A508 to Northampton.

➤ **At Brixworth roundabout,** turn left to Scaldwell. At T-junction, turn right and then left again towards Sywell.

➤ **Cross A43** and in Sywell turn right then left to Ecton.

➤ **Turn left on A4500,** then right at the lights on B573 to Earls Barton.

➤ **Take first exit** at the rbt, towards Castle Ashby. Ignore A45 and at the T-junction, turn left to Grendon.

➤ **Stay on this road** to Bozeat, to pick up A509 to Olney.

➤ **At the large roundabout,** turn left on A422 then take the first right to North Crawley.

➤ **At T-junction,** turn left to Cranfield.

➤ **Look out:** on a sweeping turn in Cranfield, turn left to Wootton and Bedford. Then go straight at the T-junction. Follow this road back to Bedford.

WHAT TO VISIT

Lyveden New Bield (NT)
An Elizabethan manor house, virtually unaltered since it was left incomplete in 1605. Discover the garden lodge and explore the garden, with its spiral mounts, terracing and canals, and wander through the apple orchard.
www.nationaltrust.org.uk

ROUTE TYPE Loop	DISTANCE 150 miles

TOUR ⑤ Woodstock Loop

THE COTSWOLDS is a revelation. Leafy lanes link sleepy stone-built hamlets where often the only signs of the modern world are the cars parked by the village green. Our route starts from Woodstock and heads out through the heart of England. From Banbury Cross to historic Warwick and Shakespeare's Stratford-upon-Avon, beautiful Broadway and Bourton-on-the-Water, it's a route that's as rich in sights as it is in corners.

START/FINISH Woodstock
VIA Warwick, Broadway, Tewkesbury and Bourton-on-the-Water
DISTANCE 170 miles
RIDING TIME 5 hours

Route Description

➤ **Leave Woodstock** on A44 towards Oxford. At the rbt, right on A4095 towards Bicester.
➤ **At T-junction,** turn left on A4260 to Banbury.
➤ **Go through Banbury**. After Banbury Cross rbt, take left turn signed Warmington (B4100).
➤ **Banbury outskirts,** at traffic lights, left on A422 to Wroxton.
➤ **Look out:** on long straight after the hairpin, take the easily missed right turn on minor road to Kineton.
➤ **In Kineton,** turn right at the first T-junction, left by pub and straight over mini-roundabout.
➤ **Stay on minor road,** straight across B4100 (it becomes B4451), over M40 and through Bishop's Itchington. At T-junction, left towards Royal Leamington Spa on B4452.
➤ **At A425 junction,** turn left towards Leamington then at rbt turn left on B4455 (Fosse Way) towards Cirencester.
➤ **After 2 miles,** right on minor road to Warwick. Right at A425.
➤ **If not stopping at Warwick Castle,** turn left at lights after rbt. Head to M40 rbt, picking up A429 towards Cirencester.
➤ **After about 3 miles,** right on minor road to Charlecote. First right to Hampton Lucy to A439.
➤ **Turn left on A439,** towards Stratford-upon-Avon.
➤ **In Stratford,** follow signs for Banbury, then Shipston. Right at rbt after river for A3400.
➤ **At rbt by superstore,** turn right on B4632 to Broadway.
➤ **Look out:** 2 miles after 2nd mini-rbt in Mickleton, left on B4035 to Chipping Campden.
➤ **Chipping Campden,** turn left towards Moreton-in-Marsh on B4081.
➤ **At A44,** turn right for epic descent of Fish Hill.
➤ **Bottom of Fish Hill,** turn left at rbt to go into Broadway.
➤ **End of Broadway main street,** turn right at rbt. After a mile, left down Pennylands Bank. At end of road, turn right.
➤ **Right then left** at staggered crossroads, across A46, carrying on through Elmley Castle.
➤ **In Pershore,** pick up A4104 to Upton until A449 in Little Malvern. Left towards Ledbury.
➤ **Look out:** after 3½ miles, take the easily missed left turn for A438 to Tewkesbury (brown sign for Eastnor Castle).
➤ **When A438 meets A38,** turn right into Tewkesbury. Follow signs for M5 through the town, but at rbt go across the motorway and take A46 towards Evesham.
➤ **At next rbt,** take third exit – B4077 to Stow.
➤ **Turn right at lights in Stow,** on A429 towards Cirencester. After 4 miles, turn left through Bourton-on-the-Water.
➤ **Go through Bourton** until A424, then right to Burford.
➤ **At mini-roundabout** on edge of Burford, turn left through Fulbrook on A361.
➤ **Look out:** after 2 miles, turn right on B4437 to Charlbury.
➤ **In Charlbury,** turn left then right. Follow signs for Woodstock, to stay on B4437. At A44, right to finish route.

WHAT TO VISIT

Warwick Castle
Learn about the history of the castle from William the Conqueror to Queen Victoria and visit the world's largest siege engine, see jousting tournaments and the castle dungeons.
www.warwick-castle.com

TOUR 5 Woodstock Loop

| ROUTE TYPE Loop | DISTANCE 170 miles |

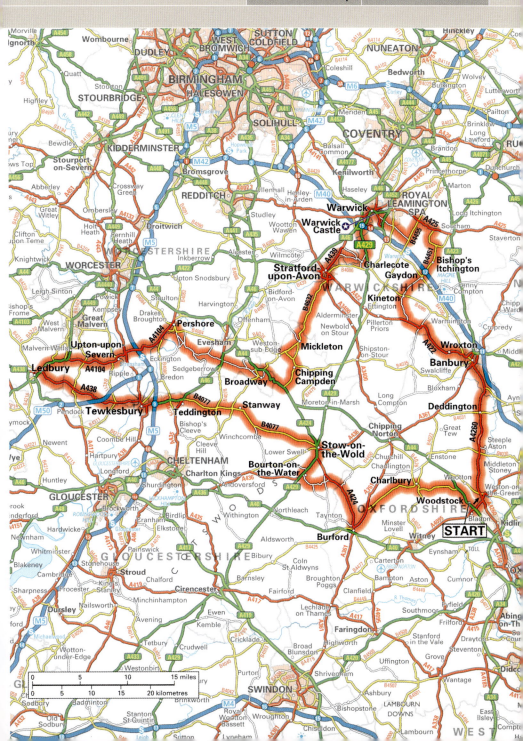

TOUR (6) Salisbury Loop

YOU NEVER forget the first time you see Stonehenge – the iconic complex of standing stones is genuinely mesmerizing. It's not the only jaw-slackening ancient site on this route, though.

This full day's ride starts by rushing past Old Sarum, takes in the standing stones of Avebury, the white horses of Uffington,

Hackpen and Alton Barnes, the Dragon Hill Iron-Age hill fort and Wayland's Smithy. Taking any time to visit these – never mind Stonehenge – makes this a full day's trip.

It's still an amazing day's riding. The roads are fantastic – the knowledge that people have been using this landscape since pre-historic times just adds to the experience.

START/FINISH Salisbury
VIA Avebury, Burford, Royal Wootton Bassett and Devizes
DISTANCE 175 miles
RIDING TIME 5 hours

Route Description
➤ **Leave Salisbury** on A345 (passes Old Sarum hill fort).
➤ **At Amesbury,** go left on A303 towards Stonehenge.
➤ **Long Barrow rbt,** turn right on A360 towards Stonehenge (visitor centre at next rbt).
➤ **Carry on north** on the B3086, then at the crossroads turn right towards Durrington.
➤ **At Larkhill rbt,** turn left on A345 towards Marlborough.
➤ **Go straight across** the rbt, 1½ miles after Upavon, on minor road signed for Woodborough.
➤ **Stay on this road** for 7½ miles, passing Alton Barnes White Horse, then turn left to East Kennett.
➤ **At A4,** turn left then right on B4003: it isn't signed, but leads to Avebury past West Kennett Avenue. (For The Sanctuary, turn right on A4 for a few hundred metres. To see Silbury Hill, carry on past the West Kennett turning for ½ mile).
➤ **At Avebury T-junction,** carry on, joining A4361 to Swindon.

➤ **Look out:** 4 miles after Avebury, take the easily missed right turn to Rockley, passing the Hackpen White Horse.
➤ **On minor road** take first left (The Common) then turn left on A346 to Swindon.
➤ **In Chiseldon** take first right, towards Hinton Parva. At B4192, go right then left and follow it for 2 miles.
➤ **At T-junction in Hinton Parva,** turn right towards Uffington on minor road and then B4507.
➤ **After 5 miles,** turn right at signs for Wayland's Smithy and Uffington White Horse. Follow to the left, cross cattle grid, passing Dragon Hill Iron-Age fort and the White Horse.
➤ **At bottom of the hill,** turn right on B4507 again. At B4001, left towards Childrey.
➤ **At A417,** left to Faringdon.
➤ **At A420 rbt,** left towards Swindon. Right at next rbt on A417 to Lechlade on Thames.
➤ **At Lechlade,** right on A361.
➤ **At Burford,** turn left on A40 to Cheltenham.
➤ **After 1 mile,** turn left on B4425 to Bibury.
➤ **Cross Cirencester** following signs for A429 to Chippenham.
➤ **Don't miss** the left turn 1 mile after last Cirencester rbt, to stay on A429.

WHAT TO VISIT

Stonehenge
Britain's greatest prehistoric monument and a World Heritage Site.
www.english-heritage.org.uk

➤ **At second Malmesbury rbt,** turn left on B4042.
➤ **At Wootton Bassett,** turn right at rbt on A3102 to Calne.
➤ **At Cross Calne** follow signs for Melksham (A3102).
➤ **At A342 junction,** turn left.
➤ **In Devizes,** follow signs for Salisbury, picking up A360.
➤ **Don't miss** right-turn in Shrewton on minor road to Winterbourne Stoke.
➤ **In Winterbourne,** turn right on A303, then left on B3083 to Berwick St James.
➤ **In Stapleford,** turn left on A36 to return to Salisbury.

TOUR ⑥ Salisbury Loop

ROUTE TYPE Loop	DISTANCE 175 miles

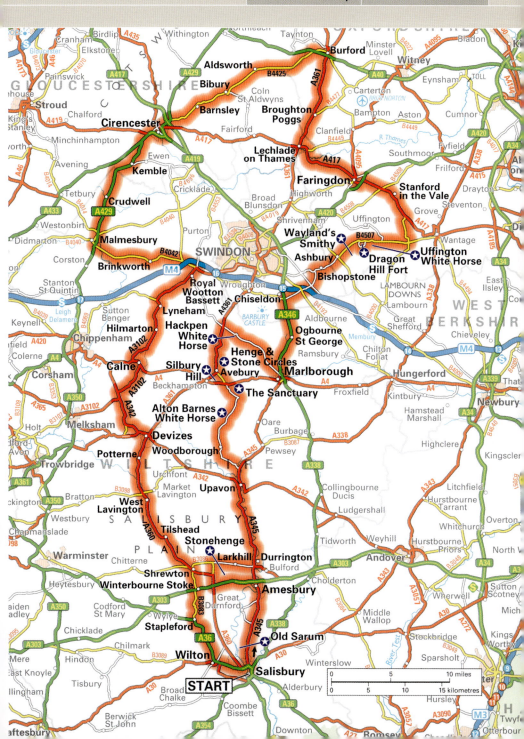

TOUR (7) Brighton Loop

WATCHING THE Speed Trials on Brighton's Marine Drive only whetted my appetite for a ride. Luckily, my friend Jane is a local rider with some great routes up her sleeves. As she led the way up Ditchling Hill, I knew I was in for a treat.

Riding in the Southeast can be tricky, with plenty of traffic and regular speed limits, but Jane's route flowed smoothly, linking old favourites like the A272 and the A285 with little lanes I'd never have found on my own. We stopped for a bite to eat in Petworth (at the highly recommended Hungry Guest cafe) before heading back to Brighton past Goodwood – the home of British motorsport.

START/FINISH Brighton
VIA Seaford, Haywards Heath, Petworth and Goodwood
DISTANCE 145 miles
RIDING TIME 4 hours

Route Description

➤ **Leave Brighton city centre** on A23. At A27, turn right towards Lewes.
➤ **Take the first exit** off A27 to Coldean. Cross rbt and take first left, to Ditchling.
➤ **In Ditchling** turn right, then right again at the mini-roundabout, joining B2116 to Lewes.
➤ **At A275,** turn right to Lewes. Keep going straight through town, following signs for Kingston and then Newhaven.
➤ **In Newhaven,** follow A259 to the left, towards Seaford and Eastbourne.
➤ **Coming into Friston,** turn left on minor road to Jevington.
➤ **In Polegate,** pick up A22 towards London – a few miles of dual carriageway to bypass Hailsham's traffic.
➤ **Go straight over** third rbt on the A267 to Heathfield.
➤ **Look out:** don't miss the left turn for A272 to Hadlow

Down, 1½ miles after the Cross in Hand roundabout.
➤ **At roundabout,** go straight across into Maresfield. After a mile, turn right on B2026 to Fairwarp
➤ **Look out:** don't miss the sharp left turn for the minor

road to Nutley, 2 miles further on.
➤ **In Nutley,** turn left on A22, then first right on minor road to Chelwood Gate.
➤ **At A275,** turn left to Danehill.
➤ **At A272,** turn right towards Haywards Heath. Stay on A272 all the way to Petworth.
➤ **From Petworth,** take A285 to Chichester.
➤ **Look out:** don't miss the right turn signed for Goodwood, 7 miles outside Petworth. At the end of the road, turn left to Chichester then, at the roundabout, turn left again towards Petworth.
➤ **At A285,** turn right then turn left on A27 towards Worthing.

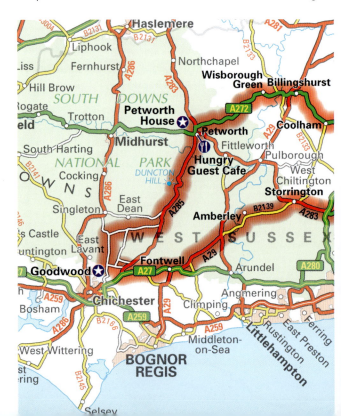

TOUR ⑦ Brighton Loop

| ROUTE TYPE Loop | DISTANCE 145 miles |

Ride 4 miles on the dual carriageway, then at the third roundabout turn left on A29 to Dorking.

➤ **At the next roundabout,** take B2139 to Storrington.

➤ **In Storrington,** turn right on A283 to Steyning.

➤ **Cross A24,** staying on A283. Cross one roundabout and when you reach the second roundabout, turn left on A2037 to Henfield.

➤ **At Henfield,** turn right on A281.

➤ **At the roundabout,** go straight over to Devil's Dyke. Stay on this road all the way back into Brighton city centre, where the route ends.

WHAT TO VISIT

Goodwood The Sussex Downs and 12,000-acre working country estate provide a glorious backdrop to the magnificent Regency house. Each June, the estate hosts the Festival of Speed – a heady mix of cars, stars and motor-sport royalty to create the largest car-culture event in the world. In September, the Goodwood Revival (usually three days) celebrates the road racing cars and motorcycles from the circuit's heyday.
www.goodwood.com

TOUR ⑧ Central/Southeast Tour Day 1

DAY 1 MORNING

WHEN THERE'S such good riding in the Southeast, it would be a shame to sit in traffic jams on the main roads. Our morning route sticks to the quiet roads, combining great corners with superb views.

FROM Brighton
TO Stockbridge
DISTANCE 90 miles
RIDING TIME 2.5 hours

Route Description

➤ **From A27** junction with the A2038, head north to Devil's Dyke. Keep going straight to the viewpoint (a dead end) then return, or follow the road round to the right, past the golf club.

➤ **At T-junction** after the golf club, turn left.

➤ **At A281 roundabout,** go straight across to Henfield.

➤ **In Henfield,** turn left on A2037 to Shoreham.

➤ **In Upper Beeding,** turn left at mini-roundabout, then right on A283 towards Steyning.

➤ **In Storrington,** turn left at second roundabout on B2139 to Bognor Regis.

➤ **At the major roundabout,** join the A29 to Bognor.

➤ **Look out:** after 2½ miles, take the easy-to-miss right turn by the flint/stone cottage on a left-hand corner – if the sign's visible, it's Baycombe Lane.

➤ **At end of the lane**, turn right and follow the road all the way to a T-junction, turning right to Eartham.

➤ **At A285,** turn right towards Guildford, then take the first left towards Goodwood.

➤ **Turn left** at end of the road, still towards Goodwood. At the roundabout, turn right to East Lavant.

➤ **In East Lavant,** turn left, then left at the mini-roundabout, then take first right: a small lane called Hunters' Race.

➤ **Turn right** on B2178 to Funtingdon. This road soon becomes B2146.

➤ **Look out:** don't miss the right turn in Funtingdon, to stay on B2146 to Petersfield. You also need to make a left turn in South Harting to stay on B2146.

➤ **From Petersfield,** take A272 to Winchester.

➤ **In Winchester,** follow signs for Basingstoke (A33) to get on A34 ring road. About three miles after the main M3 roundabout, take the exit signed for A30 to Salisbury.

➤ **At the roundabout,** take the fourth exit for A272 to Stockbridge. Turn left when it meets A30 and continue to Stockbridge, where the morning's route ends.

ROUTE TYPE Tour	DISTANCE 90 miles morning	110 miles afternoon

DAY 2 AFTERNOON

THIS IS a cracking afternoon ride with plenty to see and great places to stop. As well as the ancient monuments of Old Sarum, Avebury and the Broad Town white horse, it's a chance to enjoy the more recent charms of Bibury and Burford in the Cotswolds.

FROM Stockbridge
TO Woodstock
DISTANCE 110 miles
RIDING TIME 3 hours

Route Description

➤ **From Stockbridge,** continue along A30 to Salisbury.
➤ **At A338 roundabout,** turn right towards Swindon. At next roundabout, turn left towards Old Sarum.
➤ **At A345 roundabout,** turn right towards Amesbury.
➤ **Look out:** 1½ miles after Upavon, go straight across the roundabout on the minor road signed for Woodborough.
➤ **Stay on this road** for 7½ miles, then turn left to East Kennett.
➤ **Turn left on A4,** then take the first right on B4003: it isn't signed, but leads to Avebury.
➤ **Carry on straight** in Avebury, joining A4361 to Swindon.
➤ **Look out:** 4 miles after Avebury, turn left on the minor road to Broad Hinton. Follow to Royal Wootton Bassett.
➤ **In Royal Wootton Bassett,** turn left on A3102, then go straight over the main

roundabout on B4042 to Malmesbury.
➤ **At A429,** turn right to Cirencester. Take the Cirencester ring road, following signs for Swindon then Stow-on-the-Wold to stay on A429.
➤ **At traffic lights** after the services, turn right on B4425 to Burford.
➤ **Turn right** on A40, then left at the roundabout to go through Burford. At the

roundabout after the bridge, turn right on A361 to Chipping Norton.
➤ **Look out:** after 2 miles, take the easy-to-miss right turn on B4437 to Charlbury.
➤ **Look out:** don't get lost in Charlbury. Turn left, then right, then go straight over crossroads to stay on B4437 towards Woodstock.
➤ **At the A44,** turn right to Woodstock, to end the route.

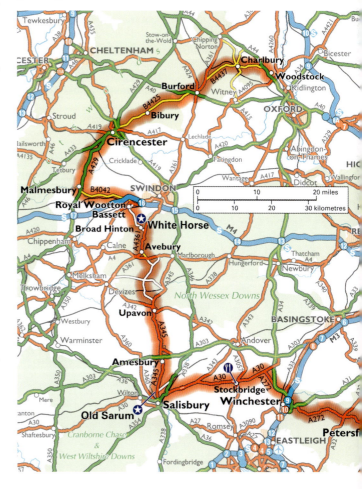

TOUR ⑧ Central/Southeast Tour Day 2

DAY 2 MORNING

A SPECTACULAR WAY to start the day on beautiful roads – with a bit of city work to get past Milton Keynes and through Bedford. Don't worry: the A413 and B660 more than make up for the need to cut through the town sections on this cracking morning's ride.

FROM Woodstock
TO Kimbolton
DISTANCE 90 miles
RIDING TIME 2.5 hours

Route Description

➤ **Leave Woodstock** on A44, towards Oxford. At the rbt, turn left on A4095 towards Bicester, going left then right when it meets A4260.

➤ **After the humpback bridge,** carry on straight as the road becomes B4027 to Wheatley.

➤ **Turn left on A40.** After 2 miles, join A418 to Aylesbury.

➤ **At the second roundabout,** turn left on B4011 to Long Crendon.

➤ **In Long Crendon,** turn right at the mini-roundabout towards Waddesdon.

➤ **Look out:** carry on straight in Chearsley, still heading for Waddesdon.

➤ **Go straight across** A41, towards Whitchurch.

➤ **In Whitchurch,** turn left on A413 to Winslow.

➤ **In Buckingham,** turn right at the third roundabout, towards Milton Keynes, following signs for Milton Keynes North (A422).

➤ **At Old Stratford,** join A5 south towards Milton Keynes – for one junction. Then rejoin A422 and follow to Bedford, via a short section on A509 and A422 again.

➤ **Go through Bedford centre,** following signs for Cambridge (A4280) until you see signs for B660.

➤ **Follow B660** to Kimbolton, turning left when the road meets B645 to Kimbolton village centre. This ends the morning's ride.

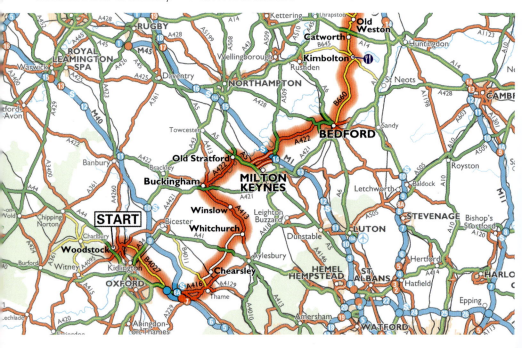

ROUTE TYPE Tour	DISTANCE 90 miles morning	110 miles afternoon

DAY 3 AFTERNOON

AFTER THE fireworks of the B660's final leg, there are some open roads across the Fens, to get to the spectacular North Norfolk coast. The A149 may get busy at times, so don't rush it: sit back and enjoy the views and the fresh breeze from the North Sea.

FROM Kimbolton
TO Cromer
DISTANCE 110 miles
RIDING TIME 3 hours

Route Description

➤ **Continue along** Kimbolton High Street (B645) then turn right on B660 to Catworth. After crossing A14, turn right at T-junction to stay on B660 to Old Weston.

➤ **Look out:** don't miss the right turn after Old Weston to stay on B660 to Great Gidding.

➤ **At T-junction** with B1040, turn left to Whittlesey.

➤ **In Whittlesey,** turn right on A605 to March.

➤ **At A141 traffic lights,** turn left to Wisbech. Go straight over the roundabout, as the road to Wisbech becomes the A47 and stay on it all the way to King's Lynn.

➤ **At King's Lynn roundabout,** turn right on A47 towards Swaffham. Take the second exit from this ring road, following signs for A149 and Cromer.

➤ **Follow A149** for 4 miles, then at the roundabout turn right on A148 to Fakenham.

➤ **In Hillington** turn left on B1153 to Flitcham.

➤ **In Docking,** turn right then left (by the church) to stay on B1153 to Brancaster.

➤ **In Brancaster,** turn right on A149 towards Wells-next-the-Sea. Take A149 all the way to Cromer, where the day's route ends.

TOUR (8) Central/Southeast Tour Day 3

DAY 3 MORNING

FROM ONE great east-coast town to another, our morning ride hugs the coast from Cromer to Aldeburgh – diving inland only to take in some unmissable roads through the unspoilt and quiet countryside.

FROM Cromer
TO Aldeburgh
DISTANCE 95 miles
RIDING TIME 3 hours

Route Description

➤ **Leave Cromer** on A149 to Great Yarmouth.

➤ **In Stalham,** turn left by the supermarket and cross the town centre, following signs for Sea Palling.

➤ **Look out:** don't go straight on by The Swan – the road turns right. At the T-junction, turn right towards Sea Palling.

➤ **Stay on this road** through Sea Palling, to Winterton-on-

Scallop sculpture, Aldeburgh beach

Sea and on, all the way to Great Yarmouth.

➤ **At A149 roundabout**, go straight towards Great Yarmouth. Stay on the main road through Yarmouth, following signs for Beccles (A143).

➤ **At A146 roundabout,** turn right towards Diss. Turn left at the next roundabout to stay on A143.

➤ **After 10 miles,** turn right at roundabout and ride through Harleston. Turn left first on

B1116 and then B1123 to Halesworth.

➤ **Leaving Harleston,** keep going straight on B1116 to Fressingfield. At T-junction, turn left to stay on B1116 to Framlingham.

➤ **From Framlingham,** take B1119 to Saxmundham.

➤ **At A12,** turn right towards Ipswich. After 2 miles – after the speed camera – turn left on A1094 to beautiful Aldeburgh, where the morning route ends.

| **ROUTE TYPE** Tour | **DISTANCE** 95 miles morning | 100 miles afternoon |

DAY 3 AFTERNOON

FROM THE shingle beaches of Aldeburgh, we head inland for the glorious back roads of Suffolk and Essex, through quaint half-timbered villages and quiet country lanes. An ice cream in Finchingfield is practically compulsory…

FROM Aldeburgh
TO Brentwood
DISTANCE 100 miles
RIDING TIME 3 hours

Route Description

➤ **Leave Aldeburgh** on A1094. After about 5 miles, turn left on B1069 to Snape Maltings.

➤ **At Tunstall T-junction,** right then left, to A1152 to Ipswich.

➤ **Join A12** towards Ipswich for one junction, turning right at second roundabout on B1079 to Grundisburgh.

➤ **Look out:** take the easy-to-miss left turn for B1078 to Needham Market, about 3 miles after Grundisburgh.

➤ **Turn left on A140**. At A14 rbt, turn right and keep going straight to stay on B1078.

➤ **At Needham Market,** turn left then right on B1078.

➤ **In Bildeston,** turn left then right on B1115 towards Sudbury.

➤ **At A1141 junction,** turn right to Lavenham.

➤ **In Lavenham,** turn left on B1071 and then right on a minor road to join A134. At A134 T-junction, turn left.

➤ **After 1 mile,** turn right on A1092 to Clare. Turn right again, on Long Melford village green to stay on A1092.

➤ **In Baythorpe End,** turn right on A1017 to Haverhill.

➤ **Turn left** towards Cambridge at the first Haverhill rbt, then left at the second rbt on B1057 to Saffron Walden.

➤ **Look out:** turn left in Steeple Bumpstead to stay on B1057 to Finchingfield.

➤ **In Finchingfield** turn right to stay on B1057 to Great Dunmow.

➤ **From Great Dunmow,** take B184 to Chipping Ongar.

➤ **At A1060 mini-rbt,** turn right to Bishop's Stortford, then after one mile turn left, back on B184 to Ongar.

➤ **Cross A414** and ride through Ongar. At the mini-roundabout, turn left on A128 to Brentwood, where the day's route ends.

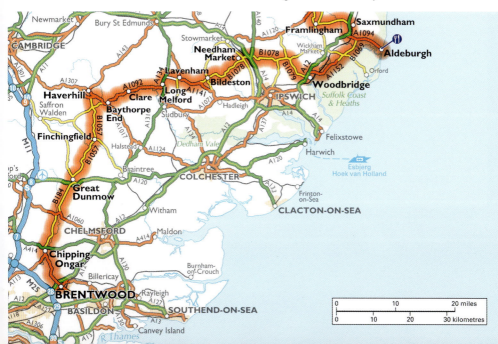

Southwest England

The Southwest of England is a special place – quiet, charming and blessed with the warmest average temperatures on mainland Britain. Better still, there are some spectacular roads, whether winding out from the Mendip Hills, across the Somerset Levels or along Devon's Jurassic coast and out onto the Cornish Peninsula. These tours reveal the riding secrets of this magical corner of England.

TOUR (9) Wells Loop

WELLS IS a surprising city – for one thing, it's the size of a small market town not a huge built-up area. But it qualifies as a city as it has a cathedral, plus a certain chic metropolitan charm. It's a lovely place.

It's also surrounded by lovely roads – not least the majestic Cheddar Gorge. If you've ever approached Wells from across the Somerset Levels, you'd never guess that

such Alpine splendour lurked in the relatively low-lying Mendip Hills.

This route takes in the gorge, before romping out to the coast at Weston-Super-Mare, then looping south through Somerset. Despite being just 150 miles, it's full day's ride – especially if you take the time to stop and enjoy some of the beautiful towns the route crosses.

START/FINISH Wells
VIA Weston-Super-Mare, Taunton, Crewkerne, Castle Cary and Glastonbury.
DISTANCE 150 miles
RIDING TIME 5 hours

Route Description

➤ **Leave Wells on A39** towards Bath.
➤ **After 3 miles,** turn left on B3135 to Cheddar.
➤ **In Cheddar,** turn right at the roundabout (towards M5), but keep going straight, passing the garage and staying on the minor road to Shipham.
➤ **At A38,** turn right to Bristol.
➤ **After a mile or so,** take the left fork for B3133 to Clevedon.
➤ **In Congresbury,** turn left at lights on A370 to Weston-Super-Mare.
➤ **At M5 roundabout,** go straight across towards Weston-Super-Mare, but take the first exit off the dual carriageway for B3440 to Sand Bay.
➤ **Follow signs for Sand Bay,** crossing three roundabouts. The road gets smaller, once it leaves the suburbs.
➤ **At Sandy Bay,** turn left at seafront, towards Weston.
➤ **At T-junction** by Kewstoke, turn right.

➤ **Go along Weston seafront** and join A370 to Taunton.
➤ **At A38 roundabout,** turn right towards Highbridge. Stay on the road all the way through Bridgwater and Taunton.
➤ **Look out:** don't miss the left turn for B3391 to Culmstock, about 3 miles after the Rockwell Green roundabout.
➤ **Follow the road** round, through Hemyock. At T-junction at the top of the long hill, turn right towards Taunton.
➤ **Go over crossroads.** A mile later at fork, turn left to Staple Fitzpaine and Chard. Go over next crossroads.
➤ **Cross A303** at the staggered crossroads, continuing on minor road to Chard.

Cheddar Gorge

➤ **Turn left on A30** to Chard.
➤ **Go into Chard** centre, following signs for A358 to Axminster. Turn left by the church, on B3162 to Forton.
➤ **When B3162 meets B3167,** turn left then right. Stay on B3162 though Winsham.
➤ **At crossroads,** turn left onto B3165 to Clapton.
➤ **From Crewkerne,** take A356 to Ilchester.
➤ **Join A303** towards Andover.
➤ **After 12 miles,** take A359 to Bruton.
➤ **At crossroads,** turn left on A371 to Shepton Mallet.
➤ **Turn left on A37** then first right for A361 to Glastonbury.
➤ **From Glastonbury,** turn right on A39 to return to Wells.

WHAT TO VISIT

Haynes International Motor Museum
Britain's largest motor museum with more than 400 cars and bikes displayed, including modern classics such as the Dodge Viper, Jaguar XJ220 and the Ferrari 360, plus the classic Jaguar E Type and AC Cobra.
www.haynesmotor
museum.com

TOUR (9) Wells Loop

ROUTE TYPE Loop	DISTANCE 150 miles

TOUR ⑩ Lyme Regis Loop

LYME REGIS is a town with real atmosphere. Built around the sweep of sandy beach from the clocktower to the Cobb – the famous harbour with its built-up wall – it's the kind of Victorian seaside resort that has aged gracefully.

Yet behind the narrow streets, above the fossil-rich cliffs, there is some fabulous riding.

The trick is steering clear of the convoys of caravans and other holidaymakers. That means avoiding the school holidays and riding on smaller lanes.

You could pass a morning devouring tiny lanes between Lyme and Crewkerne. But this full-day route is all about rolling through leafy countryside.

START/FINISH Lyme Regis
VIA: Taunton, Sherborne, Bridport Harbour
DISTANCE 141 miles
RIDING TIME 4.5 hours

Route Description

➤ **Leave Lyme** on B3165 (from Broad Street it's signed for Axminster).

➤ **At A35,** right then left to continue on B3165.

➤ **In Crewkerne,** turn left on A30.

➤ **2 miles later, turn right** on the minor road towards Dowlish Wake (brown sign for Perry's Cider Mill) and take this to Illminster.

➤ **Go straight on** through Illminster.

➤ **At A303 roundabout,** take second exit for A358 to Horton, past the services.

➤ **In Horton,** take second right after the pub: Pound Road.

➤ **After 3 miles,** turn right at first T-junction, then left at the next one.

➤ **At crossroads** in Staple Fitzpane, turn right and into Taunton.

➤ **Go through Taunton,** past station, then when A358 goes left, go straight on towards Kingston St Mary for morning coffee at Pines Café.

➤ **Turn left** out of café, towards Enmore,

➤ **In Bridgwater,** turn right onto town centre dual carriageway.

➤ **Turn right** after crossing the bridge to pick up A372.

➤ **At A361,** go right then left to carry on along A372 to Langport.

➤ **At T-junction** turn left towards Wincanton, then go

straight over the roundabout on B3153 to Somerton.

➤ **Go straight** through Somerton and, at T-junction, right to Ilchester on B3151.

➤ **At the T-junction** above a railway, turn right on A371 around Castle Cary. This bypasses Wincanton.

➤ **Half a mile** after passing under A303, turn right on B3145 to Sherborne and a lunch stop.

➤ **Head south** from Sherborne on A352.

➤ **Look out:** as you arrive in Cerne Abbas, park on left to get a good picture of the giant (see below).

➤ **Turn right** on A37, then left on A356 back towards Crewkerne (first turning after leaving the 30mph limit).

➤ **At crossroads** 6 miles after Maiden Newton, turn right on B3163 to Beaminster.

➤ **At T-junction** in village, turn left on A3066 to Bridport for an optional ice cream on the beach.

➤ **Or carry on** straight through Bridport, following signs for West Bay and B3157.

➤ **From Bridport,** continue along A35, turning onto A3059 at the roundabout for the final sweep down into Lyme Regis once again.

WHAT TO VISIT

Cerne Abbas Giant

See all 180ft (55m) of this well-know chalk outline (the viewing area is close to DT2 7AL). A tribute to Hercules or a a warning to enemies – the fact that no one is quite when or by whom he was made is part of his mystery.
www.nationaltrust.org.uk

TOUR ⑩ Lyme Regis Loop

ROUTE TYPE Loop	DISTANCE 141 miles

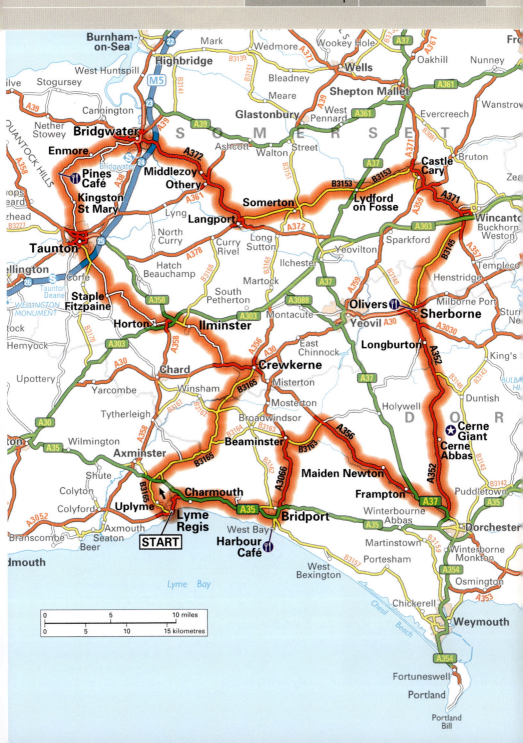

TOUR (11) St Austell Loop

THERE'S A wild romance to the Cornish coast that can go unnoticed if you're unlucky enough to get stuck behind a convoy of caravans. Timing is the key to unlocking the true beauty of this route – so avoid high-summer, school-holiday weekends and ride it in the spring or autumn, preferably on a weekday when it's much quieter.

You'll experience flowing A-roads leading into tighter B-roads that give way to narrow, twisty lanes. There's even a ferry crossing (make sure you take cash for the fare). As well as the must-see visit to Land's End, our route takes in the Arthurian gem of Tintagel and the beautiful seaside town of Padstow. With this combination of roads and sights, you're sure to fall in love with Cornwall.

START/FINISH St Austell
VIA Helston, Land's End, Newquay and Tintagel
DISTANCE 190 miles
RIDING TIME 5.5 hours

Route Description

➤ **Leave St Austell on A390**, heading towards Truro.
➤ **Look out:** a mile after Trewithen roundabout, turn left on A3078 towards St Mawes.
➤ **In St Just-in-Roseland**, turn right on B3289 to the King

Stop for lunch at Land's End

Harry Ferry. (Carry cash for the King Harry chain ferry crossing, which runs every 20 minutes).
➤ **Continue along B3289,** turning right at crossroads, to A39. Turn left at the roundabout towards Falmouth.
➤ **At double roundabout,** go right on A394 to Helston.
➤ **Stay on A394** round Helston (following signs for hospital) and head to Penzance.
➤ **At A30,** keep going straight, signed first for Penzance and then for Land's End.
➤ **Look out:** after half a dozen Penzance roundabouts, don't miss the left turn for B3315 towards Newlyn (there's red tarmac at the junction).
➤ **In Newlyn,** turn right on B3315 to Porthcurno. Follow to A30 and Land's End for lunch.
➤ **From Land's End,** ride 3 miles back along A30 and turn left on B3306, then left on A3071 through St Just (it becomes B3306 again). Stay on it all the way to St Ives.
➤ **From St Ives,** take A3074 to Hayle.
➤ **Turn left at A30 rbt**, then left at second rbt to go back into Hayle. At double rbt, right towards Gwithian on B3301.
➤ **Stay on B3301** until Portreath, picking up B3300.

➤ **Look out:** about a mile outside Portreath, take easily missed left turn to Porthtowan.
➤ **At B3277 x-roads,** turn right.
➤ **Turn left** at Chiverton Services rbt and take the first exit at main A30 rbt: A3075 to Newquay.
➤ **Go through Newquay** following signs for B3276 to Padstow.
➤ **From Padstow,** take A389.
➤ **Look out:** turn left after 2 miles, signed for Wadebridge, to stay on A389.
➤ **At A39,** left to Wadebridge.
➤ **At rbt,** right into Wadebridge, then right at mini-roundabout on B3314 to St Minver.
➤ **After 14 miles,** turn left on B3263 to Tintagel.
➤ **To visit castle,** turn left in Tintagel. Otherwise, turn right on B3263 to Boscastle, and pick up B3266 to Camelford.
➤ **In Camelford,** turn right on A39 then left to carry on along B3266 to Bodmin.
➤ **At T-junction,** turn left on A389 to Bodmin.
➤ **In Bodmin,** at double rbt by clock tower, turn right on A389 to St Austell (becomes A391).
➤ **After about 5 miles,** go straight at rbt on B3274 to Carthew. Stay on this road to reach St Austell once more.

TOUR ⑪ St Austell Loop

ROUTE TYPE Loop	DISTANCE 190 miles

WHAT TO VISIT

Lost Gardens of Heligan At the end of the 19th-century the garden's thousand acres were at their zenith, but only a few years after the Great War, bramble and ivy were rampant. Today the 200 acres includes pleasure grounds, a sub-tropical jungle, wetlands and ancient woodlands. www.heligan.com

TOUR (12) Porlock Loop

ONLY A handful of places can match Exmoor's wild splendour – and this trip takes in one of them, as this long day's ride heads south to cross Dartmoor, not once but twice.

This route takes in both the north and south shorelines of Devon, as well as the two magnificent moors. It skirts the city of Exeter and the busy tourist towns of Paignton and Barnstaple, sticking to the quiet roads that show off the beauty of the landscape. Riding the final stretch across Exmoor in the late afternoon sun is a truly special experience.

A39 towards Porlock Hill

START/FINISH Porlock
VIA Tiverton, Paignton, Tavistock and Ilfracombe
DISTANCE 240 miles
RIDING TIME 5.5 hours

Route Description

➤ **Leave Porlock on A39,** towards Bridgwater.

➤ **At traffic lights** after Minehead, turn right on A396 and stay all the way to Tiverton.

➤ **Go through Tiverton** following signs for A396 to Bickleigh. Stay on A396 all the way to Exeter.

➤ **At A377 roundabout,** go straight (signed City Centre). Stay in right-hand lane crossing the river, going right, then take first left for B3212 to Moretonhampstead.

➤ **At crossroads** in Moretonhampstead, turn left on A382 to Bovey Tracey.

➤ **In Newton Abbot,** pick up A380 to Torquay.

➤ **Go straight over rbt,** on A3022 to Torquay.

➤ **At Torquay seafront,** turn right on A3022 to Brixham.

➤ **In Paignton,** follow one-way system to seafront. Turn right at the mini-roundabout at the end of esplanade, then turn left on A379 through Goodrington.

➤ **Look out:** after golf club and petrol station, turn right on A379 to the Higher Ferry.

➤ **Dartmouth Higher Ferry** is a continuously running shuttle. Carry cash for the crossing.

➤ **Leave Dartmouth on A379** (turn left at mini-roundabout at top of the hill).

➤ **Follow A379** for 25 miles

➤ **Look out** for right-turn at second mini-roundabout in Kingsbridge (signed Plymouth).

➤ **A mile after Modbury,** turn right on A3121 to Ermington.

➤ **At T-junction** with B3213 turn left to Ivybridge.

➤ **In Ivybridge,** go straight over the rbt, cross river and follow road round to right, then turn left. At T-junction, turn right. At the mini-roundabout, turn left towards Cornwood.

➤ **Look out:** after 6 miles, take easy-to-miss turn to Yelverton.

➤ **In Yelverton,** pick up B3212 to Princetown.

➤ **In Princetown,** turn left on B3357 to Tavistock. After passing the prison, turn left at T-junction to stay on this road.

➤ **Turn right in Tavistock,** picking up A386 to Okehampton.

➤ **At roundabout,** turn right staying on A386 towards Hatherleigh.

➤ **In Great Torrington,** turn right at first roundabout and left at second one to pick up B3232 to Barnstaple.

➤ **At A39 roundabout,** turn right towards Barnstaple. Follow signs for Lynton (A39) through the town.

➤ **Look out:** going up the hill, after the hospital, take the easily missed left turn for B3230 to Ilfracombe.

➤ **In Ilfracombe,** turn right on A399 to Combe Martin.

➤ **Look out:** don't miss the turn left for A39 to Lynton, about 4 miles outside Combe Martin.

➤ **Stay on A39** all the way back to Porlock.

TOUR ⑫ Porlock Loop

ROUTE TYPE Loop	DISTANCE 240 miles

TOUR (13) Okehampton Loop

AS SOON as the weather picks up head for Okehampton, gateway to the West Country. Depending on where you live, this can be anything from a Sunday blast (for locals) to part of a much longer tour of the West Country in general.

A lot of travellers heading for the West Country tend to zip through Okehampton on the A30, or regard it as just a base for exploring Dartmoor, to the south. It's a nice town with a pleasant centre and, if you have time, has a fascinating ruined castle to visit. There's good riding north of Okehampton as well as to the south – and that's the direction this clockwise route takes.

START/FINISH Okehampton
VIA Hartland, Ilfracombe and Dulverton
DISTANCE 180 miles
RIDING TIME 5.5 hours

Route Description

➤ **From Okehampton,** head up the sweeping A386 to Hatherleigh, turning left onto A3072.

➤ **About 5 miles** after Holsworthy, turn right onto B3254 towards Kilkhampton.

➤ **Pick up A39** towards Bideford (if you miss B2354 turn, turn right to reach A39).

➤ **After 8 miles,** take left turn – on a sweeping right-hand bend – to Hartland on B3248.

➤ **In Hartland,** turn left towards Hartland Quay for a coffee.

➤ **Leave Hartland on B3248** towards Bideford and A39 – not the stretch you took into the village.

➤ **Turn left** on A39 and follow to Barnstaple.

➤ **Look out:** don't follow signs for Ilfracombe, but stay with A39 towards Lynton.

➤ **Half a mile past hospital,** turn left on B3230 and take to Ilfracombe. Follow the signs for the aquarium and a car park. Try Lynbay Fish and Chip Shop for lunch (the second one you come to).

➤ **Leaving Ilfracombe,** turn left by bus station along the south side of the harbour.

➤ **At A399,** turn left.

➤ **At Blackmoor Gate** turn left on A39 to Lynton, staying on this road through Porlock and Minehead.

➤ **At traffic lights** leaving Minehead, turn right onto A396 towards Tiverton.

➤ **Look out:** the right turn for B3222 to Dulverton is easy to miss – it's about 8 miles after Wheddon Cross, marked by a fingerpost on left-hand verge, so keep your eyes peeled.

➤ **Continue along B3222** until you rejoin A396, turning right to carry on to Tiverton.

➤ **Avoid Tiverton centre:** stay on A396 towards Bickleigh, then turn right on A3072 to Crediton.

➤ **In Crediton** centre, turn right on A377 towards Barnstaple.

➤ **In Copplestone,** keep straight ahead at lights (road bears right): A3072 to Okehampton.

➤ **Keep going straight** as road becomes B3215 back to Okehampton.

Stop for lunch in Ilfracombe

TOUR 13 Okehampton Loop

ROUTE TYPE Loop | **DISTANCE** 180 miles

TOUR ⑭ West Country Tour Day 1

DAY 1 MORNING

FROM CHARMING Wells and the glorious gorges of the Mendip Hills, this tour of the West Country heads out through magical Glastonbury to the North Devon coast. Porlock village has plenty of eateries, but for the full seaside experience we'd recommend following the signs to go down to Porlock Weir, where there's a good café overlooking the harbour.

FROM Wells
TO Porlock
DISTANCE 105 miles
RIDING TIME 3 hours

Route Description
➤ **From Wells,** take A371 to Cheddar.
➤ **In Cheddar,** right at memorial, then right at mini-rbt, following signs for Cheddar Gorge.

Riding in north Devon

➤ **Leaving Gorge,** take first left (B3371). At crossroads, turn left on B3134 to Burrington.
➤ **Right on A368** towards Bath at end of the Combe.
➤ **At A37 roundabout,** turn right to Shepton Mallet.

➤ **Just south of Shepton,** turn right on A361 to Glastonbury, joining A39 to Bridgwater.
➤ **Go through Bridgwater** following the signs to Minehead (A39).
➤ **Stay on A39** to Porlock, where the morning's route ends.

| ROUTE TYPE Tour | DISTANCE 105 miles morning | 135 miles afternoon |

DAY 1 AFTERNOON

AFTER LUNCH, climb Porlock Hill with its hairpin corners to reach the wildly beautiful Exmoor. Rather than heading into busy Barnstaple, from Lynmouth take the quieter inland roads. There's a short stretch of dual carriageway around Liskeard, but otherwise it's flowing roads all the way to St Austell.

FROM Porlock
TO St Austell
DISTANCE 135 miles
RIDING TIME 4 hours

Route Description
➤ **From Porlock,** continue along A39 towards Lynmouth.

➤ **In Lynmouth**, turn left to stay on A39 (signed for Blackmoor Gate).
➤ **2½ miles later,** turn left on B3223 to Simonsbath.
➤ **Coming into Simonsbath,** turn sharp right on B3358 to Blackmoor Gate.
➤ **At A399 junction,** turn left.

➤ **In South Molton,** turn right on B3227 to Great Torrington.
➤ **Cross river at Umberleigh**, turn right on A377 then left again, to continue on B3277.
➤ **In Great Torrington,** join A386 towards Bideford and then, just as you leave town, turn left on B3227 to Langtree.
➤ **In Stibb Cross,** this becomes A388. Stay on it, through Holsworthy and Launceston.
➤ **In Launceston,** follow signs for Plymouth (A388).
➤ **About a mile** after crossing A30 at Launceston, turn left on B3362 to Tavistock.
➤ **Look out:** don't miss the right turn to stay on B3362, just by the Art Deco garage after long uphill right-hander.
➤ **At Gulworthy rbt,** turn right on A390 to Gunnislake.
➤ **The A390** merges with A38 at Liskeard: follow the signs for St Austell.
➤ **At roundabout** at end of dual carriageway, take the second exit for A390 to St Austell, where the route ends.

TOUR (14) West Country Tour Day 2

DAY 2 MORNING

COULD THIS be the best morning's ride in the south of England? Quite possibly. Heading out to the coast, our morning route loops around Hayle to take the stunning coast ride from St Ives to Land's End – both places where a good cup of coffee can be found. The back roads between Land's End and Penzance are narrow and rewarding to ride, though there is a bit of dual carriageway to get swiftly past Penzance. The morning's ride finishes with the relaxed run in to the lovely fishing village of Porthleven for lunch.

FROM St Austell
TO Porthleven
DISTANCE 90 miles
RIDING TIME 3 hours

Route Description
➤ **Leave St Austell** on A3058 to Newquay.
➤ **After 6 or so miles,** at rbt, turn left on B3275 to Probus.
➤ **At A390 T-junction,** turn right towards Truro.
➤ **When A390** meets the A30, go straight over large rbt and turn right at the second one, taking B3277 to St Agnes.
➤ **Look out:** after 1½ miles, turn left to Porthtowan. Go straight over next x-roads. Follow road through Porthtowan, until it meets B3300.
➤ **Turn right on B3300** to Portreath. Carry on along B3301 to outskirts of Hayle.

➤ **Join A30,** follow signs for St Ives. After 3 miles, turn right on A3074.
➤ **In St Ives,** follow signs for 'Through traffic (B3306)'. Stay on B3306 to St Just.
➤ **Leaving St Just,** turn right to stay on B3306. When this road meets A30, turn right to Land's End.
➤ **After visiting Land's End,** get back on A30 for just under a mile, then turn right on B3315 to Porthcurno. Stay on this road all the way to Newlyn.
➤ **In Newlyn,** turn right following signs for Penzance, then turn right on A30.
➤ **After bypassing Penzance** on A30, join A394 to Helston.
➤ **After 8 miles,** turn right on B3304 to Porthleven, where the morning route ends.

Stunning scenery draws all kinds of holidaymakers

DAY 2 AFTERNOON

ONE OF the highlights of the afternoon ride is crossing the River Fal on the King Harry Ferry, to reach the sleepy Roseland Peninsula. Well-shaded lanes lead us back past St Austell, to the fringes of Bodmin Moor and the Cornish north coast. Crossing into Devon, we head to scenic Hartland Quay before the run to our overnight stop in Okehampton.

FROM Porthleven
TO Okehampton
DISTANCE 150 miles
RIDING TIME 5 hours

Route Description
➤ **Take the B3304** to Helston, turning right on A394, following signs for Falmouth.
➤ **At A39 double roundabout,** turn left to Truro.

➤ **After 5 miles,** turn right at rbt on B3289 to King Harry Ferry. Carry cash for the crossing.
➤ **From ferry,** continue on B3289 to St Just-in-Roseland.
➤ **Turn left** on A3078 to Truro.

TOUR ⑭ West Country Tour Day 2

| ROUTE TYPE Tour | DISTANCE 90 miles morning | 150 miles afternoon |

➤ **In Tregony,** turn right (signed village centre) to join B3287.

➤ **At A390,** turn right to St Austell.

➤ **Take A391** towards Bodmin. Cross A30 and take the third exit at roundabout for A389 to Wadebridge.

➤ **Look out:** turn left by clock tower in Bodmin to stay on A389 to Wadebridge.

➤ **At roundabout,** turn left to go into Wadebridge, then turn right at mini-roundabout on B3314 to St Minver.

➤ **At crossroads,** turn left on B3266 to Boscastle. Continue along the road (now B3263).

➤ **At A39,** turn left towards Bude.

➤ **After 20 miles,** turn left on B3248 to Hartland, then follow the signs towards Hartland Quay.

➤ **From Hartland Quay,** follow the signs for Bideford (A39). Rejoin A39, turning left.

➤ **In Bideford** join A386 to Great Torrington.

➤ **Stay on A386** all the way to Okehampton, where the route ends.

TOUR ⑭ West Country Tour Day 3

DAY 3 MORNING

THIS BREATHTAKING morning's ride takes in both the wide-open wilderness of Dartmoor and the stunning seaside run along Slapton Sands. Dropping down into Dartmouth, the Higher Ferry speeds the way into Paignton – the perfect place for a lunch stop as there are plenty of cafés. If you have time, the bustling Victorian pier is also well worth a visit.

FROM Okehampton
TO Paignton
DISTANCE 90 miles
RIDING TIME 3.5 hours

Route Description
➤ **Leave Okehampton** on B3215 towards Crediton.
➤ **After about 6 miles,** right on A3124 towards Exeter (A30).
➤ **Cross A30.** Turn right at T-junction, then left at the mini-roundabout to take A382 to Moretonhampstead.
➤ **In Moretonhampstead** turn right at White Hart, on B3212 to Postbridge.
➤ **At B3357,** turn right towards Tavistock. A few hundred

River Erme at Ivybridge

metres later, go left to continue on B3212 to Princetown.
➤ **In Yelverton,** go straight across roundabout and take the first left, following the signs for Cadover Bridge.
➤ **After crossing moor,** turn left at the T-junction towards Cornwood.
➤ **In Ivybridge,** head to the town centre for B3213 to Bittaford.
➤ **Look out:** don't miss the right turn for A3121 to Ugborough, about a mile after passing under a railway bridge.
➤ **At Hollowcombe Cross,** turn left on A379 to Kingsbridge. Stay on A379 all the way to Dartmouth.
➤ **Turn right in Dartmouth** centre and follow the signs for Higher Ferry (carry cash).
➤ **After the crossing** continue along A379 to Paignton.
➤ **In Paignton,** follow the signs for the Sea Front, where the morning route ends.

DAY 3 AFTERNOON

AFTER CUTTING through Torquay after lunch, the views are sublime, before the route climbs back inland – passing through Moretonhampstead for a second time and heading inland, past Exeter and out towards Exmoor. From Wheddon Cross the roads get even quieter, dropping down through Taunton and Chard to reach the tour's final destination, the perfectly preserved, picturesque Victorian resort town of Lyme Regis.

FROM Paignton
TO Lyme Regis
DISTANCE 145 miles
RIDING TIME 5 hours

Route Description
➤ **Continue along** Paignton sea front, following signs for Torquay (A3022) and turning left at both harbour-side roundabouts, taking A379.
➤ **At Teignmouth,** cross the bridge and turn left on A381 and then A383 towards Newton Abbot.
➤ **In Newton Abbott** pick up A382 to Bovey Tracey.

Stay to Moretonhampstead.
➤ **At Moretonhampstead,** turn right at White Hart, heading to Exeter on B3212.
➤ **Head for Exeter centre,** cross the river and turn left on A377 to Crediton.
➤ **In Crediton,** right on A3072, then left on A396 to Tiverton.

TOUR ⑭ West Country Tour Day 3

| ROUTE TYPE Tour | DISTANCE 90 miles morning | 110 miles afternoon |

➤ **Cross Tiverton** following signs for Barnstaple. At A361 roundabout, go straight over on A396 to Dulverton.

➤ **Stay on A396** to Wheddon Cross. Turn right on B3224 to Taunton.

➤ **At A358,** turn right to Taunton.

➤ **To get around Taunton,** turn left at first roundabout and right at the second roundabout. At A38 rbt, turn right towards Exeter (M5).

➤ **Look out:** Don't miss the left turn on the minor road to Ford Street and Chard, a mile after A38/M5 roundabout.

➤ **At the end of this road,** turn left to Chard.

➤ **From Chard,** take A358 to Axminster. Stay on A358 through the town, to Seaton.

➤ **At the junction with A3052,** turn left to Lyme Regis, where this tour comes to an end.

Northern England

Yorkshiremen will tell you they come from God's country – but the whole of Northern England has been blessed with an amazing landscape, rich in great riding roads. There are also large culturally rich cities to visit in the Midlands and the North, though our tours concentrate on the rural riding, getting you to great roads in the most beautiful areas: the Moors, Dales, Wolds and Lakes.

TOUR (15) Richmond Loop

GET UP into the Dales and you're surrounded by nature at its grandest – all rolling hills and big skies. And those hills are crisscrossed by some astonishing roads.

This route starts in Richmond in North Yorkshire, a beautiful town dominated by its spectacular medieval castle. It's easily reached from the rest of the country, just a few miles from the Great North Road, the A1. It's a perfect place for a weekend break – especially as it has such good riding on its doorstep.

It's not all about the roads in Yorkshire, though. Our route loops round into the North Pennines, on some equally fabulous roads that pass through an even quieter, wilder landscape. This is our idea of getting away from it all.

FROM/TO Richmond
VIA Hawes, Kendal, Middleton-in-Teesdale
DISTANCE 145 miles
ALLOW 4–5 hours

Route Description

➤ **From Richmond's** cobbled Newbiggin Square, head down the hill and over the bridge, towards Hudswell and Leyburn.

➤ **At a T-junction,** turn right and follow road that becomes A6108 to Leyburn.

➤ **Coming into Leyburn,** after King's Head take the first right, signed for Grinton.

➤ **At Grinton,** carry straight on along B6270 through Reeth.

➤ **After about 11 miles** – after Muker – take left turn signed for Hawes. This road is Buttertubs Pass: a true Dales classic.

➤ **After 5 or 6 miles,** turn left at T-junction, then right, following signs to Hawes.

➤ **Ride through Hawes** centre following signs for Sedbergh.

➤ **At national speed limit signs,** turn left on B6255 to Ingleton. This epic road passes the iconic Ribblehead Viaduct and White Scar Cave.

➤ **Ingleton village** – go straight over the first street, then right on A65 to Kirkby Lonsdale.

➤ **Coming into Kirkby Lonsdale,** take the right turn for B6254 to reach the town centre.

➤ **Follow one-way system** round and at T-junction, turn left following signs for Old Hutton.

➤ **Stay on the B6254** all the way to Kendal, then follow signs for centre and lunch. There's parking for bikes on level 1 of Kendal's underground town-centre car park (on the left where A6 one-way system meets the river).

➤ **From car park,** follow A6 round towards the train station.

➤ **After passing under** the railway bridge, take the right turn for A685, signed Tebay. If you need fuel, try Tebay services. Otherwise continue along A685 to Brough.

➤ **At Brough clocktower,** turn right and then, about half a mile further, carry on straight as the road bends to the right, taking the B6276 to Middleton-in-Teesdale.

➤ **When you drop down** from the high moors, turn left at T-junction and go into Middleton for coffee.

➤ **From Middleton,** take the B6282 to Eggleston. Follow the road round, as it becomes B6278 to Barnard Castle.

➤ **In Barnard Castle,** turn right on A67 for the town centre.

➤ **As soon as you've crossed the river,** turn left on B6277 – signed Reeth and Scotch Corner. The fast way is to turn right then left, across dual-carriageway A66. If you're nervous about doing this, or are riding with a large group, it may be safer to turn left first, then take the first right turn. You can then do a U-turn and rejoin the A66, heading back towards Penrith.

➤ **Go past** the Barnard Castle turning, then turn left to Scargill.

➤ **After 7 miles** on the Scargill road, turn left towards Reeth. In Reeth, go more or less straight on B6270 to Richmond.

➤ **Stay on this road** to A6108. Turn left to return to Richmond.

TOUR (16) Skegness Loop

DROPPING DOWN the hill, the road turns sharply right, then kinks back to the left as it starts to rise again. The freshly laid tarmac is grippy, the tyres are hot, so I turn confidently, scything through this latest sequence of bends with a huge grin on my face. There's a short straight, but I know it's followed by another rewarding complex of corners.

Since moving to Lincolnshire, I've been blown away by the quality of the roads.

This ride includes many of my favourites – including the stretch of the B1225 with the aforementioned corners. With the sun in the sky, a free day and these roads it's a fantastic place to be riding a bike. And when you're peckish, the local fish and chip shops are out of this world as well. Try the Oxford Street chip shop (right at the lights in Market Rasen). Great roads, great scenery, great grub – it's a great day out.

START/FINISH Skegness
VIA Sutton on Sea, Caistor, Wragby and Revesby
DISTANCE 180 miles
RIDING TIME 5 hours

Route Description

➤ **Leave Skegness** on A52 towards Ingoldmells.
➤ **At mini-roundabout** in Sutton on Sea, turn left on A1111 to Alford.
➤ **In Alford,** turn right on A1104 to Mablethorpe.

➤ **In Maltby le Marsh,** turn left on A157 to Louth.
➤ **At Louth,** join A16 to Grimsby.
➤ **After 7 miles,** turn left on A18 to Immingham.
➤ **At roundabout,** turn left on B1203 to Market Rasen.

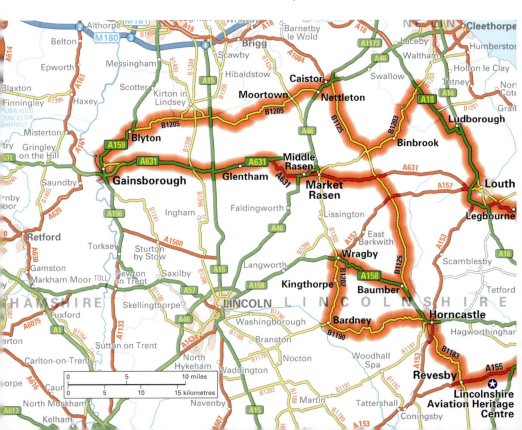

TOUR (16) Skegness Loop

| ROUTE TYPE Loop | DISTANCE 180 miles |

WHAT TO VISIT

Lincolnshire Aviation Heritage Centre
Relive a World War Two bomber airfield and experience the sights and sounds, smells and atmosphere. The only place in the country to see and ride in a Lancaster bomber on its original airfield. The largest Bomber Command museum of its kind.
www.lincsaviation.co.uk

➤ **Look out:** turn right at the x-roads at the top of the hill after Kirmond le Mire, on B1225 to Caistor.

➤ **Turn left on A46** towards Lincoln, then right in Nettleton on B1205 to Moortown.

➤ **At A15,** turn right then turn left to continue on B1205 towards Kirton in Lindsey.

➤ **In Blyton,** turn left on A159 to Gainsborough.

➤ **In Gainsborough** centre, turn left on A631 to Market Rasen.

➤ **Look out:** don't miss the right turn, 5 miles after the Caenby Corner/A15 roundabout, to stay on A631 to Market Rasen.

➤ **Note:** there's a popular bike meet on A631 at Willingham Woods, just after the racecourse.

➤ **At top of the hill** after North Willingham, turn right on B1225 to Horncastle.

➤ **At A158,** turn right to Wragby.

➤ **At traffic lights** in Wragby, turn left on B1202 to Kingthorpe.

➤ **Bardney T-junction,** go straight on B1190 to Horncastle.

➤ **In Horncastle,** turn right at T-junction. At second lights, turn right on A153 to Sleaford.

➤ **Leaving Horncastle,** take first left after national speed-limit signs, for B1183 to Scrivelsby.

➤ **At A155 T-junction,** turn left to East Kirkby.

➤ **At A16,** turn turn left towards Grimsby.

➤ **At roundabout,** turn right on A158 and head back to Skegness, where route ends.

TOUR (17) Buxton Loop

THERE'S A lot of fabulous riding in the Peak District. Cramming the best of it into one day takes a bit of doing – the roads can get busy with tourist traffic, while other stretches of pristine tarmac labour under 50mph limits. This comfortable day's ride uses all my favourite roads, while swerving the busiest ones. It's something of a 'greatest hits' trip featuring the Via Gellia, the Cat 'n' Fiddle, Snake Pass, Holm Moss – roads people dream of – along with less-well-known but equally brilliant stretches.

On the A57, Snake Pass

START/FINISH Buxton
VIA Macclesfield, Matlock, Holmfirth and Hope Valley
DISTANCE 150 miles
RIDING TIME 4.5 hours

Route Description

➤ **Leave Buxton** on A5004 to Whaley Bridge.
➤ **In Whaley Bridge,** turn left at the traffic lights on B5470 to Macclesfield.
➤ **From Macclesfield,** take A537 back towards Buxton.
➤ **Turn right** on A53 towards Leek, then first left to Grin Low and Ashbourne (A515).
➤ **Turn right on B5053** to Longnor.
➤ **Look out:** after 7 miles, take easily missed left turn on B5054 to Hartington.
➤ **Turn right on A515** to Ashbourne, then take the first left: the A5012 to Cromford.

➤ **In Cromford,** turn left and left again, following A6 through Matlock Bath towards Buxton.
➤ **After about 5 miles,** turn left on B5057 to Darley Bridge.
➤ **At B5056 x-roads,** turn right towards Bakewell. At T-junction, turn right to stay on this road.
➤ **Turn right on A6** towards Matlock, then left in Rowsley on B6012 to Beeley.
➤ **Turn right onto A619** and at the roundabout turn left on A623 to Stockport.
➤ **In Calver,** go right on A625, left on B6001 to Hathersage.
➤ **Watch out:** take a left turn in Grindleford to stay on B6001.
➤ **In Hathersage,** turn right on A6187 then second left (School Lane) onto the moors.
➤ **At T-junction,** turn left onto A625, left onto A61, left again on A57 towards Manchester.

➤ **Look out:** after about 4 miles take the easily missed right turn signed for Strines Moor.
➤ **Turn left on A616** to Huddersfield.
➤ **In New Mill,** keep going straight on A635 to Holmfirth.
➤ **From Holmfirth** take A6024 to Glossop.
➤ **At A628,** turn right towards Manchester, then take first left: B6105 to Glossop.
➤ **In Glossop,** turn left on A57 to Sheffield.
➤ **At Ladybower reservoir,** turn right at the traffic lights on A6013 to Bamford.
➤ **At traffic lights,** turn right on A6187 to Castleton. At T-junction on the moor, turn right to Chapel-en-le-Frith.
➤ **From Chapel-en-le-Frith,** take A6 back to Buxton.

WHAT TO VISIT

Chatsworth House
'The Palace of the Peak' is a veritable treasure house of works of art and one of Britain's best-loved and most-visited stately homes, set in 'Capability' Brown's glorious landscaped parkland. It's a favourite backdrop for film-makers – the gilded Palladian west front is instantly recognizable to millions.
www.chatsworth.org

ROUTE TYPE Loop   **DISTANCE** 150 miles

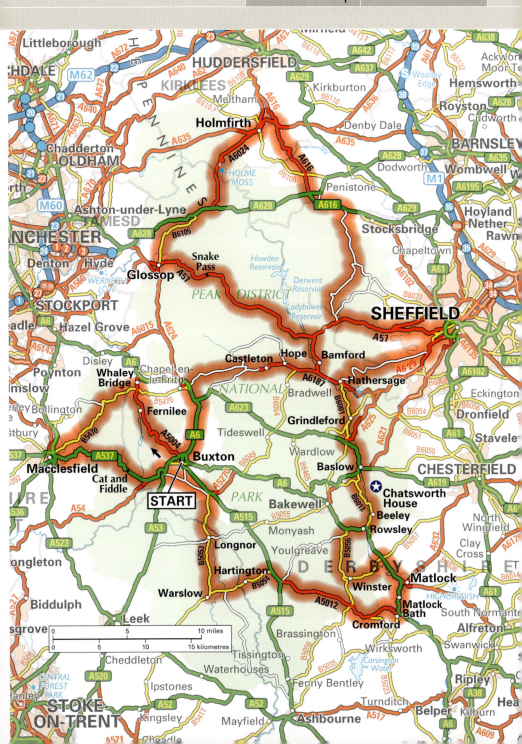

TOUR (18) Ambleside Loop

THE LAKE District is blessed not only with lakes and peaks, but also a beautiful coastline and great roads linking it all up.

As with all popular holiday areas, timing when you ride in the Lake District is critical. Weekends during the school holidays can be pretty busy and as for Bank Holidays… But if you go mid-week during term-time, chances are you'll find the roads practically empty.

This route includes the most scenic of the Lakeland passes and also heads out to the Cumbrian coast for a breath of fresh sea air. It's a full day's ride and a great trip for two, with stunning scenery and brilliant roads. There's only one narrow section of road – past Loweswater – which can be easily skipped by going back into Cockermouth to pick up the A5086.

START/FINISH Ambleside
VIA Kirkstone Pass, Silloth, Borrowdale and Broughton-in-Furness
DISTANCE 180 miles
RIDING TIME 5.5 hours

Route Description

➤ **From Ambleside,** take A591 to Windermere.

➤ **At mini-roundabout,** turn left on A592 to Penrith, over Kirkstone Pass and hugging shore of Ullswater.

➤ **Halfway round Ullswater,** turn left on A5091 to Dockray.

➤ **Turn left on A66** to Keswick.

➤ **After 4½ miles,** turn left on B5322 to Thirlmere.

➤ **At A591,** turn right to Keswick.

➤ **Ride through Keswick** centre, cross river, turn right on A591.

➤ **Turn right on A595** towards Carlisle.

➤ **After about 7 miles** turn left on B5304 to Wigton. Turn left at the memorial in Wigton.

➤ **At A596** turn right, then immediately left for B5302 to Silloth.

➤ **Look out:** at end of Silloth green, turn left for B5300.

➤ **At traffic lights** on edge of Maryport, turn left on A594 to Cockermouth.

➤ **In Cockermouth,** turn right at mini-rbt then go straight over next one on B5292. Turn right after statue, then left at lights.

➤ **Look out:** about 2 miles after B5292 passes under

A66, take a left turn to stay on B5292 back to Keswick, over Whinlatter Pass.

➤ **Join A66** towards Penrith for one junction, turning right into Keswick again. Turn right for B5289 to Borrowdale. Head around shore of Derwent Water and over Honister Pass.

➤ **At T-junction,** turn left on C2030 to Mockerkin – a very minor road along Loweswater.

➤ **At A5086,** left to Egremont.

➤ **At roundabout,** turn left on A595 to Barrow-in-Furness.

➤ **Look out:** after nearly 24 miles, turn left to stay on A595.

➤ **After 7 miles,** at top of a steep hill, turn left on A593 to Coniston. Continue to Ambleside, where the route ends.

Kirkstone Pass

WHAT TO VISIT

Lakeland Motor Museum
One of Britain largest collections of motoring memorabilia, featuring more than 30,000 exhibits, including a 1920 Grigg motor-scooter, a 1921 ABC Skootamota and several Vincent motorcycles.
www.lakeland motormuseum.co.uk

TOUR 18 Ambleside Loop

ROUTE TYPE Loop	DISTANCE 180 miles

TOUR (19) York Loop

YORKSHIRE'S HISTORIC capital is a good starting point for a spring ride on incredible roads. York is a fascinating place, crammed with interesting pubs, museums, shops, the castle and minster, all surrounded by great riding. With the Wolds to the east, the Moors to the north and the Dales to the west, it's a great destination.

You can't go wrong riding deep into the Dales, rolling out by Ribblesdale and back by Blubberhouses Moor. Or you could head over the North York Moors to the coast for fish and chips at Whitby or Scarborough. This route gives a flavour of it all, skirting the Wolds, Moors and Dales, and cuts through the beautiful Howardian Hills.

START/FINISH York
VIA Fridaythorpe, Stokesley, Leyburn
DISTANCE 169 miles
RIDING TIME 4.5 hours

Route Description

➤ **At Hull Road rbt** on A64 ring road, take B1228 past Elvington.
➤ **When B-road** turns right at the Rossmoor garage, carry on to Pocklington.
➤ **At A1079,** go straight at the rbt.
➤ **In Pocklington,** turn right on B1246 towards Driffield.
➤ **At Bainton roundabout,** turn left on B1248 to Malton.
➤ **At Wetwang,** turn left on A166 (towards York). Seaways Café in Fridaythorpe, on the corner of B1251 is a recommended stop.

➤ **Leave Seaways** on B1251 to Bridlington.
➤ **At roundabout,** turn left on B1248 to Malton.
➤ **At lights in Malton,** turn left for York until you join A64. After 3 miles, turn right at brown sign for Castle Howard.
➤ **After Welburn,** turn right at x-roads, signed for Slingsby. This is the road to Castle Howard.
➤ **Continue north** from Castle Howard, turning left to Terrington. When this back road meets a bigger lane, turn right.
➤ **In Hovingham** turn left, then left again, to Coulton.
➤ **At B1363 crossroads,** turn right to Gilling East.
➤ **At B1257,** turn left then bear right on A170 to Helmsley.
➤ **In Helmsley** market place, turn left and then turn right

(by All Saints church) to pick up B1257 to Stokesley.
➤ **At the Stokesley** roundabout, turn right on A172 to Thirsk.
➤ **At A19** join the dual carriageway for one junction. Leave A19 for A684 to Northallerton.
➤ **In Northallerton centre,** stay on A684 to Bedale. Turn right at roundabout after the railway crossing. (Fuel up in either Northallerton and Bedale)
➤ **In Bedale,** turn right to stay on B684 to Leyburn.
➤ **In Ripon,** turn left by the clock tower. Turn right at rbt, then right at the next one on A61.
➤ **Cross one rbt.** At next one, left on B6265 to Boroughbridge. Stay on B6265 until it meets A59.
➤ **Turn left on A59** to return to York.

ROUTE TYPE Loop   **DISTANCE** 169 miles

TOUR (20) Scarborough Loop

LEANING OVER the fence, I had to shout to be heard above the noise of the bikes roaring through the hairpin in front of me. "Can you believe we were riding this road the other day?" This is Scarborough, where races are held on the Oliver's Mount circuit that is – for the rest of the year – a network of public roads through a beautiful park.

But it's not just the racing that keeps drawing me back: the riding around here is spectacular too, especially along the coast. This day-long ride heads out to Flamborough Head and Spurn Head, looping back through York and over the North York Moors to Whitby and Robin Hood's Bay. Definitely a ride worth shouting about at any pace.

START/FINISH Scarborough
VIA Bridlington, Beverley, York and Whitby
DISTANCE 215 miles
RIDING TIME 6 hours

Route Description

➤ **Leave Scarborough** on A165 to Bridlington.
➤ **About 5 miles** past Filey, turn left at rbt on B1229 to Flamborough. Follow signs to Flamborough Head lighthouse.
➤ **From Flamborough,** take the B1255 to Bridlington.
➤ **Go through Bridlington** following signs for South Beach, then Hull (A165).
➤ **After 5 miles** on A165, turn left on B1242 to Hornsea.

➤ **Stay on B1242** all the way to Withernsea, going into the town centre to pick up A1033 to Hull.
➤ **To visit Spurn Head,** turn left in Patrington on B1445. If not, stay on A1033 to Hull.
➤ **Go through Hull** on A1033, following signs for Beverley.
➤ **Take A1079 past Beverley** until picking up signs for A165 to Bridlington.
➤ **At Cherry Burton roundabout,** take B1248 to Malton.
➤ **At Bainton,** turn left on A614 to Goole.
➤ **At the roundabout,** go right on A1079 to Shiptonthorpe.
➤ **At York roundabout,** double back to take A166 towards Bridlington.

➤ **In Fridaythorpe,** turn left on B1251 to Bridlington (maybe stopping at Seaways Café, just after the junction).
➤ **At Fimber roundabout,** turn left on the B1248 to Malton.
➤ **In Malton town centre,** turn right at lights, following signs for Pickering (A169).
➤ **Take A169** all the way to Whitby.
➤ **From Whitby** take A171 south to Scarborough.
➤ **To visit Robin Hood's Bay,** turn left about 2 miles outside Whitby, on B1447. From Robin Hood's Bay, follow signs for Fylingthorpe to rejoin A171.
➤ **Take A171** all the way back to Scarborough, where the route ends.

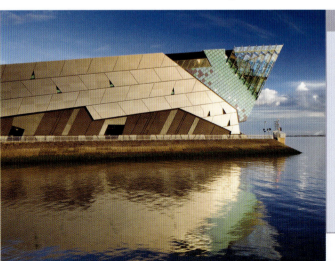

WHAT TO SEE AND DO

The Deep (Hull)
One of the deepest and most spectacular aquariums in the world, this is a blend of marine life and fun interactive presentations, which tell the dramatic story of the world's oceans. Highlights include more than 3,500 fish, a colony of Gentoo penguins, Europe's deepest viewing tunnel and a glass lift ride through a 9m deep tank.
www.thedeep.co.uk

TOUR 20 Scarborough Loop

ROUTE TYPE Loop | **DISTANCE** 215 miles

TOUR ㉑ Northern England High-Mile Tour Day 1

DAY 1 MORNING

THIS TOUR of the north of England links together some of the best roads in the country. Mileages are high – it's a trip more suited to solo riders than pillion couples – but it crams the maximum amount of riding quality into the minimum number of days.

The three-day tour starts and ends at Kegworth in Leicestershire – a central starting point, easily reached from the M1 or M42. The first morning heads out through the Peak District, taking in the famous Via Gellia, Cat 'n' Fiddle, High Peak, Hope Valley and Snake Pass roads on the way to lunch in Glossop.

FROM Kegworth
TO Glossop
VIA Macclesfied, Buxton and Snake Pass.
DISTANCE 105 miles
RIDING TIME 3 hours

Route Description

➤ **From Kegworth,** take the M1 north to J26, joining A610 to Matlock.

➤ **In Ambergate,** turn right on A6 to Matlock.

➤ **At Cromford,** turn left at the lights, then right at next lights on A5012 to Newhaven.

➤ **At A515,** turn right to Buxton.

➤ **Look out:** don't miss the left turn after 4 miles, on the minor road to Hurdlow.

➤ **In Longnor,** turn right on the B5053 to Buxton.

➤ **Look out:** after 3 miles, turn left on the minor road to Harpur Hill.

➤ **In 30 limit,** opposite the playground, turn left for Grin Low.

➤ **At A53,** turn right. Take first left: A54 to Congleton.

➤ **When the road divides,** bear right on A537 to Macclesfield.

➤ **Look out:** 5 miles after the Cat 'n' Fiddle Inn, take easy-to-miss right turn for Rainow.

➤ **At B5470,** turn right to Whaley Bridge.

➤ **In Whaley Bridge** turn right on A5004 to Buxton.

➤ **In Buxton,** join the A6 towards Stockport. After 4 miles, turn right at roundabout on A623 to Chesterfield.

➤ **Look out:** turn left on a sharp right-hand bend, following the brown sign to Edale.

➤ **At traffic lights,** turn left on A6013 to Bamford.

➤ **At A57,** turn left towards Manchester on Snake Pass to end the morning in Glossop.

DAY 2 AFTERNOON

FROM GLOSSOP, we head out across the near-Alpine curves of Holm Moss, before edging around Huddersfield and Halifax to get to the glorious Yorkshire Dales. If the ride from Grassington to Aysgarth impresses, then the B6255 from Hawes to Ribblehead will make you redefine the term 'good road'. With so many miles to cover, the A65 is a functional way to get to the overnight stop in Windermere, ready for the next day's riding.

FROM Glossop
TO Windermere
VIA Holmfirth, Addingham, Aysgarth and Ingleton
DISTANCE 135 miles
RIDING TIME 4.5 hours

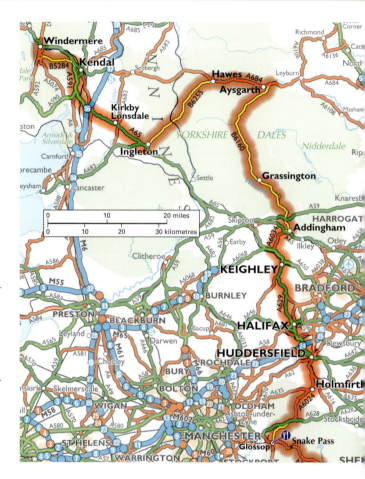

Route Description

➤ **Leave Glossop** on B6105 towards Woodhead (from A57, turn right at the lights in the town centre).
➤ **At A628,** turn right then first left on A6024 to Holmfirth.
➤ **Stay on A6024** (becomes A616) to Huddersfield. Take the Huddersfield ring road for A629 to Halifax.
➤ **Take A629** across Halifax, following the road signs for Keighley.
➤ **Cross Keighley** on A629 following signs for Skipton.
➤ **Look out:** A629 is a dual carriageway on north side of Keighley. At first rbt, turn right on A6034 to Addingham.

➤ **At the A65,** cross roundabout to B6160 into Addingham, taking B6160 to Grassington.
➤ **At A684,** turn left to Aysgarth.
➤ **Ride through Hawes** (maybe stopping for a coffee in the Penny Garth Café) and, just as you see the national speed limit signs, turn left on B6255 to Ingleton.
➤ **In Ingleton,** turn right on A65 to Kendal.
➤ **Go straight over M6 rbt** on A590 to Kendal.

➤ **After about 8 miles,** at the end of dual carriageway, turn left on B5284, following the sign for Hawkshead via Ferry.
➤ **At A5074 T-junction,** turn right to go into Windermere, where the day's route ends.

TOUR ㉑ Northern England High-Mile Tour Day 2

DAY 2 MORNING

DON'T HAVE a lie-in. This truly epic day's riding does involve a serious mileage – and some seriously mindblowing roads. The morning starts with a run along the shores of Windermere, diving out to the Cumbrian coast before cutting back to the heart of the Lake District over the wild and challenging Hardknott and Wrynose passes. After crossing Kirkstone Pass, the route climbs the scenic Hartside Pass – we'd recommend a stop for lunch at the Hartside Café (cash only – don't count on using a credit card) but you could also stop in Alston, just a few miles further on.

Buttertubs Pass (afternoon section)

FROM Windermere
TO Hartside Pass
VIA Torver, Broughton-in-Furness, Hardknott Pass and Ullswater
DISTANCE 110 miles
RIDING TIME 3.5 hours

Route Description

➤ **From Windermere,** take A592 to Newby Bridge.
➤ **At rbt, turn right on A590** to Barrow-in-Furness.
➤ **At next roundabout,** turn right on A5092 to Broughton-in-Furness. After 2 miles turn right on A5084 to Torver.
➤ **In Torver,** turn left on A593 to Broughton.
➤ **At T-junction,** right on A595 to Whitehaven. Turn right again to stay on A595.

➤ **Look out:** after 14 miles don't miss the right turn in Holmrook, signed for Irton and for Wasdale Head.
➤ **At T-junction,** turn right to Eskdale Green, then follow signs for Hardknott Pass.
➤ **At A593,** turn left to Ambleside.
➤ **From Ambleside,** take A591 to Windermere.
➤ **At mini-roundabout,** turn left on A592 to Kirkstone Pass.
➤ **At A66 roundabout,** turn right to Penrith.
➤ **Cross the M6 rbt** and at the next one, take the second exit: the A686 to Alston.
➤ **The route ends** at Hartside Café (though you could continue into Alston).

| ROUTE TYPE Tour | DISTANCE 110 miles morning | 205 miles afternoon |

DAY 2 AFTERNOON

FROM THE heart of the Pennines to the North Yorkshire coast, this is a long afternoon in the saddle (you didn't want a long lunch, did you?). The roads from Alston to Haydon Bridge and back to Stanhope seems deserted – but not compared with the road to Brough or the Buttertubs Pass to Hawes. Despite the high mileage, stop for water in Hawes: it's important to stay well hydrated, especially as there are some challenging roads ahead – not least the so-called North York TT, the B1257.

FROM Hartside Pass
TO Whitby
VIA Stanhope, Kirkby Stephen, Leyburn and Stokesley
DISTANCE 205 miles
RIDING TIME 5.5 hours

Route Description

➤ **From Hartside Café,** stay on A686 towards Haydon Bridge.
➤ **Look out:** don't miss the right turn for B6305 to Hexham, 2 miles after a hairpin corner.

➤ **After a mile,** turn right on B6295 to Allenheads. The road becomes A689 to Stanhope.
➤ **In Stanhope,** turn right on B6278 to Eggleston.
➤ **From Eggleston,** take B6282 to Middleton-in-Teesdale.
➤ **In Middleton,** turn left on B6277 and after ½ mile turn right on B6276 to Brough.
➤ **In Brough,** turn left on A685 to Kirkby Stephen.
➤ **In Kirkby Stephen,** turn left at the lights on B6259.

➤ **In Nateby,** turn left on B6270 to Swaledale.
➤ **After 11 miles,** just past Thwaite, turn right towards Hawes, over Buttertubs Pass. Turn left, then right, for Hawes.
➤ **From Hawes,** take A684 to Aysgarth and Bedale.
➤ **In Bedale,** go straight on the high street on B6258.
➤ **In Burneston,** turn left by the church, towards the A1(M).
➤ **At A6055,** parallel to A1(M), turn right towards Ripon. At rbt, turn left to Sinderby on B6267.
➤ **At A61,** turn left to Thirsk.
➤ **Take A170** from Thirsk towards Scarborough.
➤ **In Helmsley,** turn left, then right on B1257 to Stokesley.
➤ **From Stokesley,** take A172 to Middlesbrough.
➤ **In Middlesbrough,** pick up the A1043 towards Teesport.
➤ **At next roundabout,** turn right on the A171 to Whitby, where the day's route ends.

TOUR ㉑ Northern England High-Mile Tour Day 3

DAY 3 MORNING

AFTER THE demanding second day, the return run should be a breeze – it's been kept compact to allow time to return home if you don't want to stop at Kegworth. The quality of the riding doesn't diminish, though – as you cross the North York Moors and the Yorkshire Wolds, before the toll-free (for motorcycles) Humber Bridge.

FROM Whitby
TO Brigg
VIA Pickering, Bridlington and Beverley
DISTANCE 105 miles
RIDING TIME 2.5 hours

Route Description

➤ **Leave Whitby** on A171, towards Middlesbrough. At third roundabout, turn left on A169 to Pickering.

➤ **In Malton,** turn left at the lights. Cross the railway and pick up B1248 to Beverley.

➤ **At the B1251 roundabout,** turn left to Bridlington. In Sledmere turn left on B1253.

➤ **In Bridlington,** turn right on A165 to Hull.

➤ **Pick up A614** to Driffield and on to Bainton.

➤ **In Bainton,** turn left (going straight when A614 turns right) on B1248 to Beverley.

➤ **Turn right at the roundabout,** towards York. At next roundabout, take the third exit to Walkington. Stay on this road to A164.

➤ **At A164,** turn right and follow signs for the Humber Bridge. There's no toll for motorcycles.

➤ **Cross the bridge** and take the second exit from the dual carriageway. Follow B1206 to Brigg, where the morning's route ends.

| ROUTE TYPE Tour | DISTANCE 105 miles morning | 125 miles afternoon |

DAY 3 AFTERNOON

THE FINAL afternoon of riding sees the tour finishing on a high. What's the best road in Lincolnshire? Two certain candidates are the B1225, known as Caistor High Street, and the B1183 from Horncastle to Revesby – riding them back-to-back, you can assess their quality. It's all good riding though. Leicestershire's B676 to Melton Mowbray is every inch as memorable. From Melton, the run back to Kegworth flows along the sublime A6006 before meeting the A6.

FROM Brigg
TO Kegworth
VIA Horncastle, Woodhall Spa, Sleaford and Melton Mowbray
DISTANCE 125 miles
RIDING TIME 3 hours

Route Description

➤ **Leave Brigg** on A1084 to Caistor.
➤ **From Caistor,** take the B1225 to Horncastle.
➤ **At the A158,** turn left to Horncastle. At the second set of traffic lights, turn right on A153 to Sleaford.
➤ **Leaving Horncastle,** take the first left for the B1183 to Scrivelsby.
➤ **At the T-junction,** turn right to Mareham le Fen on A155.
➤ **At the roundabout,** turn left on A153 to Sleaford.
➤ **In Tattershall,** cross the bridge and turn right (after the

speed camera) on B1192 to Woodhall Spa.
➤ **In Woodhall Spa,** turn left on B1191 to Martin.
➤ **At the T-junction,** turn right on B1189 to Metheringham.
➤ **In Metheringham,** turn left on B1188 to Scopwick.
➤ **In Ruskington,** turn right at the mini-rbt. At the next rbt, join the A153 to Sleaford.
➤ **In Sleaford,** join A17 towards Newark. At the second roundabout take the A15 to Peterborough.

➤ **At A52 roundabout** turn right to Grantham.
➤ **Go straight** across the next roundabout on B6403.
➤ **Look out:** don't miss the left turn 3 miles after the railway bridge to cross the A1 into Colsterworth.
➤ **In Colsterworth,** turn right to Melton Mowbray on B676.
➤ **From Melton Mowbray,** take A6006 to Asfordby and Wymeswold.
➤ **At the A6** turn right to return to Kegworth, to end the day.

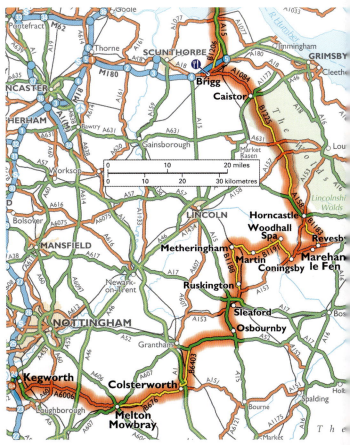

TOUR ㉒ Northern England Relaxed Tour Day 1

DAY 1 MORNING

NOT EVERY tour needs to test your endurance. In contrast to the High Mile version, the Relaxed North Tour cherry picks fine roads for a more laid-back trip. It links towns from which our other routes are based, making it easy to build a longer tour by staying two nights in one place and enjoying the daytrip ride before moving on.

The first morning starts with a relaxed jaunt through the scenic countryside of the Lincolnshire Wolds, past the Cadwell Park race track, before heading up Caistor High Street to Barton-upon-Humber for lunch.

FROM Skegness
TO Barton-upon-Humber
DISTANCE 75 miles
RIDING TIME 2 hours

Route Description

➤ **Leave Skegness** on A158, towards Lincoln.
➤ **At A16 roundabout,** turn left towards Boston.
➤ **Descending the hill** after a tight right-hander in East Keal, turn right on A155 to Sleaford.
➤ **After 5 miles,** turn right on B1183 to Horncastle.
➤ **At A153 junction,** turn right. Follow road through Horncastle to Louth.
➤ **Turn left on A16** towards Grimsby.
➤ **At the roundabout,** turn left on A157 to Lincoln. After a few hundred metres, turn right on A631 to Market Rasen.
➤ **Look out:** don't miss the right turn half a mile after Ludford for B1225 to Caistor.
➤ **At A46,** go straight over the staggered crossroads on A1173 to Immingham.
➤ **Look out:** when road turns sharply right, keep going straight on minor road to Great Limber.
➤ **Cross A18,** taking the minor road to Brocklesby.
➤ **Left on B1211** to Ulceby.
➤ **In Ulceby,** turn left on A1077 to Barton-upon-Humber.
➤ **Look out:** don't miss the right turn immediately before the national speed limit signs, for A1077. Stay all the way to Barton-upon-Humber, where the morning's route ends.

ROUTE TYPE Tour	**DISTANCE** 75 miles morning	75 miles afternoon

DAY 2 AFTERNOON

THE ROADS of the Wolds of the East Riding of Yorkshire are similar to the roads across the Lincolnshire Wolds: both are quiet and flowing, linking charming villages. It's worth holding on for Fridaythorpe before stopping for tea on this afternoon run, as the Seaways Café there is a popular biking venue. The run from there to Staxton Hill might just be our favourite part of the route, before the final leg into Scarborough.

FROM Barton-upon-Humber
TO Scarborough
DISTANCE 75 miles
RIDING TIME 2 hours

Route Description

➤ **From Barton-upon-Humber,** join A15 across the Humber Bridge. There is no toll for motorcycles.

➤ **Go straight across roundabout** on north bank of Humber, on A164 to Beverley.

➤ **After 6 miles,** turn left on minor road to Walkington. Go straight on at the traffic lights in Walkington, towards Bishop Burton.

➤ **At roundabout,** take second exit for A1035 towards Bridlington.

➤ **At the next roundabout,** go straight on B1248 to Malton.

➤ **In Bainton,** turn right on A614 towards Bridlington.

➤ **At the roundabout,** turn left to on B1246 to Pocklington.

➤ **Turn right in Pocklington,** still on B1246. Take minor road through Bolton to Full Sutton.

➤ **Look out:** don't miss right turn in Full Sutton, signed for Stamford Bridge (A166).

➤ **Turn right** on the A166 towards Driffield.

➤ **In Fridaythorpe,** turn left on B1251 to Bridlington.

➤ **In Sledmere,** turn left on B1253 to Bridlington.

➤ **At the roundabout,** turn left to Foxholes.

➤ **Turn right** at the bottom of Staxton Hill on A64 and continue on this road all the way to Scarborough, where the day's route ends.

TOUR 22 Northern England Relaxed Tour Day 2

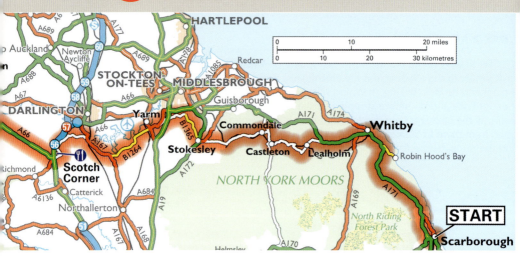

DAY 2 MORNING

THE RIDE from Scarborough to Whitby is as relaxing as it is scenic – if you have time, a detour to Robin Hood's Bay is always pleasant. From Whitby the tour takes to even quieter roads across the moors to Stokesley and Yarm. Though the route only skirts these towns, both have charming independent cafes if you'd prefer an earlier lunch to the scheduled stop at the Scotch Corner services.

Enjoy fabulous empty roads

FROM Scarborough
TO Scotch Corner
DISTANCE 75 miles
RIDING TIME 2 hours

Route Description

➤ **Leave Scarborough** on A171 to Whitby. Stay on A171 towards Guisborough.
➤ **Look out:** take the easily missed left turn to Lealholm, 5 miles after A171/A169 rbt.
➤ **Stay on minor road** to x-roads. Turn right towards Fryup.
➤ **Look out:** 1 mile later, take the easily missed right turn towards Houslake.

➤ **At the T-junction,** turn left to Danby.
➤ **In Danby,** go straight over the crossroads on the minor road to Castleton.
➤ **In Castleton,** don't miss the right turn (by the café) towards the station.
➤ **Look out:** on the high moor, take the left turn to Commondale and stay on this road all the way to Stokesley.
➤ **At A173,** turn left to Stokesley. Turn right at first roundabout (A172), then go

straight across the next one on B1365 to Helmington.
➤ **Cross A174** and turn left on B1380 to Yarm (after a few miles, road becomes A1044).
➤ **Go straight across** the roundabout in Yarm, on B1264 to Richmond.
➤ **Turn right** on the A167 to Darlington.
➤ **In Croft-on-Tees,** take the first left to Barton. Stay on minor road to Scotch Corner services at Middleton Tyas, where the morning route ends.

TOUR 22 Northern England Relaxed Tour Day 2

ROUTE TYPE Tour	DISTANCE 90 miles morning	110 miles afternoon

DAY 2 AFTERNOON

FROM THE bustle of Scotch Corner and the A66, the tour peels off to a favourite road: the B6277 between Middleton-in-Teesdale and Alston. The High Force waterfall – a five-minute walk from the car park – is worth a visit. From Alston, the route descends over Hartside Pass with majestic views out across the Lake District. Hugging the shores of Ullswater, before scrambling over Kirkstone Pass on the way to Ambleside, the day's route finishes on a real high.

High Force waterfall

FROM Scotch Corner
TO Ambleside
DISTANCE 95 miles
RIDING TIME 3 hours

Route Description

➤ **From Scotch Corner/A1 roundabout,** take A66 towards Brough.

➤ **After 10 miles,** turn right to Barnard Castle.

➤ **Turn right at roundabout.** At the end of the high street, take the left fork for B6278 to Middleton-in-Teesdale.

➤ **Stay on this road** through Middleton to Alston.

➤ **In Alston,** at bottom of the cobbled hill, turn left on A686.

➤ **In Penrith,** join A66 to Keswick.

➤ **Cross M6 and at the next roundabout,** turn left on A592 to Ullswater.

➤ **Go over Kirkstone Pass.** At rbt on edge of Windermere, turn right on A591 to Ambleside, where the day's route ends.

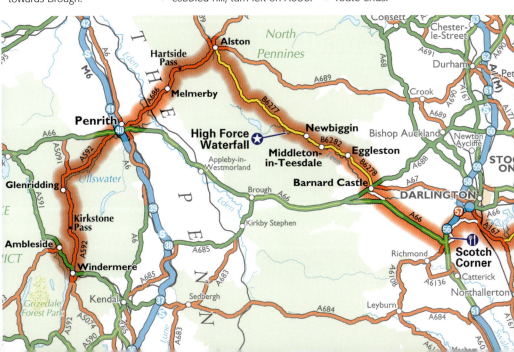

TOUR (22) Northern England
Relaxed Tour Day 3

DAY 3 MORNING

DON'T BE sad – you may have reached the final day of the tour, but the riding is still spectacular. After the Lake District, the route heads into the Yorkshire Dales. The show caves at White Scar on the B6255 outside Ingleton are fascinating – but the riding is every bit as impressive, as the road writhes through Ribbledale to Hawes. Lunch at the Pennygarth Café is practically compulsory for bikers.

Wensleydale: home of great riding (and cheese)

FROM Ambleside
TO Hawes
DISTANCE 70 miles
RIDING TIME 2 hours

Route Description

➤ **Leave Ambleside** on A593 to Coniston.

➤ **In Torver,** turn left on A5084 to Greenodd.

➤ **Turn left** on A5092 to Greenodd.

➤ **At roundabout,** turn left on A590 to Kendal, then follow signs for M6.

➤ **Go straight across M6,** taking A65 to Kirkby Lonsdale.

➤ **In Ingleton,** turn left on B6255 to Hawes.

➤ **In Hawes,** turn right to the town centre, where the morning's route ends.

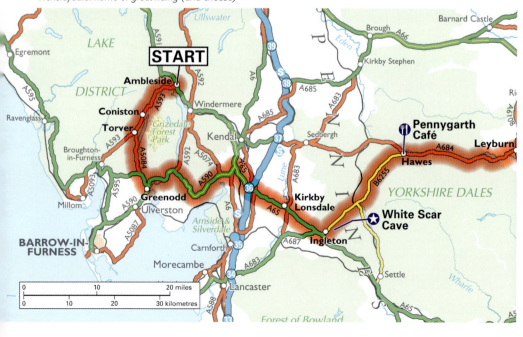

ROUTE TYPE Tour	DISTANCE 70 miles morning	90 miles afternoon

DAY 3 AFTERNOON

FROM HAWES the route continues through Leyburn and Northallerton, returning to Stokesley. The run down the B1257 to Helmsley is one of Yorkshire's most famous, nicknamed the North York TT. Don't get carried away on it, though: you'll want to save some energy for the final run into York on the B1363.

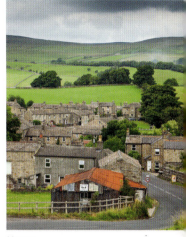

Hawes

FROM Hawes
TO York
DISTANCE 90 miles
RIDING TIME 2.5 hours

Route Description

➤ **From Hawes,** take A684 to Leyburn and Bedale.
➤ **Look out:** turn left in Bedale to stay on A684 to Northallerton.
➤ **Cross Northallerton** following the signs for Teesside A684 (A19).

➤ **After 5 miles,** join A19 to Teesside.
➤ **After 1½ miles** on dual carriageway, turn left and take A172 to Stokesley.
➤ **At roundabout,** turn right on B1257 to Great Broughton.
➤ **In Helmsley,** turn right on A170 to Thirsk.
➤ **In 1 mile,** turn left on B1257.
➤ **In another 2 miles,** turn right on B1363 to York.
➤ **Look out:** don't miss left turn by the church in Stillington to stay on B1363.

➤ **Turn right** at the mini-roundabout, then left in Sutton-on-the-Forest to stay on B1363 to York, where the tour ends.

Wales

Wales has a very different character to England. It's more rural, wild, its low mountains packed with spectacular riding – and the best bit is, the roads are astonishingly quiet. From the geological marvel of Great Orme's Head on the north coast, through Snowdonia and the Brecon Beacons, to St Davids on the beautiful Pembroke coast, our tours take in the finest riding in Wales.

TOUR (23) Ystradgynlais Loop

EVERYONE HAS favourite rides – ones with a certain nostalgic value. This is one of mine, as I spent my first few years in Llangadog and came back to visit my grandmother until I was well into my twenties. Those visits were best once I'd passed my test and could come over on a bike… so I could ride these amazing roads.

You don't need to be tripping down Memory Lane to enjoy this ride, though – it's crammed with genuinely world-class riding.

The Upper Chapel to Lower Chapel road is as challenging as it is scenic, but you won't get more bends-per-mile in Wales than with the A483 – though the A482 comes close. And as for the run from Llangadog to Brynamman, over the Black Mountain, that has everything from huge elevation changes and majestic views to hairpin bends and flowing straights. That road alone means this day-long route is sure to become one of your favourite rides, too.

START/FINISH Ystradgynlais
VIA Brecon, Newtown, Devil's Bridge and Lampeter
DISTANCE 190 miles
RIDING TIME 5.5 hours

Route Description

➤ **Leave Ystradgynlais** on A4067 towards Sennybridge.

➤ **At A40,** turn right towards Brecon.

➤ **At rbt, turn left into Brecon** (signed B4601 to Llanfaes).

➤ **At the third set of traffic lights** (next to the Cotswold camping shop) turn left on B4520 to Upper Chapel.

➤ **Look out:** don't miss the left turn for B4519 to Garth, 9 miles outside Brecon.

➤ **Turn right on A483** and follow it through Builth Wells and Llandrindod Wells, all the way to Newtown.

➤ **At Newtown traffic lights** turn left on A489 to Machynlleth. (This road becomes A470 when it crosses the railway, about 5 miles later).

➤ **At the Llangurig rbt,** turn right on A44 to Aberystwyth.

➤ **After 13 miles,** in Ponterwyd, turn left on A4120 to Devil's Bridge.

➤ **At A487 junction,** turn left to Cardigan.

➤ **Turn left in Llanfarian,** on A485 to Tregaron.

➤ **Turn right** at the mini-rbt in Llanilar to stay on A485 and

follow this road all the way to Lampeter.

➤ **From Lampeter,** take A482 to Llandovery.

➤ **At Llanwrda,** turn right on A40 towards Llandeilo.

➤ **At the roundabout,** turn left to Llangadog.

➤ **Look out:** in the village centre, carry straight on when the road bears round to the left, taking A4069 to Brynamman.

➤ **At the mini-roundabout** in Brynamman, turn left on A4068 to Ystalyfera.

➤ **Take this road** all the way back to Ystradgynlais, where the route ends.

On the A483

TOUR 23 Ystradgynlais Loop

ROUTE TYPE Loop | **DISTANCE** 190 miles

TOUR (24) Tenby Loop

THE PEMBROKE Coast is a wonder – sunshine brings out the beauty of its sandy bays, towering cliffs and blue, blue waters. The roads aren't half bad, either… and we'd far prefer messing about near the water to bobbing up and down on it.

This route from *RiDE* magazine gets the best from the area, heading out from Tenby on twisty lanes on its way from the Pembrokeshire's south coast to Cardigan Bay on the north. We'd stop for lunch in New Quay before cutting into the Preseli mountains, though the route returns to the sea at Fishguard.

The run from Fishguard, through St Davids and onto Haverfordwest delivers great views and great bends in equal measure – though a wander round Solva is highly recommended. This full day's ride will make you wonder why so many people here seem to have boats: bikes make much more sense when the roads are so great.

'Babs' – the 1926 land speed record holder at the Pendine Museum

START/FINISH Tenby
VIA Cenarth, Aberaeron, New Quay and St Davids
DISTANCE 190 miles
RIDING TIME 5.5 hours

Route Description

➤ **Leave Tenby** on A478 to Narberth.
➤ **Follow the one-way system** through Narberth, to stay on A478 towards Cardigan.
➤ **Look out:** don't miss the right turn in Blaenffos (quite a way into the village) for B4332 to Boncath and Newcastle Emlyn.
➤ **At the T-junction,** turn right on B4332 to Cenarth.

➤ **Turn right in Cenarth** on A484 to Newcastle Emlyn.
➤ **In Newcastle Emlyn,** take the right turn for B4333 to Cynwyl Elfed.
➤ **Turn right** in Cynwyl Elfed, rejoining A484 to Carmarthen.
➤ **From Carmarthen,** take A485 to Lampeter.
➤ **At A482,** turn left to go into Lampeter. Turn right at the mini-roundabout in the centre, taking A482 to Aberaeron.
➤ **In Aberaeron,** turn left on A487 to Cardigan.
➤ **In Llanarth,** turn right on B4342 to New Quay.
➤ **From New Quay** take A486 to Llandysul.

➤ **Rejoin A487,** turning right to carry on past Cardigan.
➤ **Look out:** don't miss the left turn, by the garage on the far side of Eglwyswrw, for B4329 to Haverfordwest.
➤ **After 7 miles,** turn right on B4313 to Fishguard.
➤ **From Fishguard,** take A487 to St Davids, following this road all the way to Haverfordwest.
➤ **Join A40** from Haverfordwest to St Clears.
➤ **At the roundabout,** turn right towards Pembroke Dock on A4075.
➤ **At A477 roundabout,** turn left towards St Clears.
➤ **At next roundabout** turn right on B4318 to return to Tenby, where the route ends.

TOUR ㉔ Tenby Loop

ROUTE TYPE Loop	DISTANCE 190 miles

| 0 | 5 | 10 | 15 miles |
| 0 | 5 | 10 | 15 | 20 kilometres |

TOUR 25 Aberystwyth Loop

I'M SURE most people would envy the pilot of the RAF Hawk jet threading his way through what aviators call 'the Mach Loop'. But as the plane screams along the almost Alpine valley while I'm riding down A487, I think I'm having more fun at ground level.

This extended day's ride has so many outstanding roads – and you don't need to be nudging the sound barrier to enjoy them. True, these are the kind of flowing roads that encourage a spirited ride, but rush them and you'll miss so much as they carve their way across majestic hills, through fragrant woodlands and beside a jewel-bright sea.

This long trip is easily made shorter. Carrying on to Tywyn from Dolgellau (rather than heading to Bala) makes a nice half-day ride, while heading to Harlech from Blaenau Ffestiniog can save an hour… but who'd want to shorten this route? It's just too much fun.

START/FINISH Aberystwyth
VIA Llangurig, Bala, Capel Curig and Harlech
DISTANCE 230 miles
RIDING TIME 6.5 hours

Route Description

➤ **Leave Aberystwyth** on A44 to Llangurig.
➤ **At Llangurig roundabout,** turn left on A470 to Llanidloes.
➤ **Look out:** turn left at level crossing to stay on A470, now signed to Caersws.
➤ **At Cemmaes Road rbt,** turn left on A489 to Machynlleth.
➤ **In Machynlleth,** turn right on A487 to Dolgellau.

➤ **At Cross Foxes junction,** turn left on A470 to Dolgellau.
➤ **After 3 miles,** turn right on A494 to Bala.
➤ **In Bala,** turn left on A4212 to Trawsfynydd.
➤ **After about 10 miles** (once you've passed the lake), turn right on B4391 to Ffestiniog.
➤ **At A470,** turn right on to Betws-y-Coed.
➤ **Turn left** on A5 towards Betws-y-Coed and Bangor.
➤ **In Capel Curig** turn left on A4086 to Caernarfon. It becomes A498 to Porthmadog.
➤ **In Beddgelert,** turn left (across the bridge) to stay on A498 to Porthmadog.

➤ **Look out:** don't miss the left turn, after a mile and a half, for A4085 to Penrhyndeudraeth.
➤ **A487** turn left to Dolgellau.
➤ **Look out:** 4 miles later, after crossing the bridge, take the easy-to-miss right turn for A496 to Harlech.
➤ **When A496** rejoins A470 in Llanelltyd, turn right to head towards Dolgellau.
➤ **A mile later,** turn right on A493 to Tywyn.
➤ **In Tywyn,** turn left to stay on A493 to Aberdyfi.
➤ **At A487,** turn right (across the bridge) to Machynlleth, taking A487 back to Aberystwyth once more.

WHAT TO VISIT

Harlech Castle
This great castle was part of Edward I's 'iron ring'. Harlech was completed within just seven years (1283-90). Master builder James of St George personally supervised the building – it doesn't take much imagination to envisage the remarkable feat of engineering required to erect such a vast fortress.
www.cadw.gov.wales

TOUR (26) Pwllheli Loop

YOU DON'T need a bucket and spade to enjoy the seaside – not with a motorbike and the views on this route. From our base in the seaside resort town of Pwllheli, it sweeps majestically through two colossal view points.

First destination, after riding the narrow, quiet lanes to the tip of the Llyn Peninsula, is Uwchmynydd (pronounced Uch-men-ith) with its commanding vistas out over Bardsey Island. From there we head north, zig-zagging through Snowdonia, over the pass of Llanberis and up to Llandudno to take the scenic drive around Great Ormes Head. It's well worth going to the very top for the spectacular panorama.

The views on the ride back to Pwllheli may not be so vast, but the roads are just just as satisfying, passing Conwy Castle and flowing through Blaenau Ffestiniog and Porthmadog. After this, you'll never see beach holidays in the same light again.

WHAT TO VISIT

Conwy Castle
One of the best castles in Wales and Edward I's most expensive fortress. Built 1283–1287, it features some three quarters of a mile of walls, with 22 towers and 3 gateways.
www.cadw.gov.wales

START/FINISH Pwllheli
VIA Aberdaron, Llanberis, Llandudno and Porthmadog
DISTANCE 185 miles
RIDING TIME 5.5 hours

Route Description

➤ **Leave Pwllheli** on A499 to Abersoch.
➤ **Turn right** in Llanbedrog on B4413 to Aberdaron.
➤ **Look out:** after 2½ miles, take the easily missed left turn to Y Rhiw and Aberdaron.
➤ **For the view to Bardsey Island,** turn left after bridge in Aberdaron, then left to Uwchmynydd.
➤ **Otherwise,** carry on through Aberdaron on B4413, signed for Pwllheli.
➤ **Look out:** don't miss the left turn for B4417 to Nefyn.

➤ **At the mini-roundabout** in Nefyn, turn left to stay on B4417.
➤ **At A499 roundabout,** turn left to Caernarfon.
➤ **At next rbt,** go straight towards Caernarfon on A487.
➤ **Turn right** at Bontnewydd rbt, towards Llanberis (A4086).
➤ **At A4085 roundabout,** turn right to Beddgelert.
➤ **In Beddgelert,** go straight (where the road turns right across the bridge) towards Capel Curig on A498.
➤ **After 7 miles,** turn left on A4086 to Llanberis.
➤ **At end of the lake,** turn right on A4244 to Bangor.
➤ **At A5,** turn right to Betws-y-Coed.
➤ **Cross the river** on A5 at Betws-y-Coed and turn left on A470 to Llandudno.

➤ **In Llandudno,** follow signs for the Scenic Drive, to visit Great Ormes Head (toll).
➤ **Turn left** a mile after the toll. Complete the scenic drive.
➤ **Follow signs** for Conwy (A546) to leave Llandudno.
➤ **At mini-roundabout** next to Conwy Castle, turn left on B5106 to Trefriw. Take that road to Betws-y-Coed.
➤ **Turn left on A5,** cross the river again and turn right on A470, this time to Dolgellau.
➤ **In Blaenau Ffestiniog,** turn right on A496 to Porthmadog.
➤ **Turn right on A487** to Porthmadog.
➤ **At Tremadog roundabout,** turn left on A497 to Criccieth, then return to Pwllheli.

TOUR 26 Pwllheli Loop

ROUTE TYPE Loop	DISTANCE 185 miles

TOUR (27) Wrexham Loop

EVERY SPRING, my friend John organises a reunion event for the customers of his touring company Alpine TT. They all meet in a nice hotel, enjoy a couple of ride-outs, have a slap-up meal and recapture that summer-holiday-on-tour feeling.

This year, John asked me for some route suggestions. While he led the big group ride on one of the shorter options, I set off to ride this longer 'ultimate North Wales ride-out'. It's a

belting day in the saddle – as long as you want a long ride.

If you want a shorter version, there are a couple of easy ways to reduce the mileage. From the Betws-y-Coed, take the A470 through Blaenau to cut out the Beddgelert section. From Oswestry, take the A5 all the way to Llangollen – just don't miss out Horseshoe Pass. That ends the route on a high, giving that special on-tour feeling to the ride.

START/FINISH Wrexham
VIA Denbigh, Beddgelert, Ellesmere and Horseshoe Pass
DISTANCE 190 miles
RIDING TIME 5.5 hours

Route Description
➤ **Leave Wrexham** on A541 to Mold.
➤ **From Mold,** take A494 to Ruthin.
➤ **From Ruthin,** take A525 to Denbigh.
➤ **In Denbigh,** join A543 to Pentrefoelas.
➤ **At A5,** turn right to Betws-y-Coed.
➤ **In Capel Curig,** turn left on A4086 to Caernarfon.
➤ **Keep going straight** as this road becomes A498 to Porthmadog.

➤ **In Beddgelert,** turn left (across the bridge) to stay on A498 to Porthmadog.
➤ **Look out:** don't miss the left turn, after 1½ miles, for A4085 to Penrhyndeudraeth.
➤ **In Garreg,** turn left on the B4410 to Llanfrothen.
➤ **At A487,** turn left to Dolgellau.
➤ **Look out:** after 5 miles take the easy-to-miss left turn for A4212 to Bala.

➤ **In Bala,** go straight over the staggered crossroads on B4391 to Llangynog.
➤ **After Pen-y-bont-fawr,** turn left on B4396 to Llangedwyn. When this road meets A495, turn left again.
➤ **At A483,** turn left towards Oswestry.
➤ **At A5 roundabout,** carry on straight, joining A5 to North Wales.

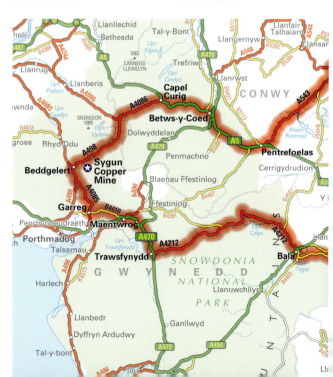

WHAT TO VISIT

Sygun Copper Mine
Learn about Welsh industrial heritage and try panning for gold at this award-winning family attraction in the Snowdonia National Park.
www.syguncoppermine.co.uk

TOUR (27) Wrexham Loop

ROUTE TYPE Loop	DISTANCE 190 miles

➤ **At the next roundabout,** turn right on A495 to Whitchurch.

➤ **Look out:** don't miss the left turn to stay on A495 to Whitchurch, a mile after roundabout in Ellesmere town centre.

➤ **At A525,** turn left to Wrexham.

➤ **Look out:** after 3 miles, turn left on A539 to Hanmer.

➤ **In Overton,** join A528 to Wrexham.

➤ **After 2 miles,** turn left on A539 to Llangollen.

➤ **In Llangollen,** carry straight on along A542 to the famous Horseshoe Pass.

➤ **At the roundabout,** turn right on A5104 to Chester.

➤ **At the traffic lights,** turn right on A525 to Wrexham, where the route ends.

Stopping off at the Ponderosa Cafe on the Horseshoe Pass

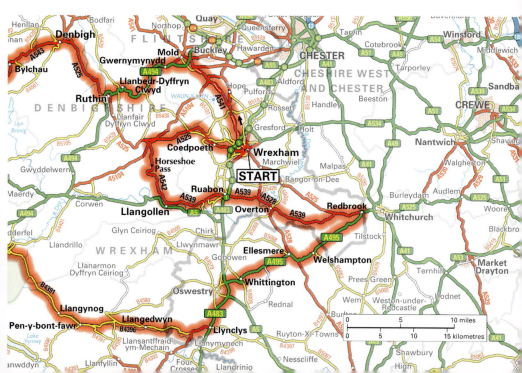

TOUR 28 Wales High-Mile Tour Day 1

DAY 1 MORNING

THIS TOUR crams the maximum possible number of the best roads in Wales into three long days. It places the emphasis on riding, not stopping for tea or photo opportunities. Mileages on this tour favour the solo rider, rather than the pillion couple.

The route starts with the fabulous run down the A466 on the England/Wales border, before heading inland, to the riding paradise of the Brecon Beacons. A little dual carriageway along the Heads of the Valleys covers the ground before the route cuts through the National Park to the recommended lunch stop in Brecon.

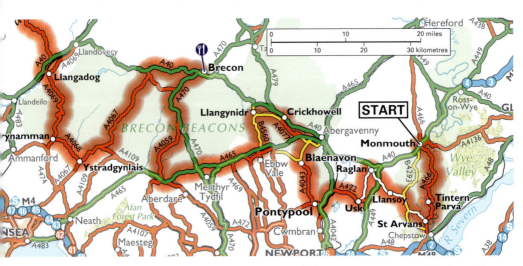

FROM Monmouth
TO Brecon
VIA Tintern Parva, Pontypool, Crickhowell and Merthyr Tydfil
DISTANCE 100 miles
RIDING TIME 3 hours

Route Description

➤ **Leave Monmouth** on A466 to Chepstow.
➤ **In St Arvans,** turn right to Devauden (where the road becomes B4293).
➤ **Look out:** don't miss the left turn 1½ miles outside Devauden, towards Llansoy. Take this road to Raglan.
➤ **At A40 roundabout** in Raglan, take the first exit for the minor road to Gwehelog. Stay on it all the way to A472, turning right to Usk.
➤ **Follow A472** through Usk to A4042.
➤ **At A4042** turn left towards Pontypool. At third roundabout, turn right to continue on A472 to Pontypool.
➤ **At the next rbt,** turn right on A4043 to Pontypool.
➤ **In Blaenavon,** turn right on B4246 to Abergavenny.
➤ **At the T-junction** turn left to Govilon, then go straight across A465 rbt on A4077 to Crickhowell.
➤ **Look out:** don't miss the right turn, by the pub, to stay on A4077 to Crickhowell.

➤ **At Legar traffic lights** (by old bridge) go straight on the minor road towards Talybont-on-Usk.
➤ **Look out:** about 3 miles past the traffic lights take the very easily missed left turn for B4560 to Garnlydan. If you get to Llangynidr, you've missed the turn.
➤ **In Garnlydan,** join the Heads of the Valleys Road – A465. Stay on this towards Merthyr Tydfil and then Neath, until you pick up A4059 to Brecon.
➤ **Turn left** on A470 to Brecon, where the morning's route ends. There are several good cafes in the town for lunch.

ROUTE TYPE Tour	**DISTANCE** 100 miles morning	130 miles afternoon

DAY 1 AFTERNOON

THE AFTERNOON leg of the first day starts with more of the magical Beacons roads, culminating in the rollercoaster Black Mountain road, the A4069 – a favourite location for magazine road tests and *Top Gear* TV shoots. From there the ride climbs towards Lampeter and the quiet roads to Cardigan, on the coast.

While the day's end is by the sea, it's not in Cardigan. The route heads back inland, across the Preseli Mountains – it's a landscape rich in standing stones, but there's little time to stand about and admire them on this tour. There's still some quality riding to be done to reach the end of the route in the picture-postcard walled seaside town of Tenby.

FROM Brecon
TO Tenby
VIA Ystradgynlais, Newcastle Emlyn, Cardigan and Narberth
DISTANCE 130 miles
RIDING TIME 4 hours

Route Description
➤ **From Brecon,** take A40 towards Llandovery.
➤ **After 7 miles,** turn left on A4067 to Swansea.
➤ **Turn right at double-rbt** in Ystradgynlais, then turn right at the next roundabout on A4068 to Brynamman.
➤ **At the mini-roundabout** in Brynamman, turn right on A4069 to Llangadog.
➤ **Go straight through** Llangadog. Cross the railway and turn right at the rbt on A40 towards Llandovery.
➤ **After 2 miles,** turn left on A482 to Lampeter.
➤ **At the mini-roundabout** in Lampeter town centre, go straight – taking A475 to Newcastle Emlyn.

➤ **From Newcastle Emlyn,** take A484 to Cardigan.
➤ **At A487 roundabout,** turn left to Fishguard.
➤ **Look out:** don't miss the left turn, by the garage on the far side of Eglwyswrw, for B4329 to Haverfordwest.
➤ **After 7 miles,** turn left on B4313 to Narberth (go left then right when crossing the A40).
➤ **From Narberth,** take A478 to Tenby, where the day's route ends.

TOUR (28) Wales High-Mile Tour Day 2

DAY 2 MORNING

FROM THE tiny port town of Tenby to the larger seaside resort of Aberystwyth, there's not much sea to be seen on this morning's ride. Heading through the heart of South Wales and into Mid-Wales, it's a route built around magnificent roads through splendidly wooded hills, from the A483 to the A44. There are plenty of places to eat in Aberystwyth, but it's worth going right into the centre of town, as bikes often throng the sea-front promenade at weekends.

Llandovery market square

FROM Tenby
TO Aberystwyth
VIA Carmarthern, Llandovery and Rhayader
DISTANCE 120 miles
RIDING TIME 3 hours

Route Description
➤ **Leave Tenby** on A478 towards Narberth.
➤ **At A477 roundabout,** turn right to reach the village of St Clears.

➤ **Join A40** towards Carmarthen. Stay on A40 all the way to Llandovery.
➤ **In Llandovery,** cross the railway tracks and turn left on A483 to Builth Wells.
➤ **In Beulah turn left** on B4358 to Newbridge on Wye.
➤ **In Newbridge,** turn left on A470 to Rhayader.
➤ **At the Llangurig roundabout,** turn left on A44 to Aberystwyth, where the morning's route ends.

ROUTE TYPE Tour	**DISTANCE** 120 miles morning	180 miles afternoon

DAY 2 AFTERNOON

READY FOR a mindblowing ride? The afternoon route is long but so rewarding. From Aberystwyth it heads up the coast to ride the Machynlleth loop, out around the coast, before heading back inland. If short of time, you could drop the lap of Lake Vyrnwy – but it really is beautiful. From Vyrnwy the route heads to Bala and into Snowdonia, passing through the lovely village of Beddgelert on the way to the day's final destination, Caernarfon.

FROM Aberystwyth
TO Caernarfon
VIA Dolgellau, Aberdyfi, Lake Vyrnwy and Beddgelert
DISTANCE 180 miles
RIDING TIME 5 hours

Route Description

➤ **Leave Aberystwyth** on A487 to Machynlleth and then Dolgellau.
➤ **At A470 T-junction,** turn left towards Dolgellau.
➤ **After 4 miles,** turn left on A493 to Tywyn.
➤ **In Tywyn,** turn left to stay on A493 to Aberdyfi.
➤ **At A487 junction,** turn right (across the bridge) to return to Machynlleth.
➤ **By the clocktower** in Machynlleth, turn left on A489 to Newtown.
➤ **At the roundabout** in Cemmaes Road, turn left on A470 to Dolgellau.

➤ **In Mallwyd,** turn right at the roundabout on A458 to Welshpool.
➤ **After 10 miles** turn left on B4395 to Llanfyllin.
➤ **Look out:** after 7 miles take the easy-to-miss, very tight left turn for B4393 to Llanwddyn and Lake Vyrnwy.
➤ **It's worth following** signs to do a lap of the beautiful Lake Vyrnwy, before returning to Dafarn Newydd to take B4396 to Pen-y-bont-fawr.
➤ **In Pen-y-bont-fawr** turn left on the B4391 to Bala.
➤ **Go straight over** the staggered crossroads in Bala, on A4212 to Trawsfynydd.

➤ **After 10 miles,** turn right on B4391 to Ffestiniog.
➤ **At A470,** turn right on A470 to Betws-y-coed.
➤ **In Blaenau Ffestiniog,** turn left at the roundabout on A496 to Porthmadog.
➤ **At A487 T-junction,** turn right to Porthmadog.
➤ **After half a mile,** turn right on B4410 to Rhyd.
➤ **In Garreg,** turn right on A4085 to Beddgelert.
➤ **At A498 T-junction,** turn right to Beddgelert.
➤ **In Beddgelert,** cross the bridge and follow the road to the left as it becomes A4085. Stay on this road to Caernarfon.

TOUR (28) Wales High-Mile Tour Day 3

DAY 3 MORNING

THE FINAL day of the high-mile tour starts with one of the highlights of riding in Wales: the Pass of Llanberis, in the shadow of Mount Snowdon. But there's no time for a trip to the top of the mountain on the railway, as there are more brilliant roads to be ridden on the way to the Horseshoe Pass. Then the ride loops into England briefly, stopping for lunch in the beautiful market town of Oswestry.

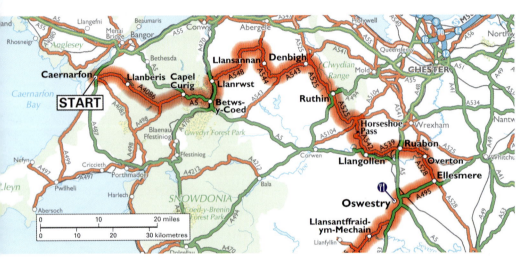

FROM Caernarfon
TO Oswestry
VIA Llanberis, Llanrwst and Llangollen
DISTANCE 100 miles
RIDING TIME 3 hours

Route Description

➤ **Leave Caernarfon** on A4086 to Llanberis. Stay on this road past Snowdon all the way to Capel Curig.
➤ **At A5 T-junction,** turn right to Betws-y-Coed.
➤ **In Betws-y-Coed,** cross the bridge and turn left on A470 to Llandudno.
➤ **In Llanrwst,** turn right on A548 to Abergele.
➤ **After 12 miles,** turn right on A544 to Llansannan.

➤ **At A543 T-junction,** turn left to Denbigh.
➤ **From Denbigh,** take A525 to Ruthin.
➤ **In Ruthin,** take A525 to Wrexham.
➤ **After 7 miles,** turn right on A542 to Llangollen.
➤ **Stay on this road** through Llangollen. It soon becomes A539 to Ruabon.

➤ **Continue on A539** through Ruabon.
➤ **In Overton,** turn right on A528 to Ellesmere.
➤ **From Ellesmere,** take A495 to Oswestry, where the morning's route ends.

Through the Pass of Llanberis

| ROUTE TYPE Tour | DISTANCE 100 miles morning | 125 miles afternoon |

DAY 3 AFTERNOON

AFTER LUNCH IN Oswestry it's back into Wales without delay, heading for one of the absolute highlights of the trip. The A483 from Newtown to Crossgates is a truly sublime road – just watch out for a couple of deceptive, tightening bends. If you need a drink, there's a popular biking café by the garage when turning left on the A44 in Crossgates. The riding continues to dazzle on the minor roads to Brecon, from where the larger but no less enjoyable A40 leads to Abergavenny. In dual-carriageway form, this road leads back to Monmouth where the tour finishes.

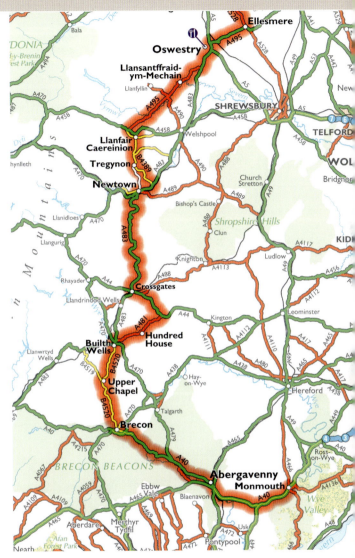

FROM Oswestry
TO Monmouth
VIA Newton, Hundred House and Brecon
DISTANCE 125 miles
RIDING TIME 3.5 hours

Route Description

➤ **From Oswestry,** take A483 towards Welshpool.
➤ **Look out:** after a few miles, turn right on A495 to Llansantffraid-ym-Mechain.
➤ **Don't miss** the turning, 2 miles later, to stay on A495.
➤ **At A458 junction,** turn left to Welshpool.
➤ **In Llanfair Caereinion,** turn right then left by church on B4389 to Newtown. At junction with B4390, turn right.

Two miles later, in Tregynon, turn left to stay on B4389.
➤ **At A483 T-junction,** turn right to Newtown.
➤ **At the lights in Newtown,** turn left to stay on A483 to Llandrindod Wells.
➤ **At the rbt in Crossgates,** turn left on A44 to Leominster.

➤ **After 7 miles,** turn right on A481 to Hundred House.
➤ **Go into Builth Wells,** cross the river and turn right. At the end of the high street turn left to Upper Chapel on B4520.
➤ **From Brecon,** join A40 back to Monmouth.

TOUR 29 Wales Relaxed Tour Day 1

DAY 1 MORNING

IN CONTRAST to the high-mile tour, which delivers lots of brilliant corners but doesn't allow time for visiting attractions, long lunches or stopping to smell the flowers, our two-day low-mile tour is designed to give a relaxed weekend on the best roads in Wales. As it links three of the towns where our daytrips start, it's easily expanded to be come a full tour, simply by stopping two nights in each destination to ride those trips as well.

The first day starts with the sensational Black Mountain road, followed by our favourite stretch of the A40, through the wooded twists around the hamlet of Halfway. From Brecon it climbs up to the million-dollar panorama of the Garth viewpoint, before swinging back to Llandovery on the spectacular A483.

FROM Ystradgynlais
TO Llandovery
VIA Llangadog, Brecon and Garth
DISTANCE 80 miles
RIDING TIME 2.5 hours

Route Description

➤ **Leave Ystradglynais** on the A4068 to the village of Brynamman.

➤ **At the mini-roundabout** in Brynamman, turn right on A4069 to Llangadog.

➤ **In Llangadog,** turn right to stay on A4069 to Llandovery.

➤ **In Llandovery,** carry on straight (making a right turn) on A40 to Brecon.

➤ **At the roundabout,** turn left into Brecon (signed for B4601 to Llanfaes).

➤ **At the third set** of traffic lights (next to the Cotswold camping shop) turn left on B4520 to Upper Chapel.

➤ **Look out:** don't miss the left turn for B4519 to Garth, 9 miles outside Brecon.

➤ **In Garth,** turn left on A483 to Llandovery, where the morning route ends. Note: turn left at the T-junction in Llandovery to get to the popular West End Café.

New Quay (afternoon)

ROUTE TYPE Tour	**DISTANCE** 80 miles morning	90 miles afternoon

DAY 1 AFTERNOON

FROM LLANDOVERY to the coast, we have some fabulous riding. We start on quiet roads, but they get quieter heading out from Lampeter, through Newcastle Emlyn to Cardigan.

Cardigan's a nice town to explore, but if that's too early for a break, the seaside village of New Quay is also a great place for a coffee before the final run through Aberaeron, to the day's destination in Aberystwyth.

FROM Llandovery
TO Aberystwyth
VIA Lampeter, Cardigan and New Quay
DISTANCE 90 miles
RIDING TIME 3 hours

Route Description

➤ **Leave Llandovery** on A40, towards Llandeilo (from the town centre, go back towards A483 junction, but carry straight on past the garage, across the railway track).

➤ **In Llanwrda,** turn right on A482 to Lampeter.

➤ **Carry on straight ahead** at the mini-roundabout in the centre of Lampeter, on A475 to Newcastle Emlyn.

➤ **In Newcastle Emlyn,** turn right on A484 and head towards Cardigan.

➤ **At roundabout with A487,** turn right to Aberystwyth.

➤ **After 15 miles,** turn right on A486 to New Quay.

➤ **Follow the road** through New Quay (or stop for coffee), as it loops around becoming B4342 to Llanarth.

➤ **Turn left** on A487 and stay on this road all the way to Aberystwyth, where the day's route ends.

TOUR ㉙ Wales Relaxed Tour Day 2

DAY 2 MORNING

DON'T HURRY away from Aberystwyth in the morning: there may be a little rush-hour traffic, but once that's died down you'll probably have the A44 to yourself. Get a good run down that road and you'll be asking yourself if that's the best one you've ridden so far… at least until you get to Crossgates.

It might be worth crossing the over the roundabout at Crossgates to get a strong coffee, just to steady yourself before taking the epic A483 to Newtown. You could also get an early lunch in Newtown but (especially if you stopped in Crossgates) we would rather keep going, taking the ultra-quiet B4389 to Llanfair Caereinion, which is our preferred lunch stop.

FROM Aberystwyth
TO Lanfair Caereinion
VIA Llangurig, Crossgates and Newtown
DISTANCE 80 miles
RIDING TIME 2 hours

Route Description

➤ **Leave Aberystwyth** on A44 and ride on towards Llangurig.

➤ **At the Llangurig roundabout,** turn right on A470 to Rhayader.

➤ **In Rhayader,** turn left on A44 to Leominster.

➤ **At the mini-roundabout** in Crossgates, turn left on A483 to Newtown.

➤ **Turn right** at the traffic lights in Newtown, on A483 towards Welshpool.

➤ **After 3 miles,** turn left on B4389 to Llanfair Caereinion. Turn right at the T-junction in Tregynon to stay on this road.

➤ **Look out:** take the easily missed left turn in New Mills to stay on B4389 all the way into the small town of Llanfair Caereinion, where the morning's route ends.

TOUR 29 Wales Relaxed Tour Day 2

ROUTE TYPE Tour	DISTANCE 80 miles morning	95 miles afternoon

DAY 2 AFTERNOON

THE AFTERNOON ride is very relaxed – lovely, flowing roads with spectacular views. If you do want to extend it, the scenic coastal loop through Barmouth and Harlech is easily added from Dolgellau. But for a more easy-going day, stick with this route, taking the seven-mile straight to Trawsfynydd.

The A4212 from Trawsfynydd to Bala is a real classic, flying along a valley floor before climbing to swoop across the moors and around Llyn Celyn. From there we head on flowing roads to Llangollen and the highlight of the afternoon ride, the Horseshoe Pass. It's only a gentle canter from there to Wrexham, the largest town in north Wales, where the day's ride ends.

FROM Llanfair Caereinion
TO Wrexham
VIA Dolgellau, Trawsfynydd and Llangollen
DISTANCE 95 miles
RIDING TIME 2.5 hours

Route Description

➤ **From Llanfair Caereinion** town centre, cross the river and take A458 to Dolgellau.

➤ **At the Mallwyd,** turn right on A470 to Dolgellau. Stay on this road for 23 miles.

➤ **In Trawsfynydd,** turn right on A4212 to Bala.

➤ **In Bala,** turn left on A494 to Llangollen.

➤ **At the traffic lights,** turn right on A5 to Llangollen.

➤ **Look out:** after 10 miles take the tight left turn (by a black-and-white timber-frame house)

on B5130 to Horseshoe Pass. It's also signed for Ruthin (A542).

➤ **Turn left** on A452, Horseshoe Pass.

➤ **At the roundabout,** turn right on A5104 to Wrexham and Chester.

➤ **At the traffic lights,** turn right to take A525 into Wrexham, where the day's route and the tour ends.

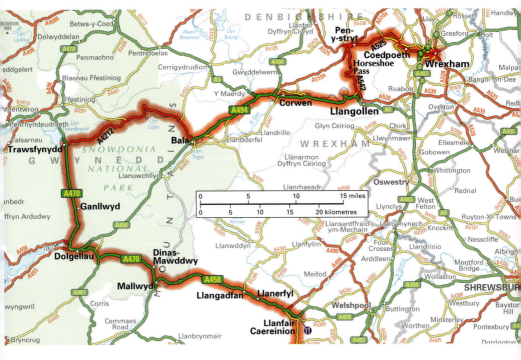

Scotland

Scotland is riding heaven. From its highest peaks to its wildest shores, this is a beautiful country best appreciated on two wheels. With romantic castles, peaceful lochs and sleepy islands to visit along the way, our tours cover every corner of Scotland so you can discover it all for yourself.

TOUR (30) Dundee Loop

SPECTACULAR SCENERY, low levels of traffic, superbly twisty roads – often with good surfaces… This route from *RiDE* magazine is close to heaven. Some of it's close to the cities, too, with main roads making it easily accessible for travellers from the rest of the UK.

The route starts in Dundee – a great place to visit, with loads of historic attractions. But we're here for the riding, which gets better the further north you go, into the Cairngorms. The day's ride starts out on a popular route through Glen Shee, before peeling off to Alford and Banchory. Through the lower hills, you're even more likely to have the roads entirely to yourself.

WHAT TO VISIT

Balmoral Castle

Queen Victoria and Prince Albert first leased the castle in 1848. Albert bought it four years later and completed a new castle by 1856. It is still the Royal Family's Highland residence today. Explore the grounds, gardens and trails between April and July.
www.balmoralcastle.com

START/FINISH Dundee
VIA Glenshee, Alford and Fettercairn
DISTANCE 185 miles
RIDING TIME 5 hours

Route description

➤ **Leave Dundee** on A90, towards Forfar and Aberdeen.
➤ **After 5 miles** of dual carriageway, turn left on A928 towards Kirriemuir and Glamis Castle.
➤ **At A94,** turn left towards Coupar Angus.
➤ **After about 7 miles,** you'll pass through Meigle; turn right onto B954 to Alyth.
➤ **At A926 roundabout,** turn left to Blairgowrie.
➤ **In Blairgowrie,** turn right on A93 to Bridge of Cally – see

brown signs for the Ski Centre for a break.
➤ **For a coffee,** stop at the Glen Shee Ski Centre, which has the only cafe for miles around.
➤ **Continue along A93,** through Braemar and towards Ballater (perhaps stop at Balmoral Castle).
➤ **Look out:** take the easy-to-miss left turn for A939 to Tomintoul 6 miles after Balmoral Castle.
➤ **At the T-junction** 10 miles later, turn right on A944 to Alford (it becomes A97).
➤ **At the next T-junction,** turn right on A944 to Alford and Aberdeen. We recommend stopping for lunch in Alford.
➤ **Leave Alford** the way you came in, on A944. After half a mile, turn left on A980 to Banchory.
➤ **After 7 miles,** at B9119, go right then left across staggered x-roads to stay on A980.

➤ **In Lumphanan,** turn left at the T-junction, still on A90.
➤ **In Torphins,** turn right on B993 towards Kincardine O'Neil.
➤ **At T-junction** with A93, turn left towards Aberdeen.
➤ **At traffic lights** in Banchory, turn right on B974 to Fettercairn.
➤ **Look out:** turn left in Strachan to stay on B974.
➤ **Leave Fettercairn** on B966 to Edzell, passing under A90 into Brechin.
➤ **At mini-roundabout,** turn left and cross Brechin following signs for A933 to Arbroath (turn right after a tight left).
➤ **8 miles outside Brechin,** turn right on B961 to Redford.
➤ Go straight at the staggered crossroads with B9218, staying on B961 towards Newbigging.
➤ **Look out:** leaving Newbigging, turn right on B961 to Kingennie, following this road back to Dundee.

TOUR 30 Dundee Loop

ROUTE TYPE Loop | **DISTANCE** 185 miles

TOUR (31) Oban Loop

I'M NOT often given to moments of guilt about riding bikes – it's a pleasure, but not a guilty one. But I had a second's pause as I reached for my crash helmet after stopping for an ice cream at Inverary. It was so quiet, so peaceful, the mirror-shined waters of Loch Fyne reflecting the perfect blue sky, the only sounds an occasional melody of birdsong. And I was about to fire up a noisy motorbike…

The moment passed and I carried on, going from quiet roads to silent ones, listening to the birds singing again while waiting for the Bute ferry. After a quick circuit of the island, I got back on the ferry to ride more quiet roads through the unspoilt scenery around Loch Eck. And if I was the only vehicle disturbing the sounds of nature, I was fine with that. The riding here is simply too good to resist – and there's no need to feel guilty about enjoying it.

START/FINISH Oban
VIA Lochgilphead, Rothesay, Inveraray and Lochawe
DISTANCE 225 miles
RIDING TIME 7 hours

Route Description
➤ **Leave Oban** on A816 towards Campbeltown.

➤ **At the mini-roundabout,** turn left on A83 to go into Lochgilphead. Stay on this road for 35 miles, through Inveraray and round Loch Fyne.
➤ **Look out:** don't miss the right turn for A815 to Dunoon and the Isle of Bute ferry.
➤ **After nearly 10 miles,** turn right on A886 to Colintraive and the Isle of Bute ferry. Stay on this road to take the ferry to Rhubodach on Bute, which runs twice an hour (for timetable, see www.calmac.co.uk).
➤ **Get off the ferry,** turn left and then ride 6 miles on A886 towards Bannatyne.
➤ **Turn right on A844** to Ettrick Bay. On reaching a T-junction, turn left to stay on A844 – now signed for Rothesay.
➤ **Continue through Rothesay** to take A886 back to Rhubodach and take the ferry back to the mainland.
➤ **From Colintraive,** ride 5 miles back along A886, then turn right on B836 to Sandbank.
➤ **Turn left on A815** towards Glasgow and Kilmu, passing Loch Eck and the A886, all the way to A83.
➤ **Turn left** at A83, retracing your tyre tracks to Inveraray.
➤ **Turn right** by Inveraray Castle, on A819 to Oban.
➤ **At A85 junction,** turn left to return to Oban, where the route ends.

WHAT TO VISIT

Inveraray Castle
This magnificent castle is the ancestral home of the Duke of Argyll and one of the country's finest stately homes. Most of what you see today was planned by the 3rd Duke, including the township and the beautiful surrounding parkland. The State Dining Room and the Tapestry Room are highlights.
www.inveraray-castle.com

TOUR ㉛ Oban Loop

ROUTE TYPE Loop | **DISTANCE** 225 miles

TOUR (32) Falkirk Loch Loop

THERE'S SO much great riding in Scotland and much of it is pretty famous – from Glen Coe and the road to Skye to the Bealach na Ba pass to Applecross. But there's more to see and even more great roads to ride.

Our route starts and ends in Falkirk. It's a charming town on the tourist trail into Scotland and makes a good base if you don't want to go into the cities of Edinburgh, Glasgow or Stirling. This route is all about the glorious shores of the lochs. However, it's a full day's ride, especially if you include the optional loop all the way out to Rannoch Station.

VIA: Loch Katrine, Kinloch Rannoch and Dunkeld
START/FINISH: Falkirk
DISTANCE: 218 miles
RIDING TIME: 6.5–7 hours

Route Description

➤ **Leave Falkirk on A883,** skirting Denny town centre to pick up B818 to Fintry.

➤ **At B822 T-junction,** turn right, still heading to Fintry. Carry straight on as road becomes B818 again.

➤ **In Kilearn,** turn right, in front of the church, on B834.

➤ **At A81 roundabout,** turn right to Aberfoyle.

➤ **At Rob Roy roundabout,** turn left on the A821 (Trossachs Trail) to Stronachlachar.

➤ **Look out:** turn right at the end of Aberfoyle high street to stay on A821 over Duke's Pass.

➤ **A good coffee stop** is at Loch Katrine: turn left when the road bends sharply right beside Loch Achray. Then return and continue along A821.

➤ **At A84,** turn left to Crianlarich. The road becomes the A85 at Lochearnhead.

➤ **Turn right on A827** to Killin, 5 miles after Lochearnhead.

➤ **In Kenmore,** turn left on the minor road to Kinloch Rannoch.

➤ **At the B846 T-junction,** turn left, still towards Kinloch Rannoch.

➤ **Look out:** after 4 miles take the easily missed left turn for Schiehallion Road.

➤ **In Kinloch Rannoch,** turn left for optional loop to Rannoch Moor. After visiting it, backtrack to this point.

➤ **Alternatively,** just turn right on B846 to Pitlochry. We recommend getting lunch in Kinloch Rannoch.

➤ **Leave Kinloch Rannoch** on B846 to Pitlochry.

➤ **At Tummel Bridge,** bear left on B8019, still for Pitlochry.

➤ **At the next T-junction,** turn right, following signs for A924.

➤ **In Pitlochry,** turn left on A924 to Blairgowrie.

➤ **At Bridge of Cally,** turn right on A93 to Blairgowrie.

➤ **In Blairgowrie,** cross the river and bear right on at the traffic lights on the A923 to Dunkeld.

➤ **If you need** a coffee stop, we'd recommend Palmerston's on Dunkeld High Street.

➤ **At A9,** turn right then immediately left on A822 to Crieff.

➤ **At A85 junction,** turn right to Crieff.

➤ **In Crieff** town centre, pick up A822 to Stirling.

➤ **Look out:** 5 miles outside Crieff take the easily missed left turn on A823 to Dunfermline. Cross A9 to stay on A823.

➤ **At A91 junction,** turn right then left again to stay on A823.

➤ **In Rumbling Bridge,** turn right on A977 to Kincardine Bridge.

➤ **Cross one roundabout,** then turn right on A876 to Falkirk.

➤ **Cross the river,** turn right at the roundabout and take the first slip road for A905 to return to Falkirk, where the route ends.

WHAT TO VISIT

Scottish Hydro Electric Visitor Centre
The visitor centre in Pitlochry features an exhibition showing how electricity is brought from the power station to the customer, and there is access to the turbine viewing gallery. The salmon-ladder viewing chamber allows you to see the fish as they travel upstream to their spawning ground.
www.scottish-hydro-centre.co.uk

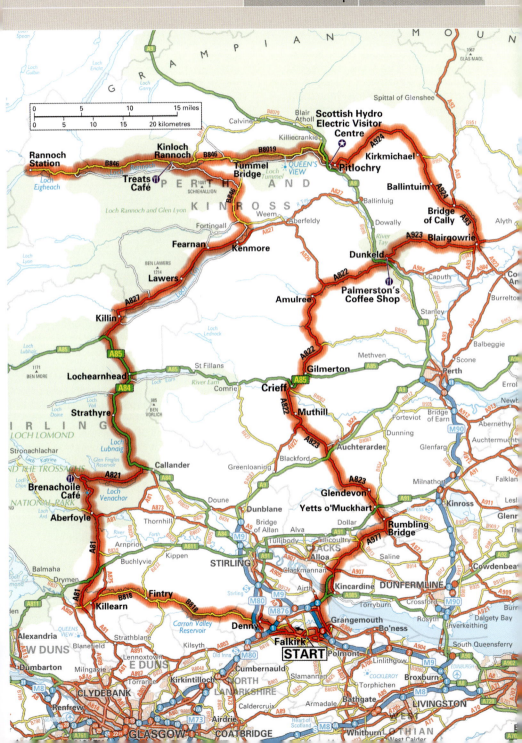

TOUR (33) Skye Loop

THE ISLE of Skye is one of the jewels of Scotland's West Coast – a ruggedly mountainous, atmospheric place that draws walkers, climbers and bikers throughout the summer. It's well set up to cater to visitors… but actually we'd stay on the mainland, in the welcoming, bike-friendly Strathcarron Hotel. Not only because the ride from Strathcarron to Skye is great, but also because you always pay a premium for staying on Skye itself.

This full-day's ride takes in not only all the main, well-known riding highlights and sights of Skye but also an extra destination – one recommended to us by Andrew, the landlord at Strathcarron. The road to Elgol may be a dead-end but it's perhaps the most scenic road on the island, a challenging ribbon of tarmac that gift-wraps a series of stunning panoramas, like a selection of impressive presents on Christmas morning.

Above: Across the Skye Bridge

START/FINISH Strathcarron
VIA Portree, Uig, Dunvegan and Elgol
DISTANCE 225 miles
RIDING TIME 6 hours

Route Description
➤ **From Strathcarron,** take A890 to Kyle of Lochalsh.
➤ **Turn right** on A87 to Kyle of Lochalsh.
➤ **Cross the Skye Bridge**.
➤ **Turn right** at the roundabout, staying on A87 to Portree.
➤ **In Portree,** bear right through the town centre and take A855 to Staffin. Take this road all the way to the village of Uig.
➤ **From Uig,** continue on A87 back towards Portree.
➤ **After about 10 miles,** turn right on A850 to Dunvegan.

➤ **In Dunvegan,** turn left to ride along the shore of the loch on A863.
➤ **To visit the Talisker distillery,** turn right after about 18 miles, on B8009 to Carbost (the distillery is well signposted).
➤ **After the detour to Carbost,** return to A863 and turn right, continuing to Sligachan.
➤ **At A87,** turn right to return to Broadford.
➤ **In Broadford,** take the right turn just before the petrol station, the B8083 to Elgol.
➤ **This 15-mile road** might just be the highlight of a trip to Skye – it's narrow, challenging and amazingly scenic. It's also a dead end – so after drinking in the views from Elgol harbour, return to Broadford.

➤ **In Broadford,** turn right on the A87 to Kyle of Lochalsh.
➤ **About 7 miles** after passing the Skye Bridge, turn left on A890 to Gairloch. Return to Strathcarron to end the route.

WHAT TO VISIT

Talisker Distillery
A working distillery on the Minginish Peninsula in the village of Carbost with a long history (it's the oldest on Skye) with great views of the Cuillins. Tours and tastings are available, though when riding our best advice is to take a sample home with you.
www.malts.com/talisker

| ROUTE TYPE Loop | DISTANCE 225 miles |

TOUR 34 Applecross Loop

SOMETIMES, IT'S all about the weather. The Pass of the Cattle – also known as the Bealach na Ba – clambers over the mountains of the Applecross peninsula, rough and narrow and poorly surfaced yet utterly mesmerizing. Even in the rain.

But on a day like this, with the sun high in a cloudless sky and a gentle breeze to keep temperatures moderate rather than sweltering... On a day like this, it's one of the best places in the world to ride a bike and it's as rewarding as any Alpine pass, and the views over the sea to Skye are awe-inspiring.

And then there's the coastal road from Applecross to Shieldag which – whisper it – might actually be better than Bealach na Ba. After hugging the coast, our route heads to Ullapool before backtracking to Strathcarron. It's a superb ride at any time of year, but on a summer's day it's unbeatable.

START/FINISH Strathcarron
VIA Applecross, Kinlochewe, Ullapool and Achnasheen
DISTANCE 200 miles
RIDING TIME 6 hours

Route Description

➤ **From Strathcarron,** take A890 towards Gairloch.
➤ **At the T-junction,** turn left on A896 to Lochcarron.

➤ **After 9 miles,** turn left on the road to Applecross, Bealach na Ba. This is the famous – and challenging – Pass of the Cattle.
➤ **In Applecross,** turn right to Shieldaig.
➤ **After 24 amazing miles,** turn left at the T-junction, rejoining A896 to Shieldaig. Stay on this road all the way to Kinlochewe.

➤ **In Kinlochewe,** turn left to Gairloch on A832. Stay on this road for about 60 miles.
➤ **At A835 junction,** turn left to Ullapool – where there's a petrol station and plenty of places to grab a snack.
➤ **From Ullapool,** return along A835 towards Inverness and Garve.
➤ **After about 30 miles,** turn right on A832 – again signed for Gairloch.
➤ **At the Achnasheen roundabout,** turn left on A890 to Lochcarron.
➤ **After 18 miles,** turn left on A890 to return to Strathcarron, where the route ends.

WHAT TO VISIT

Applecross Walled Garden
Sitting in the heart of the Applecross Estate, the garden dates from 1675 and has been restored since 2001. Discover herbaceous borders, fruit trees, raised vegetable beds and a really good café.
www.applecrossgarden.co.uk

Twists and turns near Applecross

TOUR ㉞ Applecross Loop

| ROUTE TYPE Loop | DISTANCE 200 miles |

TOUR (35) Inverness Loop

IF YOU'VE never been to the Highlands, there are some sights you need to see. Loch Ness is one, Eilean Donan – the castle that featured in the movie *Highlander* – is another. But for bikers, the real must-see is the A87 from Invergarry to Skye, the Road to the Isles.

This balloon route from Inverness, the capital of the Highlands, covers these bases but it's no mere box-ticking exercise. This is a sublime ride, with all kinds of roads – from the relaxed cruise along the A82, keeping one eye on the waters to spot Nessie, to the majestic rollercoaster of the A87, and the narrow and wild A896 from Lochcarron to Kinlochewe. It's everything that's great about riding in the Highlands condensed into 200 memorable miles.

START/FINISH Inverness
VIA Fort Augustus, Strathcarron, Kinlochewe and Muir of Ord
DISTANCE 200 miles
RIDING TIME 5 hours

Route Description

➤ **Leave Inverness** on A862 to Beauly.
➤ **Look out:** after about eight miles take the easily missed left turn on A833 to Kiltarlity and Drumnadrochit.
➤ **Turn left** on A831 to Drumnadrochit.
➤ **In Drumnadrochit,** turn right on A82 towards Fort William. Stay on it all the way along Loch Ness, passing through Fort Augustus.
➤ **After about 25 miles,** in Invergarry, turn right on A87 to Kyle of Lochalsh. When it reaches a T-junction, turn left to stay on A87 towards the Skye Bridge.
➤ **After 30 miles,** turn right on A890 to Lochcarron.
➤ **Cross the railway** line at Strathcarron and, a mile later, turn left on A896 to Lochcarron. If you're low on petrol, top up in Lochcarron.
➤ **Stay on A896** all the way through Shieldaig to Kinlochewe.

Urquhart Castle overlooking Loch Ness

➤ **If you need fuel,** turn left in Kinlochewe for the petrol station (the last one for miles). Otherwise, turn right on A832 to Achnasheen.
➤ **Go straight over** the Achnasheen roundabout, on A832 to Inverness.
➤ **At A835 T-junction,** turn right towards Inverness.
➤ **At the large roundabout,** turn right on A862 to Maryburgh. Stay on this road through Muir of Ord to Beauly – and then all the way back to Inverness, where this route ends.

WHAT TO VISIT

Urquhart Castle
You may spot Nessie from Urquhart's tower house – it affords spectacular views over the famous loch.
www.historic-scotland. gov.uk

TOUR (36) Dornoch Loop

WHEN WE stopped to take a few snaps beside the blue waters of Loch Eriboll, I could tell the lads were enjoying themselves. Crash helmets came off to reveal huge grins. None of them had ridden in the far north of Scotland before – and they simply couldn't believe how good the roads were.

"Just wait," I promised them. "It just gets better and better."

Every year I organize a trip for my mates and our first foray to the Highlands formed the basis of this route. Most of the roads are wide and sweeping, though a few are more challenging. They all have two things in common: spectacular views and little traffic. That means, whoever you ride them with, you're always guaranteed to enjoy the journey.

Rush hour on the scenic A838 country coast road

START/FINISH Dornoch
VIA Helmsdale, Thurso, Scourie and Bonar Bridge
DISTANCE 230 miles
RIDING TIME 6 hours

Route Description
➤ **Leave Dornoch** on B9168.
➤ **At A9,** turn right to Thurso.
➤ **In Latheron,** turn left to stay on A9 to Thurso. At the junction with A882, turn left again.
➤ **Follow A9** through Thurso town centre, towards the ferry, but then carry straight on along A836 to Tongue.

➤ **In Tongue,** keep going straight as the road becomes A838 to Durness.
➤ **You're on this road** for 50 miles – and still need to keep going straight at Laxford Bridge, where it becomes A894 to Scourie.
➤ **Keep going** on A894, over the curving Kylesku Bridge and all the way to Loch Assynt.
➤ **Turn left** on A837 to Ullapool. Stay on this road all the way to A836.
➤ **At the T-junction,** turn right to Bonar Bridge on A836.

➤ **Turn left** in Bonar Bridge, on A949 to Spinningdale.
➤ **At A9 junction,** turn left to Thurso.
➤ **After 1 mile,** turn right on A949 to return to Dornoch, where the route ends.

WHAT TO VISIT

Smoo Cave
Located 1¼ miles east of Durness, Smoo Cave is set in limestone cliffs and is the most dramatic coastline cave in Britain.
www.smoocave.org

TOUR (37) Moffat Loop

IT'S EASY to think that motorcycling in Scotland means Glen Coe, Skye and the West Coast. That's a terrible error – there are some fantastic roads to be found just as soon as you cross the border from England. Roads like the A708 from Moffat to Selkirk, for example.

We've become regular visitors at Moffat's Buccleuch Arms Hotel over the years, as it's supremely bike friendly and makes the perfect base for exploring these spectacular roads. You'd have thought that any route starting with the A708 couldn't sustain that level of brilliance, but this ride delivers thrill after thrill – a full day of superb riding, without the bother of fighting your way round Glasgow and Edinburgh to get to the Highlands. Superb.

START/FINISH Moffat
VIA Selkirk, Biggar, Cumnock and Carronbridge
DISTANCE 170 miles
RIDING TIME 4.5 hours

Route Description

➤ **From Moffat** town centre, take A708 to Selkirk, past St Mary's Loch.

➤ **Coming into Selkirk,** turn left on A707 to Peebles.
➤ **At The Nest roundabout,** carry straight ahead on A72 to Peebles.
➤ **Go straight** through Peebles town centre, following signs for Glasgow (A72).
➤ **After 10 miles,** when A72 meets A701, turn left to stay on A72 towards Glasgow.

➤ **Look out:** don't miss the right turn, half a mile later, onto A721.
➤ **At A702 T-junction,** turn left towards Carlisle.
➤ **Ride through Biggar,** then turn right on A72 to Glasgow.
➤ **Turn right** on A73 to Lanark.
➤ **At the traffic lights** by the old stone bridge, go straight ahead on A70 to Ayr.

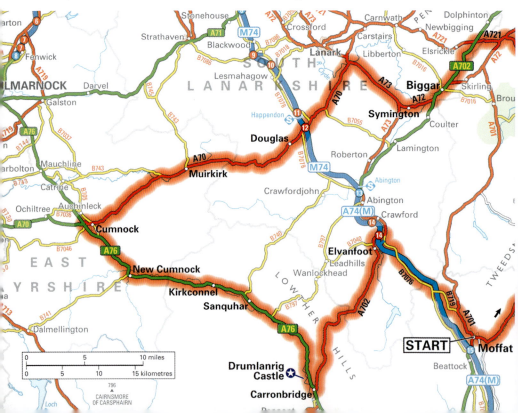

TOUR (37) Moffat Loop

ROUTE TYPE Loop	DISTANCE 170 miles

WHAT TO VISIT

Drumlanrig Castle

This unusual pink sandstone castle was built in the late 17th century in Renaissance style and is surrounded by a glorious country estate. It contains a collection of fine art, French furniture, as well as silver and relics of 'Bonnie' Prince Charlie. The old stable block has a craft centre and the grounds offer woodland walks. There's also a recently renovated Scottish Cycle Museum and shop.
www.drumlanrigcastle.co.uk

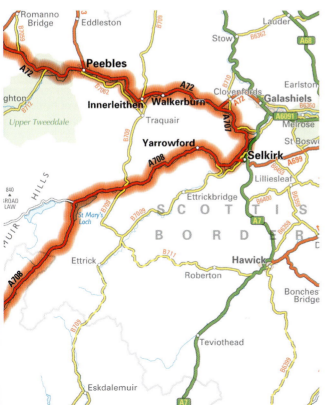

➤ **In Cumnock,** turn right at the mini-roundabout on A70.

➤ **At the large roundabout,** turn left on A76 to Dumfries.

➤ **Look out:** don't miss the very sharp left turn in Carronbridge, for A702 to Edinburgh.

➤ **At Elvanfoot,** go straight over the roundabout and pass under the motorway.

➤ **At the T-junction,** turn right on B7076 to Beattock.

➤ **After 7½ miles,** turn left on B719 to Greenhillstairs, passing over the motorway, then turning right.

➤ **At A701 T-junction,** turn right to return to Moffat, where the route ends.

TOUR (38) Scotland High-Mile Tour Day 1

DAY 1 MORNING

LIKE OUR other high-mile tours, this trip from *RiDE* magazine aims to cram three days with as many amazing roads as possible. Distances are daunting – it's not so suitable for touring couples, but solo riders prepared to put the hours will get three days of unforgettable riding.

The tour starts from Moffat and though it uses the Edinburgh ring road and the motorway across the Forth Road Bridge, the emphasis is on quality corners and quiet roads as it swoops past the Knockhill race track to our lunch stop in Crieff.

FROM Moffat
TO Crieff
VIA Selkirk, Galashiels and Dunfermline
DISTANCE 125 miles
RIDING TIME 3.5 hours

Route Description

➤ **Leave Moffat** on A708 to Selkirk.

➤ **From Selkirk,** take A7 to Galashiels and Edinburgh.

➤ **Join A720** City Bypass West towards Glasgow and the Forth Road Bridge. Keep following signs for the Forth Road Bridge (A90).

➤ **Cross the Firth of Forth** and join M90 North.

➤ **Leave M90** at Junction 2 on A823(M) to Dunfermline.

➤ **At the end** of the motorway, continue along A823 to Dunfermline.

➤ **Cross Dunfermline** following signs for A823 to Crieff.

➤ **At A977,** turn right. After 1 mile, turn left to continue on A823 still to Crieff.

➤ **At A91,** turn right then carry straight on to continue on A823 to Crieff.

➤ **At A822 junction,** turn right to Crieff, where the morning's route ends.

| ROUTE TYPE Tour | DISTANCE 125 miles morning | 150 miles afternoon |

DAY 1 AFTERNOON

FROM CRIEFF into the Cairngorms, the High-Mile Tour blasts through the ski resort areas of Glenshee and the Lecht. This means huge elevation changes, enormous vistas and mile after mile of thrilling, empty roads. It's important to keep a weather eye on your fuel consumption here – petrol stations are few and far between, so make sure you don't leave Blairgowrie without a full tank or you could be in trouble. You can top up again in Grantown-on-Spey for the final run into Inverness.

FROM Crieff
TO Inverness
VIA Dunkeld, Blairgowrie and Grantown-on-Spey
DISTANCE 150 miles
RIDING TIME 4.5 hours

Route Description
➤ **Leave Crieff** on A85 towards Perth.
➤ **After 1½ miles,** turn left on A822 to Dunkeld.
➤ **At A9,** turn right then immediately left into Dunkeld.
➤ **From Dunkeld,** take A923 to Blairgowrie.
➤ **Cross Blairgowrie** and turn left on A93 to Braemar.
➤ **Look out:** don't miss the left turn for B976 to Tomintoul, about 9 miles after Braemar.
➤ **At Garnashiel Lodge,** turn left on A939 to Tomintoul. Stay on this road all the way to Grantown-on-Spey.
➤ **Turn left** on A95. Go across the rbt into Grantown-on-Spey.
➤ **At the traffic lights** in Grantown, turn right on A939 to Nairn.
➤ **Look out:** 7 miles outside Grantown, take the left fork (by the vintage AA box) to stay on A939 to Nairn.
➤ **From Nairn,** take A96 to the route's end at Inverness.

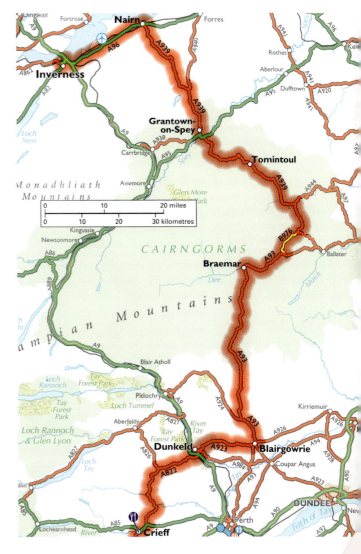

TOUR ③8 Scotland High-Mile Tour Day 2

DAY 2 MORNING

FEELING RESTED? Good. Today is a big-mile day, so an early start is essential. You'll have noticed that in this book we avoid using the A9, which is a dull, dangerous and over-restricted road, but the first stretch over the Beauly and Cromarty Firth is scenic enough.

After that, the route heads into the wild country, taking the rugged, single-track A836 to Tongue. From there it's the majestic coastal route through Durness, to Scourie. There are petrol stations in Lairg, Durness and Scourie: don't risk running out of fuel.

FROM Inverness
TO Scourie
VIA Bonar Bridge, Altnaharra and Durness
DISTANCE 140 miles
RIDING TIME 4 hours

Route Description

➤ **From Inverness,** head north on A9 towards Thurso.

➤ **After about 17 miles,** turn left on B9176 to Ardross and Lairg (A836).

➤ **At A836 T-junction,** turn left to Bonar Bridge.

➤ **Cross the bridge** in Bonar Bridge and turn left on A836 to Lairg. Stay on this road all the way to Tongue.

➤ **In Tongue,** turn left on A838 to Durness.

➤ **Stay on this road** for 50 miles – and keep going straight at Laxford Bridge, where it becomes A894 to Scourie.

The A832 road near Kinlochewe

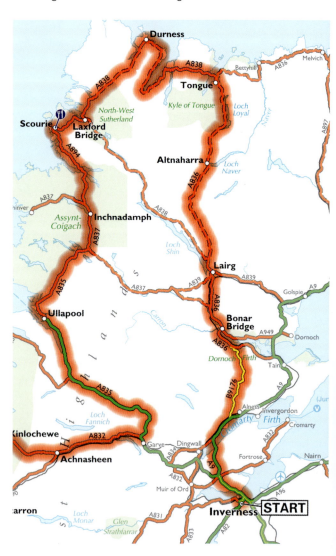

| ROUTE TYPE Tour | DISTANCE 140 miles morning | 215 miles afternoon |

DAY 2 AFTERNOON

THIS IS the big one, an Olympian afternoon route that combines spectacular views with astonishing roads. It is a long route, but don't rush it. Accept that it's a long ride and savour it, especially the coast road round the Applecross peninsula and the Pass of the Cattle. However, if you are worried about time, this is definitely the section to drop, going from Achnasheen to Strathcarron on the A890. There's fuel to be had in Ullapool, Kinlochewe, Applecross and Lochcarron, before you get to Skye.

FROM Scourie
TO Portree
VIA Ullapool, Kinlochewe and Applecross
DISTANCE 215 miles
RIDING TIME 6 hours

Route Description

➤ **From Scourie,** continue along A894 to Loch Assynt.
➤ **At A837,** turn left to Ullapool.
➤ **After 8 miles,** turn right on A835 to Ullapool.
➤ **Top up** with fuel in Ullapool. before continuing on A835 to Inverness, past Altguish Inn.
➤ **After 12 miles,** turn right on A832 to Gairloch: the second turning for A823 after Ullapool.
➤ **In Kinlochewe,** turn left on A896 to Torridon.
➤ **Look out:** don't miss the right turn 18 miles later (about a mile outside Shieldaig) for Kenmore and Applecross.

➤ **In Applecross,** turn left to Lochcarron on the Bealach Na Ba, the Pass of the Cattle.
➤ **At A896 junction,** turn right to Lochcarron.
➤ **Look out:** About 2 miles after Lochcarron, turn right on A890 to Kyle of Lochalsh.
➤ **At A87,** turn right to Kyle of Lochalsh. Go over Skye Bridge.
➤ **At the roundabout,** turn right on A87 to Portree.

TOUR 38 Scotland High-Mile Tour Day 3

DAY 3 MORNING

YOU HAVE a choice on the third day of the High Mile Tour. We favour taking the Mallaig ferry and the A830 to Fort William but a good alternative is crossing the Skye Bridge and taking the majestic A87. It adds 20 miles to the route but probably saves half an hour.

The ride through Glen Coe and across Rannoch Moor is perhaps the most iconic in Scotland, the epic scale of the landscape delivering a sense of wild beauty. We suggest stopping for lunch at the equally iconic – for bikers – Green Welly Stop in Tyndrum.

FROM Portree
TO Tyndrum
VIA Fort William and Glen Coe
DISTANCE 135 miles
RIDING TIME 4 hours

Route Description

➤ **Leave Portree** on A87 to Kyle of Lochalsh.
➤ **Look out:** a mile or so outside Broadford, turn right on A851 to Armadale – signed for the Armadale-Mallaig ferry.

➤ **Take the ferry** – we recommend pre-booking this crossing. For information, see www.calmac.co.uk
➤ **From Mallaig,** take A830 to Fort William.
➤ **Turn right** on A82, into Fort William. Stay on this road through Glen Coe and across Rannoch Moor to Tyndrum, where the morning's route ends.

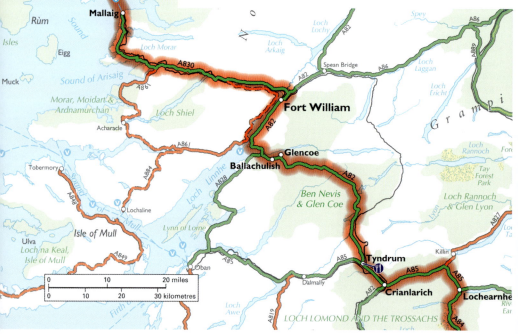

RIDE (38) Scotland High-Mile Tour Day 3

ROUTE TYPE Tour	DISTANCE 135 miles morning	190 miles afternoon

DAY 3 AFTERNOON

ANOTHER DEMANDING but rewarding afternoon. It is easily shortened if necessary: just stay on the A721 until it meets the A701, taking this fine road direct to Moffat.

FROM Tyndrum
TO Moffat
VIA Aberfoyle, Carluke and Carronbridge
DISTANCE 190 miles
RIDING TIME 5 hours

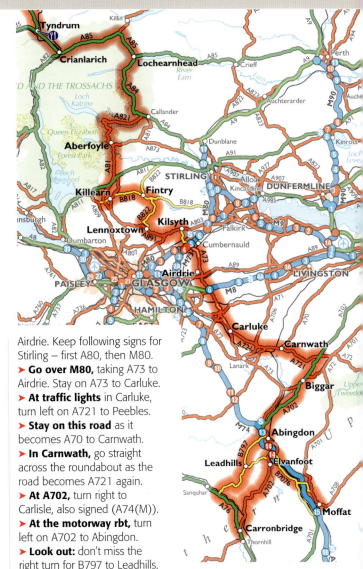

Route Description

➤ **From Tyndrum,** continue along A82 to Crianlarich.
➤ **Now take A85 to Perth.** Keep going straight in Lochearnhead, as the road becomes A84.
➤ **Look out:** don't miss the right turn 12 miles after Lochearnhead (opposite a white bungalow) for A821 to Aberfoyle.
➤ **Turn left** towards Glasgow in Aberfoyle, still on A821.
➤ **At the roundabout,** turn right on A81 to Glasgow.
➤ **At the next roundabout,** turn left on B834 to Killearn.
➤ **Turn left** by the church in Killearn, on A875.
➤ **1 mile later,** turn right on B818 to Fintry.
➤ **Go though Fintry** and stay on this road as it becomes B822 to Lennoxtown.
➤ **In Lennoxtown,** turn left on A891, then left on A803 to Kilsyth.
➤ **At the second roundabout** in Kilsyth, turn right on B802 to

Airdrie. Keep following signs for Stirling – first A80, then M80.
➤ **Go over M80,** taking A73 to Airdrie. Stay on A73 to Carluke.
➤ **At traffic lights** in Carluke, turn left on A721 to Peebles.
➤ **Stay on this road** as it becomes A70 to Carnwath.
➤ **In Carnwath,** go straight across the roundabout as the road becomes A721 again.
➤ **At A702,** turn right to Carlisle, also signed (A74(M)).
➤ **At the motorway rbt,** turn left on A702 to Abingdon.
➤ **Look out:** don't miss the right turn for B797 to Leadhills, as you leave Abingdon.
➤ **At A76,** turn left to Dumfries.
➤**Look out:** don't miss sharp left turn in Carronbridge, for A702 to Edinburgh.
➤ **At Elvanfoot,** go straight over the roundabout and pass under the motorway.

➤ **At the T-junction,** turn right on B7076 to Beattock.
➤ **After 7½ miles,** turn left on B719 to Greenhillstairs, passing over the motorway, then turning right.
➤ **At A701,** turn right to Moffat, where the route ends.

TOUR (39) Scotland Relaxed Tour Day 1

DAY 1 MORNING

IN CONTRAST to the ultra-marathon of the High-Mile Tour, the Relaxed Tour uses some of the same roads to provide a relaxed, pillion-friendly trip through the best bits of Scotland. It links towns where we have day-trip loops, making it easy to extend by staying an extra night to enjoy our circular trips. The first day begins with a gentle ride through well-tended countryside, heading for the foothills of the Cairngorm mountains.

FROM Falkirk
TO Blairgowrie
VIA Crieff and Dunkeld
DISTANCE 70 miles
RIDING TIME 2 hours

Route Description

➤ **From Falkirk,** take A905 to Stirling and the Kincardine Bridge.
➤ **At the double roundabout** for M876, turn right on A876 Kincardine Bridge.
➤ **Join A977,** signed to Perth (M90).
➤ **Look out:** don't miss the left turn, 9 miles later, for A823 to Crieff.

River Braan at Dunkeld

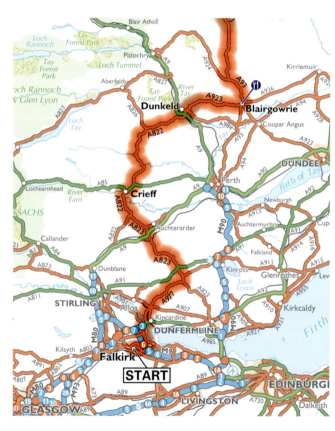

➤ **At A91,** turn right then carry straight on to continue on the A823 to Crieff.
➤ **At A822,** turn right to head to Crieff.
➤ **Turn right in Crieff** to go into the town centre, following signs for Dunkeld (A822) and Perth (A85).

➤ **Leave Crieff** on A85 to Perth. After about 1½ miles, turn left on A822 to Dunkeld.
➤ **At A9,** turn right then immediately left to go into Dunkeld.
➤ **From Dunkeld,** take A923 to Blairgowrie, where the morning's route ends.

DAY 1 AFTERNOON

THE AFTERNOON ride echoes the route used by the High Mile Tour – though this version cuts out one narrow, bumpy road. The ride through Glenshee and over the eastern shoulder of the mountains is truly unmissable, delivering spectacular views all the way. Just remember to fill up before setting off after lunch, as there's no more fuel until Grantown-on-Spey (and none between there and Inverness).

FROM Blairgowrie
TO Inverness
VIA Glenshee, Braemar and Grantown-on-Spey
DISTANCE 125 miles
RIDING TIME 3.5 hours

Route Description

➤ **From Blairgowrie,** take A93 to Braemar.

➤ **Look out:** don't miss the left turn for A939 to Tomintoul, about 6 miles after Balmoral.

➤ **At the T-junction,** turn left to stay on A939. Keep following this road for another 25 miles.

➤ **At A95 T-junction,** turn left. Go straight across the roundabout into Grantown-on-Spey.

➤ **At the traffic lights** in Grantown, turn right on A939 to Nairn.

➤ **Look out:** take the left fork 7 miles outside Grantown (by the vintage AA box) to stay on A939 to Nairn.

➤ **After 13 miles,** turn left on the B9101 to Cawdor. This road becomes B9090.

➤ **Stay on B9090** until it meets A96, then turn left to Inverness, where the day's route ends.

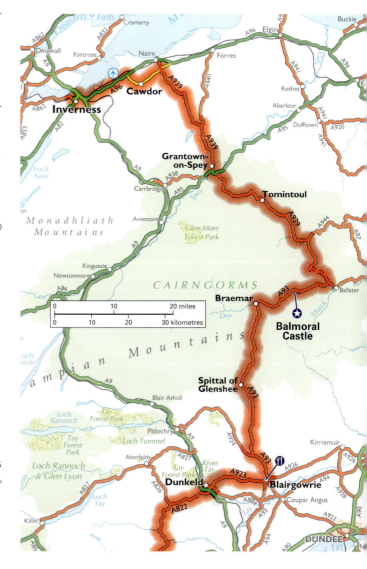

TOUR 39 Scotland Relaxed Tour Day 2

DAY 2 MORNING

FROM THE capital of the Highlands to the wilds, the morning route doesn't take long to leave civilization far behind – and if it seems like a short route, that's because there really are very few places to stop out here. Lairg may seem like a tiny place, but after you leave it you're on your own for another 40 miles until you get to Ullapool, the next place where you could stop for lunch… so we'd go for an early stop in Lairg.

FROM Inverness
TO Lairg
VIA Muir of Ord and Bonar Bridge
DISTANCE 60 miles
RIDING TIME 1.5 hours

Route Description

▶ **Leave Inverness** on A862 to Beauly. Take this road all the way through Dingwall.

▶ **At A9 roundabout,** go straight ahead, towards Thurso.

▶ **After 4 miles,** turn left on B9176 to Ardross and Lairg (A836).

▶ **At A836 T-junction,** turn left to Bonar Bridge.

▶ **Cross the bridge** in Bonar Bridge and turn left on A836 to Lairg, where the morning's route ends.

Beautiful Lochcarron

ROUTE TYPE Tour	DISTANCE 60 miles morning	135 miles afternoon

DAY 2 AFTERNOON

THE FIRST few miles out of Lairg are on a small road, but soon the views open up – a ribbon of tarmac rolling between purple hills with hardly any other signs of human life for mile after mile. From Ullapool, the roads are bigger but no busier. The final loop from Kinlochewe to Lochcarron returns to smaller, spectacular roads through the wilderness.

FROM Lairg
TO Strathcarron
VIA Ullapool, Achnasheen and Shieldaig
DISTANCE 135 miles
RIDING TIME 3.5 hours

Route Description

➤ **Leave Lairg** on the A839 and follow signs for Ullapool (A835).
➤ **At the T-junction,** turn right on the A837 towards Kylesku.
➤ **Look out:** after 18 miles, take the first left turn for A835 to Ullapool.

➤ **In Ullapool,** follow the road past the petrol station on A835 towards Inverness.
➤ **After about 30 miles,** turn right on the A832 to Gairloch. Go straight over the Achnasheen roundabout to stay on this road.
➤ **In Kinlochewe,** turn left on A896 to Torridon. Stay on this road for about 35 miles.
➤ **Look out:** don't miss the right turn 2 miles after Lochcarron, for A890 to Kyle of Lochalsh. This leads to Strathcarron, where the day's route ends.

Peaceful Ullapool

TOUR ③⑨ Scotland Relaxed Tour Day 3

DAY 3 MORNING

THE MOST scenic road of the Relaxed Tour? The final day has two of the strongest candidates, one before lunch and one after it. The morning's star road is the sublime A87. It has lochs, moors, forests and the spectacular castle Eilean Donan. It's also worth spending a few minutes at the Glen Garry viewpoint for the fantastic panorama. We'd stop for lunch in Spean Bridge, but if you want a slightly later lunch, you can hang on until Fort William where the morning's route ends.

FROM Strathcarron
TO Spean Bridge
VIA Dornie and Invergarry
DISTANCE 75 miles
RIDING TIME 2 hours

Route Description

➤ **Leave Strathcarron** on A890 to Kyle of Lochalsh.

➤ **At A87,** turn left to Fort William.

➤ **Look out:** don't miss the left turn, 9 miles after the Cluanie Inn, to stay on A87 to Invergarry.

➤ **In Invergarry,** turn right on A82 to Fort William. Stay on this road all the way to Spean Bridge.

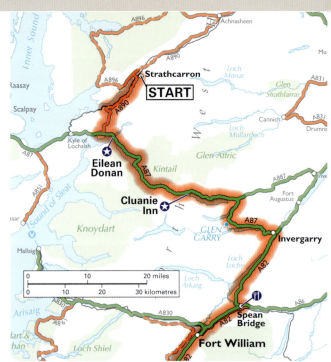

Glen Coe: the A82

RIDE 39 Scotland Relaxed Tour Day 3

| ROUTE TYPE Tour | DISTANCE 75 miles morning | 145 miles afternoon |

DAY 3 AFTERNOON

THE AFTERNOON'S candidate for the 'most-scenic' award is the A82, romping through the jaw-dropping splendour of Glen Coe and out across Rannoch Moor. It's the kind of untamed landscape that suggests dinosaurs or mammoths are lurking somewhere nearby, just out of sight. From Tyndrum the route heads down past beautiful Inveraray and alongside restful Loch Fyne, before turning north to the lovely resort town of Oban, where the tour ends.

FROM Spean Bridge
TO Oban
VIA Glen Coe, Tyndrum and Lochgilphead
DISTANCE 145 miles
RIDING TIME 3.5 hours

Route Description

➤ **From Spean Bridge,** take A82 to Fort William and continue along this road through the famous and spectacular Glen Coe.
➤ **In Tyndrum,** turn right on A85 to Oban.
➤ **After 13 miles,** turn left on A819 to Inveraray.
➤ **In Inveraray,** turn right on A83 to Campbeltown.
➤ **Go through** Lochgilphead and turn right onto A816. Take this road to Oban, where the day's route ends.

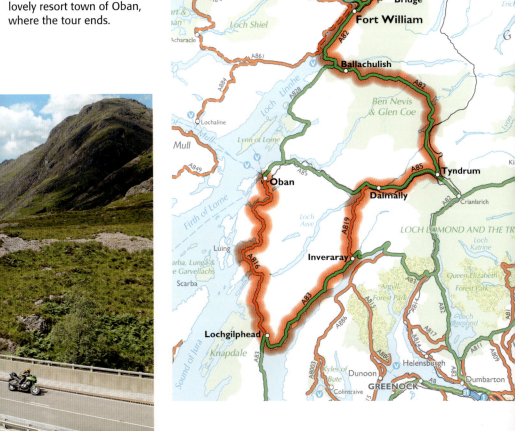

Long Tours

If you're looking for a longer bike trip, we have five tours designed to fit comfortably with taking a week off work. Including the weekends at either side, that gives you nine days for riding. You can discover an awful lot of Britain's best roads in that time.

The seven-day high-mile tours (allowing a day to reach the start and finish) head through England to Scotland and are packed with interesting roads. The more pillion-friendly relaxed tours are five days long, with lower daily mileages and allow a rest day for sightseeing to be added by staying for two nights in any location.

These tours start from Hull and from the M20 outside Dover – handy for visitors to the UK arriving at one of those ports. However, the idea is that the Dover tours are easy for Londoners and residents of the Southeast to adapt, while the Hull tours are easily picked up by anyone in the northern half of the country.

For a longer trip, we have an epic eight-day tour that was inspired by a story in *RiDE* magazine: the Maxxis Diamond Ride. Taking in the Peaks, Dales, Lakes, Borders, Highlands, North York Moors and Lincolnshire Wolds, it's a relaxed ride around some of Britain's best-loved landmarks on amazing roads.

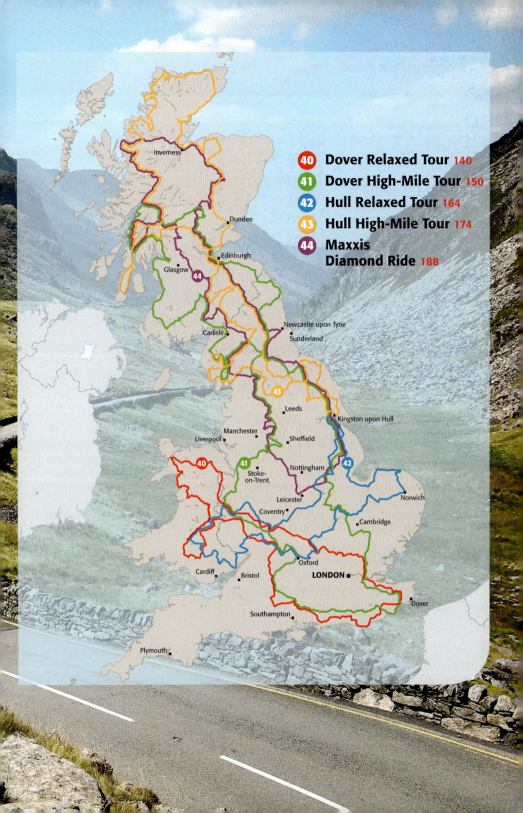

40	Dover Relaxed Tour 140
41	Dover High-Mile Tour 150
42	Hull Relaxed Tour 164
43	Hull High-Mile Tour 174
44	Maxxis Diamond Ride 188

Inverness

Dundee

Edinburgh

Glasgow   **44**

Carlisle

Newcastle upon Tyne

Sunderland

43

Leeds

Manchester

Liverpool   Sheffield

Kingston upon Hull

40   **41**

Stoke-on-Trent

Nottingham   **42**

Leicester   Norwich

Coventry

Cambridge

Cardiff   Bristol

Oxford

LONDON

Southampton

Dover

Plymouth

TOUR (40) Dover Relaxed Tour Day 1

DAY 1 MORNING

THE TWO "Dover" tours were conceived to help visitors to the UK get straight to the best roads, starting and finishing from the M20 services by the Eurotunnel. However, anyone living in London or the Southeast can easily adapt and use these routes to unlock the great riding in the rest of the country.

FROM Junction 11, M20
TO Eastbourne
DISTANCE 55 miles
RIDING TIME 2 hours

Route Description

➤ **From Junction 11 of M20,** take A20 towards Sellindge.
➤ **At the traffic lights,** turn left on B2067 to Aldington. At the T-junction, turn right to stay on B2067.
➤ **Look out:** at the next T-junction, turn right and take the first left turn to stay on B2067. Stay on this road all the way to Tenterden.
➤ **In Tenterden** town centre, turn left on A28 to Hastings.
➤ **At the A268 junction,** turn left to stay on A28.

➤ **After 4 miles,** turn right on B2165 to Staplecross.
➤ After 4 miles, at Cripps Corner x-roads, turn right on B2089 to Battle.
➤ **At the A21 T-junction,** turn right towards Sevenoaks.
➤ **At the John's Cross rbt,** turn left on A2100 to Battle.
➤ **In Battle,** take A271 towards Eastbourne.
➤ **At the junction** with A269, turn right to stay on A271.
➤ **Look out:** one and a half miles later, turn left on the minor road to Wartling and Herstmonceux Castle.
➤ **At the A259 rbt,** take the third exit and follow signs for Pevensey Bay (where William the Conquerer landed in 1066).
➤ **Pevensey Bay,** take A259 into Eastbourne, where the morning route ends.

Pevensey beach: invading Norman army not pictured

ROUTE TYPE Tour	**DISTANCE** 55 miles morning	130 miles afternoon

DAY 1 AFTERNOON

A GREAT AFTERNOON ride, exploring the back-roads across the South Downs and out to the first night's stop in the historic city of Salisbury.

FROM Eastbourne
TO Salisbury
DISTANCE 130 miles
RIDING TIME 3.5 hours

Route Description

➤ **Leave Eastbourne** on A259 to Seaford (look for signs to Beachy Head).

➤ **In Newhaven,** join A26 towards Lewes and Brighton.

➤ **At the Beddingham rbt,** turn left on A27 to Brighton.

➤ **After 8 miles** on A27, take the exit for Ditchling (as A27 passes beneath a high bridge).

➤ **At the double roundabouts,** turn right then right again. Take first left turn for Ditchling.

➤ **In Ditchling,** turn left on B2112 back towards Brighton.

➤ **Turn left** on A273 to Brighton.

➤ **After 1 mile,** turn right on A23 for Crawley and London.

➤ **Take the first exit** for A281 to Henfield.

➤ **At the rbt,** go straight across to Ponyings. Stay on this road through Fulking and Edburton.

➤ **At A2037 T-junction,** turn left to Upper Beeding.

➤ **Turn left** at first rbt then right at second rbt, to take A283 to Steyning and Horsham (A24).

➤ **Go straight across A24,** staying on A283 to Storrington.

➤ **In Storrington,** turn left at the second rbt on B2139 to Bognor Regis.

➤ **At the major rbt,** join A29 to Bognor.

➤ **At A27 rbt,** turn right to Chichester.

➤ **Cross two roundabouts,** then take the exit for A285 to Guildford.

➤ **Head north** on A285 for half a mile, then turn left on minor road to Lavant.

➤ **In Lavant,** turn left at T-junction, then right at the mini-rbt for A286 to Midhurst.

➤ **Look out:** don't miss the left turn, leaving Mid-Lavant, for B2141 to Petersfield.

➤ **In South Harting,** turn left on B2146 to Petersfield.

➤ **From Petersfield,** take A272 to Winchester.

➤ **At Winchester,** turn left onto A31. At rbt turn right towards A3 and follow the signs for Basingstoke (A33) to get on A34 ringroad. About 3 miles after the main M3 rbt, take exit for A30 to Salisbury.

➤ **At the rbt,** take the 4th exit for A272 to Stockbridge.

➤ **At A30 junction,** turn left and take this road to Salisbury where the route ends.

TOUR (40) Dover Relaxed Tour Day 2

DAY 2 MORNING

THE MORNING ride should allow time for you to make a short stop at Stonehenge – but don't worry if you make a late start and decide to skip it, as the route also passes through the Neolithic marvel of the Avebury stone circle. From the Vale of the White Horse, the route heads on into the beautiful Cotswold Hills, stopping for lunch at the picture-postcard stone-built village of Bourton-on-the-Water.

FROM Salisbury
TO Bourton-on-the-Water
DISTANCE 75 miles
RIDING TIME 2 hours

Route Description

➤ **From Salisbury,** take A360 towards Devizes.
➤ **Cross over A303** at the rbt.
➤ **At the Stonehenge rbt,** go straight across on B3086.
➤ **Rollestone** – at the crossroads, turn right to Durrington.
➤ **At the Larkhill roundabout,** turn left on the A345 towards Marlborough.
➤ **At roundabout,** 1½ miles after Upavon, go straight over on the minor road to Woodborough.
➤ **Look out:** don't miss the left turn, 7½ miles after the roundabout, signed for East Kennett.
➤ **At A4 T-junction,** turn left then take the first right (after the layby) on B4003 to Avebury.
➤ **At the T-junction in Avebury,** carry straight on, joining A4361 to Swindon.
➤ **4 miles after Avebury,** turn left on a minor road to Broad Hinton. Stay on this road all the way to Royal Wootton Bassett.
➤ **Cross Wootton Bassett** and pick up B4042 to Malmesbury.

➤ **Turn right on B4696** to Ashton Keynes after the road goes under the motorway.
➤ **Look out:** don't miss the right turn, leaving Ashton Keynes, to stay on B4696 (signed M4, M5 and Swindon).
➤ **At roundabout,** join A419, which becomes A417, towards Gloucester and M5.

➤ **At the next junction,** join A429 to Stow. Turn left at the traffic lights to stay on A429.
➤ **Stay on the Fosse Way** (A429) for 14 miles, then turn left into Bourton-on-the-Water, where the morning route ends. (The junction is immediately after the old stone bridge, with a filter lane.)

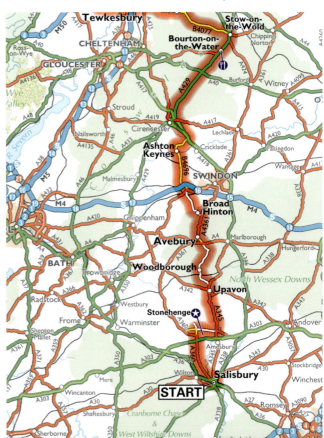

TOUR 40 **Dover Relaxed Tour Day 2**

| ROUTE TYPE Tour | DISTANCE 75 miles morning | 75 miles afternoon |

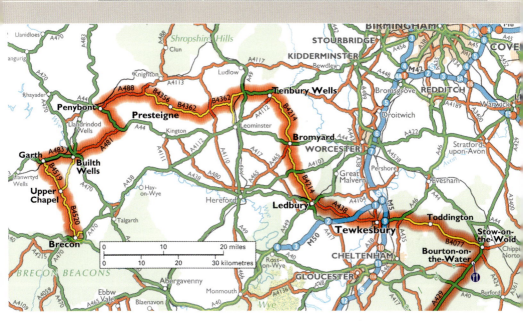

DAY 2 AFTERNOON

THE AFTERNOON ride leaves the Cotswolds to meander through the rolling hills of Shropshire's Golden Valley – a brilliant way to enter Wales. Turning west, the roads get ever quieter and the scenery more impressive, especially clambering up to the Garth viewpoint, shortly before descending to the overnight stop in the beautiful market town of Brecon.

FROM Bourton-on-the-Water
TO Brecon
DISTANCE 75 miles
RIDING TIME 2 hours

Route Description

➤ **Continue on A429** (the Fosse Way) from Bourton-on-the-Water all the way to Stow-on-the-Wold.

➤ **At the traffic lights** in Stow, turn left on A424 to Evesham.

➤ **Look out:** straight away, turn left on B4077 to Upper Swell. Stay on this road to the A46.

➤ **At the rbt,** go straight across, joining A46 to Tewkesbury.

➤ **Go straight across** Tewkesbury town centre, picking up A38 to Worcester.

➤ **Look out:** don't miss the left turn, half a mile after Tewkesbury's half-timbered pub, for A438 to Ledbury.

➤ **In Ledbury,** follow signs for the train station to pick up B4214 to Bromyard.

➤ **At A4103,** go across staggered x-roads, staying on B4214.

➤ **At A465 T-junction,** turn right to go into Bromyard.

➤ **From Bromyard** town centre, take B4214 to Tenbury Wells.

➤ **In Tenbury,** turn right to the town centre. Cross the river

and at A456 junction, turn left towards Shrewsbury.

➤ **At A49 junction,** turn right then immediately left to join B4362 to Presteigne.

➤ **At the T-junction,** turn left on B4361 to Leominster. The road becomes B4362 to Presteigne.

➤ **From Presteigne,** take B4356 to Llanbister.

➤ **At A488 junction,** turn left to Penybont.

➤ **In Penybont,** turn left on the A44 towards Hereford.

➤ **After 5½ miles,** turn right on A481 to Builth Wells.

➤ **Turn left** on A483, then left again at rbt by showground to go through Builth Wells. Stay on A483 towards Llandovery.

➤ **In Garth,** turn left on B4519 to Upper Chapel.

➤ **At junction with B4520,** turn right to Upper Chapel. Stay on this road to Brecon, where the route ends.

TOUR ④⓪ Dover Relaxed Tour Day 3

DAY 3 MORNING

THE MORNING route heads into the heart of the Brecon Beacons, swooping through the wild mountains – and passing the worth-a-visit Penderyn distillery. From Ystradgynlais it heads back across the Black Mountain, heading for the near-Alpine climb up the majestic A483. The lunch stop is at the popular biking café in Crossgates.

FROM Brecon
TO Crossgates
DISTANCE 90 miles
RIDING TIME 2.5 hours

Above right: Black Mountain

Route Description

➤ **Leave Brecon** on A470 to Merthyr Tydfil.
➤ **At the end of the Beacons Reservoir,** turn right on A4059 to Neath.
➤ **At the roundabout,** turn right to join A465 to Neath.
➤ **Take the first exit** from the dual carriageway: A4109 to Glynneath.

➤ **At the traffic lights,** go straight across on A4109 to Abercraf. This road becomes the A4221.
➤ **At A4067 T-junction,** turn left towards Swansea.
➤ **At double rbt,** turn right to Ystradgynlais, still on A4067.
➤ **At the rbt,** turn right on A4068 to Brynamman.
➤ **At the Brynamman** mini-roundabout, turn right on A4069 to Llangadog.
➤ **Look out:** in Llangadog village centre, turn right to stay on A4069 to Llandovery.
➤ **At T-junction** in Llandovery, turn left on A40. After a few hundred metres, turn right on A483 to Builth Wells (if you cross the railway line, you've just missed the turning).
➤ **In Beulah,** turn left on B4358 to Newbridge on Wye.
➤ **In Newbridge,** turn right on A470 then turn left, continuing along B4358 to Llandrindod Wells.
➤ **At T-junction,** turn right on A4081 to Llandrindod Wells.
➤ **In Llandrindod Wells,** turn left on A483 to Newtown. Stay on this road to Crossgates: turn right at roundabout on A44 for the café and petrol station.

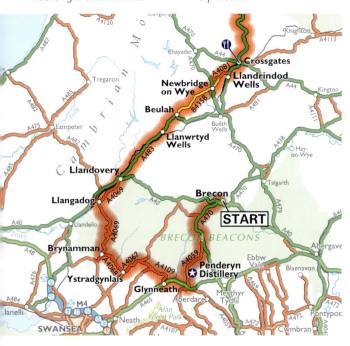

| **ROUTE TYPE** Tour | **DISTANCE** 90 miles morning | 120 miles afternoon |

DAY 3 **AFTERNOON**

THE AFTERNOON'S ride begins with one of the very best stretches of tarmac in Wales: the astonishingly serpentine A483 to Newtown. From there we head north to Snowdonia, passing Cader Idris – Wales's second-highest mountain – and swooping out to the coast in the shadow of Harlech Castle, through the fragrant woods around Beddgelert on the way to the overnight stop in Caernarfon.

FROM Crossgates
TO Caernarfon
DISTANCE 120 miles
RIDING TIME 3.5 hours

Route Description

➤ **From Crossgates,** continue north on A483 to Newtown
➤ **At traffic lights** in Newtown, turn left on A489 to Machynlleth.
➤ **Look out:** don't miss the right turn after 5 miles, just before a level crossing, to join A470 to Caersws and Machynlleth (A489).
➤ **At Cemmaes Road** rbt, turn left on A489 to Machynlleth.
➤ **In Machynlleth,** turn right on A487 to Dolgellau.
➤ **At Cross Foxes,** turn left on A470 to Dolgellau.
➤ **At Llanelltyd roundabout,** turn left on A496 to Barmouth.
➤ **At A487 T-junction,** turn left towards Porthmadog.
➤ **Take second right** turn to pick up B4410 to Rhyd.

➤ **In Garreg,** turn right on A4085 to Beddgelert.
➤ **At the T-junction** on stone bridge, turn right on A498 to Beddgelert.
➤ **In Beddgelert,** follow the road round to the left as it crosses the bridge and becomes A4085 again. Stay on this road all the way to Caernarfon, where the day's route ends.

Harlech Castle

TOUR ④ **Dover Relaxed Tour** Day 4

DAY 4 MORNING

THE MORNING route takes in two of the most famous roads in Wales: the Pass of Llanberis and Horseshoe Pass. Both are spectacularly scenic... but which one will be the highlight of your ride? Or will you prefer one of the other, less famous roads? The A543, B4501 and B5105 may not be so well-known, but they're utterly brilliant biking roads.

FROM Caernarfon
TO Oswestry
DISTANCE 90 miles
RIDING TIME 3 hours

Route Description

➤ **Leave Caernarfon** on A4086 to Llanberis.

➤ **After descending** from the pass, turn left at T-junction to Capel Curig.

➤ **At Capel Curig,** turn right on A5 to Betws-y-Coed.

➤ **In Pentrefoelas,** turn left on A543 to Denbigh.

➤ **After 8 miles or so,** turn right on B4501 to Cerrigydrudion.

➤ **In Cerrigydrudion,** turn left on B5105 to Ruthin.

➤ **At the roundabout in Ruthin** town centre, turn right on A525 to Wrexham.

➤ **Look out:** don't miss the right turn, 7 miles later, for A542 to Llangollen. This road takes you over Horseshoe Pass.

➤ **In Llangollen,** turn right to cross the bridge, then left on A5 to Oswestry.

➤ **At the second roundabout,** turn right on A5. Cross the next roundabout and at the third one, turn right on B5069 to go into Oswestry, where the morning's route ends.

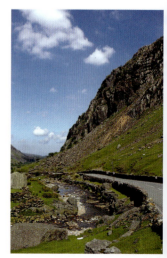

Pass of Llanberis

| **ROUTE TYPE** Tour | **DISTANCE** 90 miles morning | 130 miles afternoon |

DAY 4 AFTERNOON

THE AFTERNOON ride heads back into England but, even without big-name passes to cross, the quality of the riding remains high. Twisting through the verdant Shropshire hills, the route crosses historic Stratford-upon-Avon and skirts the edges of the Cotswolds on its way to the overnight stop in the quiet market town of Banbury.

FROM Oswestry
TO Banbury
DISTANCE 130 miles
RIDING TIME 3.5 hours

Route Description

➤ **From Oswestry** town centre, take B5069 to Morda and Trefonen.
➤ **At A483 T-junction,** turn right to Welshpool.

➤ **Stay on A483** through Welshpool. At the roundabout 1½ miles after the station, turn left on A490 to Churchstoke.
➤ **In Churchstoke,** turn left on A489 to Craven Arms.
➤ **At A488 T-junction,** turn right to Craven Arms.
➤ **Look out:** don't miss the left turn in Lydham (just past the church) to rejoin A489 to Craven Arms.
➤ **At A49 crossroads,** turn right to Leominster.
➤ **At the Ludlow rbt,** turn left on A4117 to Kidderminster.
➤ **Look out:** don't miss the right turn for B4202 to Worcester, a mile after Cleobury Mortimer (there's a garage on the corner).

➤ **Stay on B4202,** crossing A456, until it meets A443. Turn left to Worcester.
➤ **In Holt Heath,** turn left on A4133 to Droitwich.
➤ **At the Droitwich rbt,** turn right on the A38 to Worcester.
➤ **At the traffic lights** in Martin Hussingtree, turn left on A4538, towards M5 and Evesham.
➤ **At M5 roundabout,** take the second exit for A4538 to Evesham.
➤ **At the second roundabout,** turn left on A422 to Stratford.
➤ **At the T-junction,** turn right on B4088 to Evesham. Turn right at the chequer-board crossroads in Dunnington to stay on this road.
➤ **At the roundabout,** turn left on the minor road to Bidford.
➤ **Go straight over** A46 roundabout, taking B439 to Bidford. Stay on this road to Stratford-upon-Avon.
➤ **Go into Stratford** centre and pick up A422 to Banbury, where the day's route ends.

TOUR (40) Dover Relaxed Tour Day 5

DAY 5 MORNING

THE FINAL day can be shortened dramatically by using the motorway if you need to return to Dover or Folkestone for an early crossing, but why waste the final day of the trip by spending it all on dull roads? The planned route picks its way through the bustling Southeast on roads that are as rewarding as the Welsh ones, albeit potentially a little busier.

FROM Banbury
TO Hertford
DISTANCE 75 miles
RIDING TIME 2.5 hours

Route Description

➤ **Leave Banbury** on A422 to Brackley.
➤ **At Brackley,** take A43 towards Northampton.
➤ **Turn right** at the next roundabout, on A422 to Buckingham.
➤ **In Buckingham** town centre turn right at the mini-roundabout and follow the 'All routes' signs until you can join A413 to Aylesbury.
➤ **At the traffic lights** in Aylesbury, turn left towards Leighton Buzzard (A418). At the next roundabout, turn left on A418 to Milton Keynes.
➤ **Ride through Wing village** and at the rbt, turn right on A4146 to Leighton Buzzard.
➤ **At third rbt,** turn right on the A4146 to Hemel Hempstead.
➤ **After 8 miles,** at the double-roundabout, turn left towards Whipsnade on B489.

➤ **At next roundabout,** turn right on the B4506 to Dagnall.
➤ **Take first left turn** for B4540 to Whipsnade (also signed for the zoo).
➤ **When B4540 meets A5,** turn right to St Albans and M1. Stay on A5, passing under M1 where it becomes A5183 to St Albans.
➤ **At the next roundabout,** turn left on B487 and take this road to Harpenden.
➤ **Cross Harpenden,** following signs for train station and memorial hospital, to pick up B653 to Wheathampstead.
➤ **Stay on B653** to Welwyn Garden City.
➤ **Passing under A1(M),** join A414 to Hertford, where the morning's route ends.

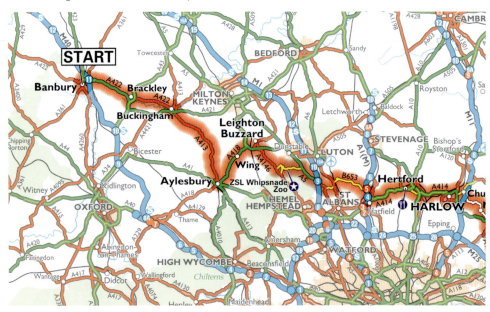

TOUR 40 Dover Relaxed Tour Day 5

ROUTE TYPE Tour	DISTANCE 75 miles morning	104 miles afternoon

DAY 5 AFTERNOON

A BIT OF motorway is needed to get around London and over the Thames: the M25, over the Dartford crossing (free for motorcycles), then a burst of the M2. However, the final canter across the Downs finishes the tour on a high, getting back to the services by the Eurotunnel, where the tour began.

FROM Hertford
TO Junction 11, M20
DISTANCE 104 miles
RIDING TIME 3 hours

Route Description

➤ **Leave Hertford** on A414 to Harlow.
➤ **At the main A10 rbt,** take B1502 to Great Amwell.
➤ **Rejoin A414** to Harlow at the next roundabout.
➤ **Stay on A414** around Harlow, until you can turn left on B183 to Hatfield Heath.

➤ **At the second rbt,** turn right towards Churchgate Street.
➤ **Turn right** at the T-junction, into Churchgate Street (name of the village, not the road).
➤ **Take first left** to Threshers Bush after the road passes beneath the motorway.
➤ **At the T-junction,** turn right to Moreton and Chipping Ongar.
➤ **In Moreton,** turn right to Ongar (next to the pub).
➤ **At B184 T-junction,** turn right to Ongar.
➤ **In Chipping Ongar,** turn left on A128 to Brentwood

(also signed for Secret Nuclear Bunker).
➤ **From Brentwood** centre, follow signs for A12 and M25.
➤ **Join M25** to Dartford.
➤ **Cross the River Thames** then leave M25 at Junction 2, following signs for (M2) Canterbury A2.
➤ **Stay on A2** as it becomes the M2.
➤ **Leave M2** at Junction 6 (Faversham), turning right on the A251 to Ashford.
➤ **After 6 miles,** turn left at the rbt on A252 to Canterbury.
➤ **Turn left** onto A28.
➤ **Look out:** after a mile turn right to Shalmsford Street.
➤ **At B2068 T-junction,** turn right to Petham and Folkestone. Stay on this road back to the services at Jctn 11 of M20, where the route ends.

TOUR (41) Dover High-Mile Tour Day 1

DAY 1 MORNING

AS WITH the Relaxed Tour, this high-mile tour aims to help visitors to the UK and those living in the Southeast get to the best riding Britain has to offer with minimal fuss. With slightly longer days, more suited to solo riders than pillion couples, this seven-day trip heads to Scotland through Lincolnshire, Yorkshire and Northumberland, before returning through the Lake District, Peak District and the beautiful Cotswold Hills.

Beautiful Essex in summer

FROM Junction 11, M20
TO Chipping Ongar
DISTANCE 80 miles
RIDING TIME 2 hours

Route Description

➤ **From Junction 11** of M20, take B2068 to Canterbury.

➤ **In Lower Hardres,** turn left on the minor road to Chartham (first left turn inside the 40 limit).

➤ **At A28 T-junction,** turn left towards Ashford.

➤ **Stay on the road** in Chilham, as it becomes A252 to Charing.

➤ **In Charing,** turn right at the roundabout on A20 to Lenham.

➤ **After 9 miles,** join M20 towards London.

➤ **Take M20 to M25.**

➤ **At Junction 1,** follow signs to M25 The North (M25 (N)) and the Dartford Crossing. The crossing is toll-free for motorcycles.

➤ **Stay on M25** to Junction 28 (for A12).

➤ **At the A12 roundabout,** take the fourth exit for A1023 to Brentwood.

➤ **At the double roundabout** in Brentwood High Street, turn left on Chipping Ongar Road (A128).

➤ **After 7 miles,** turn right at the mini-roundabout and go into Chipping Ongar, where the morning's route ends.

TOUR (41) Dover High-Mile Tour Day 1

ROUTE TYPE Tour	DISTANCE 80 miles morning	135 miles afternoon

DAY 1 AFTERNOON

ONGAR IS our lunch stop as it's so easily reached from the M25 – the morning route is easily shortened by using the motorway all the way from Folkestone or Dover to Brentwood. It means anyone living in the Southeast can reach Chipping Ongar to start the tour. From here, the real riding begins – out across Essex and Cambridgeshire to the gorgeous Lincolnshire market town of Stamford.

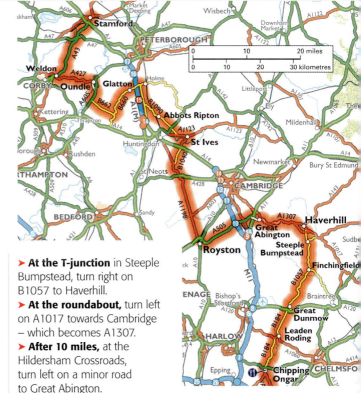

FROM Chipping Ongar
TO Stamford
DISTANCE 135 miles
RIDING TIME 3.5 hours

Route Description

➤ **From roundabout** at end of Chipping Ongar high street, take B184 to Great Dunmow.
➤ **At A1060 T-junction,** turn right towards Chelmsford.
➤ **At mini-rbt** in Leaden Roding, turn left to continue to Great Dunmow on B184.
➤ **Stay on B184** all the way through Great Dunmow town centre – don't miss the right-turn on the high street, opposite the Saracen's Head. Cross one roundabout then turn right on B1057 to Finchingfield.
➤ **In Finchingfield,** cross the bridge on the green and turn immediately left to stay on B1057 to Haverhill.
➤ **Look out:** don't miss the left turn half a mile later to stay on B1057.

➤ **At the T-junction** in Steeple Bumpstead, turn right on B1057 to Haverhill.
➤ **At the roundabout,** turn left on A1017 towards Cambridge – which becomes A1307.
➤ **After 10 miles,** at the Hildersham Crossroads, turn left on a minor road to Great Abington.
➤ **At roundabout,** go straight over towards Pampisford, to join A505 to Duxford.
➤ **From Royston** take A1198 to Huntingdon.
➤ **After 15 miles,** turn right at roundabout on B1040 to St Ives. It becomes A1096 when it crosses A14.
➤ **At the double roundabout,** turn left on A1123 towards Houghton and Huntingdon.
➤ **After two miles,** turn right on B1090 to Abbots Ripton.
➤ **At the T-junction** in Abbots Ripton, turn right to stay on B1090.
➤ **Look out:** don't miss the right turn to Wood Walton 2½ miles later, on B1090.

➤ **At the roundabout,** turn right on B1043 to Conington.
➤ **Cross three more roundabouts,** running parallel to A1(M) without joining it.
➤ **Look out:** don't miss the right turn a mile after third rbt for B660. At end of sliproad, turn left on B660 to Glatton.
➤ **At the T-junction,** turn right on B662 to Oundle.
➤ **At A605 roundabout,** turn right to Oundle. After 2 miles, turn left to go into Oundle.
➤ **In Oundle,** turn left in front of the church on A427 to Corby.
➤ **In Weldon,** turn right. At rbt turn right again on A43.
➤ **Stay on A43** to Stamford, where the day's route ends.

TOUR ④① Dover High-Mile Tour Day 2

DAY 2 MORNING

VISITORS TO the East Midlands notice one thing very quickly: the further you get from the A1, the quieter the roads become. With Britain's Great North Road carrying the bulk of traffic north, the roads across the rolling hills of the Wolds of Lincolnshire and Humberside offer fantastic, quiet riding through unspoilt countryside. The morning's route crosses the Humber Bridge, which is toll-free for motorcycles.

FROM Stamford
TO Wetwang
DISTANCE 130 miles
RIDING TIME 3 hours

Route Description

➤ **Leave Stamford** on A6121 to Bourne.

➤ **At A151 T-junction,** turn left towards Corby Glen.

➤ **Look out:** take the easily missed left turn at the top of the hill outside Corby Glen, for B1176 to Burton Coggles and Grantham.

➤ **At the roundabout,** turn right on A52 to Boston.

➤ **After half a mile,** turn left on B6403 to Ancaster.

➤ **At traffic lights in Ancaster,** turn right on A153 to Sleaford.

➤ **At Sleaford roundabout,** turn left on A15 to Lincoln. Take the second exit at the next roundabout to stay on A15.

➤ **After 4 miles,** turn right on B1191 to Ashby de la Launde and Woodhall Spa. Turn right then left in Scopwick to stay on this road.

➤ **At B1189 junction,** turn left. A quarter of a mile later, turn right to continue on B1191 to Woodhall Spa and Horncastle.

➤ **In Horncastle,** turn left at the lights on A158 to Lincoln.

➤ **After 3 miles,** turn right on B1225 to Caistor, crossing a series of crossroads.

➤ **At A46** go straight over the staggered crossroads, taking the A1173.

➤ **When A1173 turns hard right,** go straight ahead on the minor road to Great Limber.

➤ **Go straight** across A18, taking the minor road signed for Brocklesby.

➤ **Turn left** on B1211 to Ulceby.

➤ **In Ulceby,** turn left on A1077 to Barton-upon-Humber.

➤ **Look out:** don't miss right turn in Ulceby to stay on A1077.

➤ **From Barton-upon-Humber,** join A15 over Humber Bridge.

➤ **Go straight** across the roundabout on the north bank of the Humber, on the A164 to Beverley.

➤ **After 6 miles,** turn left on minor road to Walkington and carry on across the traffic lights, towards Bishop Burton.

➤ **At roundabout** take second exit for A1035 to Bridlington.

➤ **Go straight** over next rbt on B1248 to Malton.

➤ **At A614** T-junction in Bainton, turn right to Bridlington.

➤ **At roundabout,** take second exit to continue on B1248 to Malton and Wetwang, where the morning's route ends.

TOUR ④ Dover High-Mile Tour Day 2

| ROUTE TYPE Tour | DISTANCE 130 miles morning | 180 miles afternoon |

DAY 2 AFTERNOON

FROM THE Midlands into the North of England, the afternoon's route has some spectacular riding. Leaving the Wolds it skirts the North York Moors before heading into the high hills of the Pennines. This is England's border country and the route heads for the Northumbrian coast, with an overnight stop in historic Alnwick.

FROM Wetwang
TO Alnwick
DISTANCE 180 miles
RIDING TIME 4 hours

Route Description

➤ **Leave Wetwang** on A166 towards York.

➤ **Loook out:** after half a mile turn right on B1248 to Malton. Cross Malton town centre, where the road becomes B1257 to Helmsley.

➤ **At A170 T-junction,** turn right to go into Helmsley.

➤ **In Helmsley** market place, turn left and then right to take B1257 to Stokesley.

➤ **At Stokesley rbt** turn left on the A172 to Thirsk.

➤ **Join A19** for one junction, then take the A684 to Northallerton.

➤ **From Northallerton** take A167 to Darlington.

➤ **At second Darlington roundabout,** turn left on A67 to Barnard Castle.

➤ **In Barnard Castle,** go straight over mini-roundabout then turn right on B6278 to Middleton-in-Teesdale.

➤ **After 5 miles,** in Eggleston, turn right on B6278 to Stanhope.

➤ **In Stanhope** turn right then left to continue along B6278 to Edmundbyers.

➤ **At A68** turn left to Corbridge.

➤ **Join A69 towards** Hexham for one junction, then continue along A68 towards Jedburgh.

➤ **At A696 junction,** turn right to Otterburn and Newcastle.

➤ **After 3 miles** turn left on B6341 to Rothbury, then to Alnwick, where the route ends.

TOUR ④1 Dover High-Mile Tour Day 3

DAY 3 MORNING

OUR MORNING route heads out to the wild Northumbrian coast, past imposing Bamburgh Castle, before heading into Scotland. While the riding and the scenery are spectacular on the way to Edinburgh, there's no handy, scenic way to get past the Scottish capital – so we just use the Edinburgh ring road and the motorway over the Forth Road Bridge. Once off these dull roads, grab some lunch in Dunfermline before starting the infinitely more rewarding afternoon ride.

FROM Alnwick
TO Dunfermline
DISTANCE 120 miles
RIDING TIME 3 hours

Route Description

➤ **Leave Alnwick** on B1340 and take this road all the way to Bamburgh.
➤ **At road fork** in Bamburgh village, bear right on B1342 to Belford.
➤ **Look out:** don't miss the left turn for A1, 4 miles after Bamburgh.
➤ **At A1,** turn right to Berwick.

➤ **After 4 miles,** turn left on B6353 to Fenwick.
➤ **Don't miss** the right turn after 5 miles to stay on B6353 to Coldstream.
➤ **After 4 miles,** take the left turn (opposite Ford Castle's gate house) on B6353/B6354 to Cornhill-on-Tweed.
➤ **At A697** T-junction turn right to Coldstream.
➤ **Entering Coldstream,** turn right on A6112 and then take this road all the way to Duns.
➤ **In Swinton,** turn right to stay on A6112.

➤ **Go through Duns** on A6112. A mile later, turn left on B6355 to Abbey St Bathans.
➤ **At x-roads in Pencaitland,** turn left on A6093.
➤ **At A68 junction,** turn right to Edinburgh.
➤ **Join A720** Edinburgh bypass and follow signs for the Forth Road Bridge.
➤ **Keep following the bridge signs,** until you join A90 and cross the bridge, joining M90.
➤ **Leave M90** at Junction 2, taking A823(M) into Dunfermline, where the morning's route ends.

ROUTE TYPE Tour	DISTANCE 120 miles morning	175 miles afternoon

DAY 3 AFTERNOON

WITH SCOTLAND'S city belt behind us, the afternoon ride is spectacular – sweeping out across the green hills of Fife and along the shores of peaceful lochs. The landscape just gets bigger and more beautiful with every mile. Passing through the snow gate at Tyndrum, the scenery needle hits the red as the road climbs across the wilds of Rannoch Moor and into spectacular Glen Coe. Our route then turns south to hug the coast all the way to reach the overnight stop in Oban.

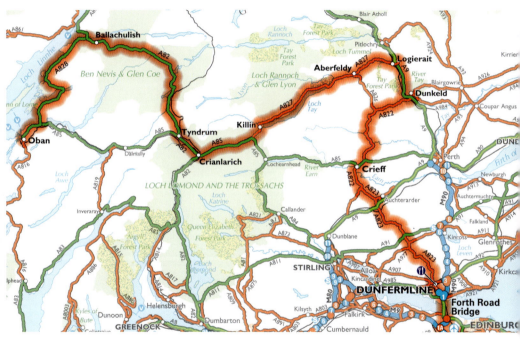

FROM Dunfermline
TO Oban
DISTANCE 175 miles
RIDING TIME 3.5 hours

Route Description
➤ **Leave Dunfermline** on A823 to Crieff.
➤ **At A977,** turn right. After 1 mile, turn left to continue on A823.
➤ **At A91,** turn right then carry straight on as the road forks to continue on A823 to Crieff.

➤ **At A822 junction,** turn right to Crieff. Turn right in the town centre to continue along A822 to Dunkeld (this road becomes A85).
➤ **Look out:** take the easily missed left turn for A822 to Dunkeld about a mile outside Crieff.
➤ **In Dunkeld, turn left** on A9 towards Inverness.
➤ **After 7 miles,** when it becomes a dual carriageway, leave A9 and join A827 to Logierait and Aberfeldy.

➤ **At A85 T-junction,** turn right to Crianlarich.
➤ **At the roundabout in Crianlarich,** turn right on A82 to Tyndrum.
➤ **After nearly 40 miles,** at the roundabout after Ballachulish, turn right on A828 to Oban.
➤ **After crossing the Connel Bridge,** turn left on A85 and continue to Oban, where the day's route ends.

TOUR (41) Dover High-Mile Tour Day 4

DAY 4 MORNING

WHEN THE sun shines on Oban, it's one of the most beautiful towns from which any touring route could start. It would be a shame to leave, if the roads weren't so good – down to Lochgilphead and up to Inverary, around gorgeous Loch Fyne. The A82 around Loch Lomond is generally busier – and it leads to bustling Glasgow: best nip past the city quickly on bigger roads from Dumbarton to Greenock, our lunch stop.

FROM Oban
TO Greenock
DISTANCE 125 miles
RIDING TIME 2.5 hours

Route Description

➤ **Leave Oban** on A816 towards Campbeltown.

➤ **At mini-roundabout,** turn left on A83 to go into Lochgilphead. Stay on this road for 35 miles, through Inverary and round Loch Fyne.

➤ **At Tarbet,** this road becomes A82, heading south to Dumbarton and Glasgow.

➤ **Look out:** as A82 becomes a two-lane road again, leaving Dumbarton, take the exit for the Erskine Bridge (A899).

➤ **Cross Erskine Bridge.** Stay on road as it becomes M898.

➤ **When A898 divides,** bear right on M8 to Greenock.

➤ **When M8** motorway finishes, continue along A8 to Greenock, where the morning's route ends.

Inverary on the banks of Loch Fyne

ROUTE TYPE Tour	DISTANCE 125 miles morning	180 miles afternoon

DAY 4 AFTERNOON

OUR AFTERNOON route hugs the coast, escaping the cities and heading out into Scotland's least populated region, Dumfries and Galloway. This area of rolling hills and fragrant forests is blessed with brilliant and traffic-free roads – and though these Southern Uplands are less famous than the Highlands, they contain beautiful passes and Scotland's highest village, Wanlockhead – through which our route passes on its way to the overnight stop in Moffat.

FROM Greenock
TO Moffat
DISTANCE 180 miles
RIDING TIME 4 hours

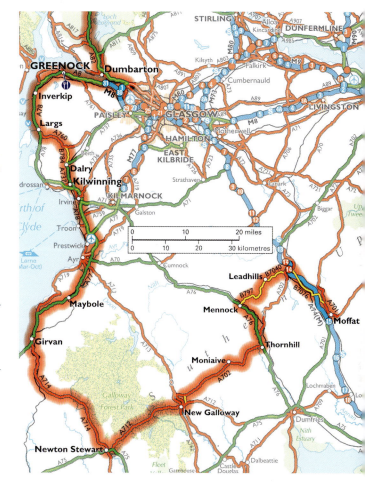

Route Description

➤ **Leave Greenock** on A78 to Inverkip, staying on this road all the way to Largs.
➤ **At the traffic lights** in Largs turn left on A760 to Kilbirnie.
➤ **After 6 miles,** turn right onto the B784 to Dalry.
➤ **At B780,** turn right to Dalry.
➤ **In Dalry,** turn right on A737 to Kilwinning.
➤ **Cross Kilwinning** and join A78 to Ayr.
➤ **At A77 roundabout,** carry on towards Ayr and Stranraer.
➤ **At second Girvan rbt,** take the second exit for A714 to Newton Stewart and Pinmore.
➤ **Cross Newton Stewart** and turn left on A75 to Dumfries.

➤ **After a mile,** turn left on A712 to New Galloway.
➤ **At A713,** go right then left across the staggered crossroads.
➤ **After half a mile,** turn left on B7075 to Moniaive.
➤ **At A702,** turn right to Moniaive.
➤ **In Thornhill,** turn left on A76 towards Kilmarnock.
➤ **In Mennock,** turn right on B797 to Wanlockhead.

➤ **In Leadhills,** turn right on B7040 to Elvanfoot.
➤ **At A702 T-junction,** turn left towards Abington.
➤ **Go straight over rbt,** under the motorway, then turn right on B7076 to Beattock.
➤ **After 7 miles,** turn left (crossing motorway again) on B719 to Greenhillstairs.
➤ **At A701 T-junction,** turn right to Moffat where the day's route ends.

DAY 5 MORNING

FROM SCOTLAND we return to England and the glorious Lake District. It's one of the best places in Britain to ride a bike, with spectacular scenery and no shortage of cafes in the tourist-friendly towns. The route stops in Coniston where a favourite lunch stop is the Bluebird Café on the shores of Coniston Water.

FROM Moffat
TO Coniston
DISTANCE 125 miles
RIDING TIME 3 hours

Route Description

➤ **Leave Moffat** on A701 to Dumfries.

➤ **From Dumfries,** take A75 to Carlisle.

➤ **At Gretna,** join A74(M) south to England. Crossing the border, this becomes M6.

➤ **Leave M6** at Junction 44, taking A689 to Workington. After crossing eight roundabouts, at the ninth the road to Workington becomes A595: stay with it.

➤ **After 20 miles,** turn left on A5086 to Cockermouth.

➤ **In Cockermouth,** cross the river, turn left at the first mini-roundabout and go straight over the next one. On the high street, take the first left after the statue, then go left at the lights on B5292.

➤ **When the road forks,** bear right on B5289 to Low Lorton and Buttermere.

➤ **Look out:** don't miss the left turn about 2 miles after Lorton to stay on B5289 to Buttermere.

➤ **Stay on B5289** over Honister Pass, all the way to Keswick.

➤ **Turn left** on Keswick high street, taking A591 to Windermere.

➤ **In Ambleside,** pick up A593 to Coniston, following the signs through the one-way system. Stay on A593 all the way to Coniston, where the morning route ends.

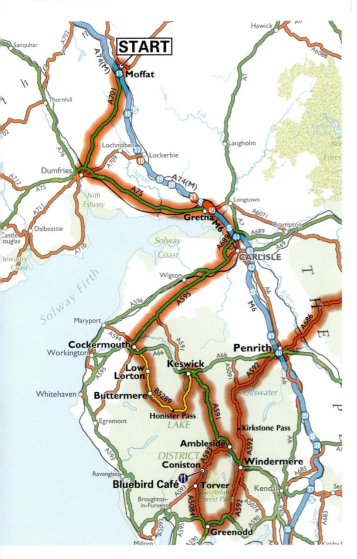

ROUTE TYPE Tour	DISTANCE 125 miles morning	165 miles afternoon

DAY 5 AFTERNOON

THE AFTERNOON'S route makes a stab at claiming the 'best half-day of the tour' award. Looping back through the Lakes, it climbs Hartside Pass to Alston, before scrolling on quiet roads through Teesdale and into the Yorkshire Dales. These are utterly brilliant roads – huge views, great corners, low traffic levels. It's riding heaven, all the way to the overnight stop in Skipton.

FROM Coniston
TO Skipton
DISTANCE 165 miles
RIDING TIME 3.5 hours

Route Description

➤ **From Coniston,** continue along A593 towards Broughton.
➤ **In Torver** turn left on A5084 to Greenodd.
➤ **At A5092 junction,** turn left to Kendal.
➤ **At A590 roundabout,** turn left to Kendal.
➤ **After 5 miles,** turn left on A592 to Bowness. Stay on this road over Kirkstone Pass and along the shore of Ullswater.
➤ **At A66 roundabout,** turn right to Penrith.
➤ **Go straight across** M6 rbt. At the second rbt, take the second exit for A686 to Alston.
➤ **In Alston,** turn right towards Scotch Corner, climbing the cobbled street by the church. At the end of the high street, go straight ahead on B6277 to Barnard Castle.

➤ **In Middleton-in-Teesdale,** turn right on B6277 to Scotch Corner. Half a mile later, turn right on the B6276 to Brough.
➤ **Turn right** at the T-junction to go into Brough. At the clock tower, turn left on A685 to Kirkby Stephen.
➤ **At the traffic lights** in Kirkby Stephen, turn left on B6259 to Nateby.
➤ **At A684 T-junction,** turn left to Hawes.
➤ **In Hawes,** take the first right turn for B6255 to Ingleton.
➤ **At Ribblehead viaduct,** turn left on B6479 to Horton-in-Ribblesdale.

➤ **Turn left** in Settle, ride through the town and turn left at the roundabout on A65.
➤ **Stay on A65** all the way to Skipton, where the day's route ends.

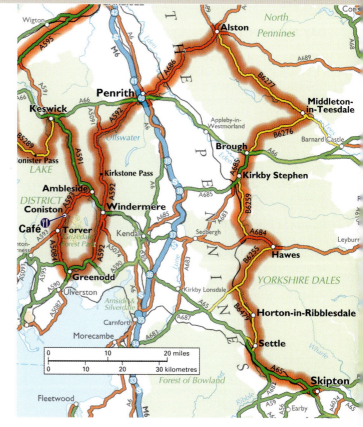

The A592 to Kirkstone Pass

TOUR (41) Dover High-Mile Tour Day 6

DAY 6 MORNING

TRAVERSING THE towns of Yorkshire takes a little delicate planning: there's great riding on the moors here, but there are a few built-up areas to be patiently negotiated. It's worth it, as from Holmfirth we're into the riding paradise of the Peak District. Our route takes in Holm Moss, Snake Pass, Hope Valley, High Peak and the Cat 'n' Fiddle. A late lunch stop is scheduled in the famous bike hangout Lynn's Raven Café at Whitchurch, but you could try Crewe for an earlier lunch.

FROM Skipton
TO Prees Heath
DISTANCE 140 miles
RIDING TIME 3.5 hours

Route Description

➤ **Leave Skipton** on A6131, picking up A629 to Keighley.
➤ **From Keighley,** continue along A629 to Halifax.
➤ **At crossroads,** turn right on A6033 to Hebden Bridge.
➤ **In Hebden Bridge,** turn left on A646 to Mytholmroyd and Halifax.
➤ **From Halifax,** take A629 to Huddersfield.
➤ **Take Huddersfield** ring-road to A616 to Holmfirth.
➤ **Look out:** at the traffic lights in Honley, bear right on A6024 to Holmfirth. Stay on this road all the way to A628.
➤ **At A628** turn right to Manchester.

➤ **Look out:** take the first left for B6105 to Glossop.
➤ **At the traffic lights** in Glossop, turn left on A57 to Sheffield (Snake Pass).
➤ **At the traffic lights by Ladybower Reservoir** – turn left on the A6013 to Bamford.
➤ **At traffic lights,** turn right on A6187 to Castleton. At T-junction on the moor, turn right to Chapel-in-le-Frith.
➤ **In Chapel-in-le-Frith,** turn right on A6 to Stockport.
➤ **At second roundabout,** turn left on A5004 to Whaley Bridge. Stay on this road all the way to Buxton.
➤ **In Buxton town centre** turn right on A53 to Leek.

➤ **At edge of Buxton,** turn right on A54 to Congleton.
➤ **When road forks,** bear right on A537 to Macclesfield (the Cat 'n' Fiddle road).
➤ **From Macclesfield,** take A536 to Congleton.
➤ **From Congleton,** take A534 to Sandbach and Crewe.
➤ **At Nantwich,** turn right on A51 to Chester. Cross two roundabouts then, at traffic lights, go straight on A534 to Wrexham.
➤ **At A49,** turn left to Whitchurch.
➤ **Join A41** around Whitchurch and follow it towards Wolverhampton. This is a short dual-carriageway leading to a roundabout, where the morning route ends at Lynn's Raven Café in Prees Heath.

| ROUTE TYPE Tour | DISTANCE 140 miles morning | 155 miles afternoon |

DAY 6 AFTERNOON

THE JOY of a full tour like this is watching the land change. The purple heather of the Scottish Glens and the Pennines, the lush Lake District and the windswept Dales and Peak District are all very dramatic, but the afternoon's route showcases a quieter kind of beauty as it winds its way into the leafy heart of England. With rolling green hills and stone-built villages, the contrast with some of the earlier landscapes couldn't be greater, but for many people, this is rural England at its beautiful best.

FROM Prees Heath
TO Oxford
DISTANCE 155 miles
RIDING TIME 4 hours

Route Description

➤ **From A41/A49 roundabout,** take A49 to Shrewsbury.
➤ **Join A5** around Shrewsbury, signed for North Wales. At the fourth roundabout, turn left on A488 to Bishop's Castle.
➤ **In Lydham,** turn left on A489 to Craven Arms.
➤ **At A49** turn left to Craven Arms.
➤ **In Woofferton,** turn left on A456 to Kidderminster.
➤ **In Burford,** turn right on A4112 to Tenbury Wells. At the end of the high street, carry straight on along B4204 to Clifton upon Teme.
➤ **In Martley,** turn left opposite the garage to stay on B4204 to Worcester.
➤ **Cross Worcester** following signs for county hospital or Evesham (A44).

➤ **Take A44** to Evesham. Follow A46 ring road towards M5 South until rejoining A44 to Oxford.
➤ **10 miles** from the Evesham ring road, turn right on A424 to Stow-on-the-Wold.
➤ **At the lights in Stow,** turn right on A429 towards Cirencester. At the bottom of the hill, take the left fork for A424 to Burford.
➤ **At Burford rbt,** turn left on A361 to Chipping Norton.
➤ **After 2 miles,** turn right on B4437 to Charlbury.
➤ **In Charlbury,** turn left then right to stay on B4437 to Woodstock.
➤ **At A44,** turn right to Woodstock. Stay on this road to Oxford, where the route ends.

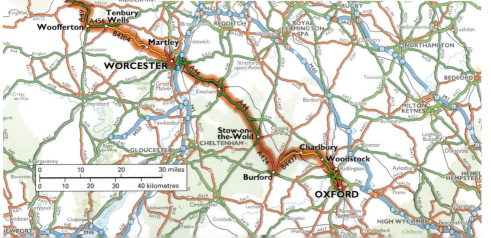

TOUR (41) Dover High-Mile Tour Day 7

DAY 7 MORNING

THE TOUR finishes with a run back into Britain's Neolithic past, along the Vale of the White Horse and into Avebury. From there it's south and east, to Winchester – former seat of Anglo Saxon kings – and then to lunch at Loomies Cafe, a biking institution in the Southeast.

Avebury's vast stone circle is a World Heritage Site

FROM Oxford
TO Loomies Café
DISTANCE 100 miles
RIDING TIME 2.5 hours

Route Description

➤ **Leave Oxford** on A420 to Swindon.

➤ **Cross Swindon** following the signs for Devizes until you pick up A4361 to Wroughton.

➤ **In Wroughton,** turn right at the roundabout after the hospital to stay on A4361 to Devizes.

➤ **Leaving Avebury,** as the road passes through the stone circle and turns sharply to the right, carry straight on along B4003 – it's not signed but will lead you past the West Kennet Avenue of standing stones.

➤ **At A4,** turn left then take the first turn on the right, the minor road to East Kennett.

➤ **At the T-junction,** turn right to Alton Barnes.

➤ **At A345 roundabout,** go straight across, taking the main road towards Salisbury.

➤ **In Upavon,** turn left on A342 to Andover.

➤ **At A338,** go left, then right, across the staggered crossroads to stay on A342.

➤ **From Andover,** join A303 towards London.

➤ **After about 8 miles,** take the exit for A34. At the bottom of the sliproad, turn right to take A34 to Winchester.

➤ **At M3 roundabout,** take the second exit for Petersfield (A272) and Alton (A31).

➤ **At next roundabout,** at the bottom of the hill, turn left on A31. At the next roundabout, take the last exit – doubling back on yourself. Then take the first left for the A272 to Petersfield.

➤ **After 9 miles,** at traffic lights, turn right on A32: Loomies Café is a few hundred metres down the road, on the right.

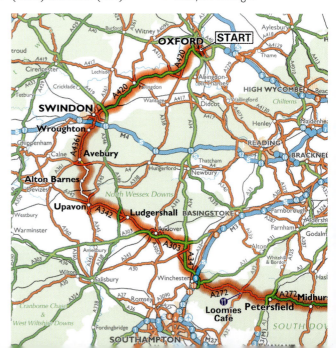

ROUTE TYPE Tour	**DISTANCE** 100 miles morning	110 miles afternoon

DAY 7 AFTERNOON

THE FINAL run back to the M20 – whether to the Eurotunnel, the Dover ferry or the road back to London – is built around one of the most popular biking roads in the south: the A272. It cuts through classic English countryside, linking picture-postcard towns and quaint villages. The last leg back to the services dives out to Rye and Camber Sands on the coast – one last chance for a seaside ice cream. Those looking for a quicker return to London could stay on the A21 from Hurst Green, through Tunbridge Wells.

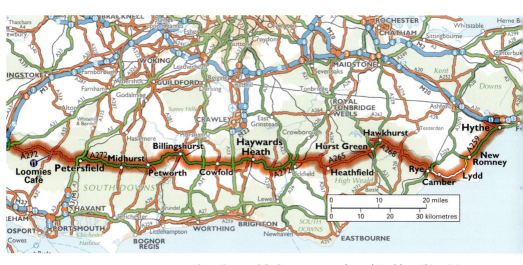

FROM Loomies Café
TO J11 M20 (Folkestone/ Eurotunnel)
DISTANCE 110 miles
RIDING TIME 3 hours

Route Description

➤ **From Loomies Cafe,** turn left on A32. Then, at traffic lights, turn right on A272 to Petersfield.

➤ **Stay on A272** for nearly 70 miles – through the towns of Petersfield, Midhurst, Petworth, Billingshurst, Haywards Heath and Maresfield.

➤ **After leaving Hadlow Down** village, the road reaches a T-junction. Turn right on A267 to Heathfield.

➤ **When the road forks,** carry straight on along A265 to Heathfield. Stay on A265 all the way to Hurst Green.

➤ **At T-junction** in Hurst Green turn left on the A21 to London.

➤ **After half a mile,** turn right on A229 to Hawkhurst.

➤ **At the traffic lights** in Hawkhurst, turn right on A268 to Rye. After 5 miles, this road becomes A28.

➤ **Look out:** don't miss the right turn just after the level crossing to continue to Rye on A268.

➤ **At mini-roundabout** in Rye, turn left on A259 to Dover.

➤ **After a mile,** turn right on the minor road to Camber and Lydd Airport. Stay on road through Lydd, until it rejoins A259 outside New Romney.

➤ **Turn right** on A259 to Folkestone.

➤ **From one-way system** in Hythe, join A261 to Junction 11 of the M20, where the tour ends.

Discover charming Rye

TOUR (42) Hull Relaxed Tour Day 1

DAY 1 MORNING

LIKE THE two Dover tours, the Hull tours were conceived to help visitors to the UK, focusing on those arriving from the Rotterdam or Zeebrugge crossing. Going to Hull cuts out the populous southeastern corner of England, which has some distinct advantages. Like the previous tours, though, these two trips also make it easy for anyone living in the northern half of the UK to get to the best riding in other parts of the country.

FROM Hull
TO Boston
DISTANCE 80 miles
RIDING TIME 2 hours

Route Description

➤ **Leave Hull** on the Humber Bridge (toll-free for motorcycles), which becomes A15 on the south bank.

➤ **At M180 roundabout,** go straight over on A18 towards the airport.

➤ **Leaving Great Limber,** take the first right turn after the national speed limit signs on the minor road to Caistor.

➤ **At A1173,** carry straight on.

➤ **At A46,** go straight over the staggered crossroads, taking B1225 to Rothwell and Horncastle.

➤ **Stay on B1225** – going over several crossroads – until it meets A158.

➤ **At A158 T-junction** turn left to Horncastle.

➤ **At second set** of traffic lights in Horncastle, turn right on A153 to Sleaford.

➤ **Look out:** don't miss the left turn, immediately after leaving Horncastle, for B1183 to Scrivelsby.

➤ **At A155 T-junction,** turn left to Skegness.

➤ **In West Keal,** turn right on A16 to Boston, where the morning's route ends.

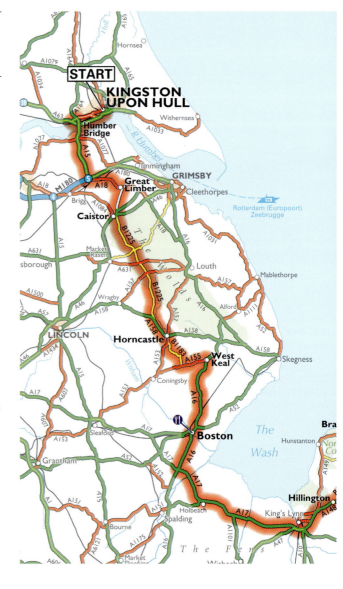

ROUTE TYPE Tour	DISTANCE 80 miles morning	105 miles afternoon

DAY 1 AFTERNOON

THIS RELAXED tour is structured around linking fascinating cities – county towns that are packed with character, making them great destinations for the touring motorcyclist. This afternoon's destination is Norwich – after a brief run across the Fens and out around the lovely North Norfolk coast. Keep an eye out for visiting celebrities if you stop for coffee in fashionable Brancaster.

FROM Boston
TO Norwich
DISTANCE 105 miles
RIDING TIME 2.5 hours

Route Description
➤ **From Boston,** continue on A16 to Spalding.

➤ **At A17 roundabout,** turn left to King's Lynn.
➤ **At large King's Lynn roundabout,** go straight over on A47 towards Swaffham.
➤ **1½ miles later,** take the exit Cromer and A149.
➤ **Cross two roundabouts** and, at the third, turn right on A148 to Fakenham.
➤ **In Hillington,** turn left on B1153 to Flitcham.
➤ **In Docking,** turn right on B1454 to Fakenham, then turn left by the church on B1153 to Brancaster.
➤ **In Brancaster,** turn right on A149 to Wells.
➤ **Sightseeing:** you can detour into Burnham Market or Wells-next-the-Sea. Otherwise, stay with A149 all the way to Sheringham.
➤ **At the roundabout in Sheringham,** turn right on A1082 to Holt.

➤ **At A148,** turn right to King's Lynn.
➤ **At rbt in Holt,** turn left on B1149 to Norwich.
➤ **At A140** turn right to continue into Norwich, where the day's route ends.

Boston's historic working windmill

TOUR (42) Hull Relaxed Tour Day 2

DAY 2 MORNING

Ely Cathedral

FROM HISTORIC Norwich, across East Anglia to the dreaming spires of Oxford, this is a relaxed day's ride. It starts heading out to the fringes of Thetford Forest (Britain's largest area of woodland). From there it cuts inland across the Fens, past the Isle of Ely with its mind-boggling cathedral and on to the lunch stop in the quaint market town of St Ives.

FROM Norwich
TO St Ives
DISTANCE 80 miles
RIDING TIME 2 hours

Route Description

➤ **Leave Norwich** on B1108 to Watton. Continue through the town.

➤ **At A1065 T-junction,** turn left towards Newmarket.

➤ **At the Mundford roundabout,** turn right on A134 to King's Lynn.

➤ **At the T-junction** opposite the Foldgate Inn, turn left

on A1122 to the town of Downham Market.

➤ **At A10 roundabout,** turn left to Ely. Unless going into town to visit the Cathedral, stay on A10 around Ely.

➤ **From roundabout** by services, take A142 to March.

➤ **Cross one roundabout** on A142 then, 3 miles later, turn left on A1421 to Haddenham.

➤ **In Haddenham,** turn right on A1123 to Huntingdon. Stay on this road to St Ives, where the morning route ends (follow the signs for the town centre to find the cafes).

| **ROUTE TYPE** Tour | **DISTANCE** 80 miles morning | 105 miles afternoon |

DAY 2 AFTERNOON

IT'S THE combination of great bends, classic English countryside views and low levels of traffic that make these roads superb – perfect for laid-back bikes but also for touring. Crossing Bedford and Milton Keynes, the route heads into the Chiltern Hills and on to the fantastic city of Oxford.

FROM St Ives
TO Oxford
DISTANCE 105 miles
RIDING TIME 3 hours

Route Description

➤ **Leave St Ives,** continuing along A1123 to Huntingdon.
➤ **A mile after the St Ives** traffic lights, turn right on the B1090 to Abbots Ripton.
➤ **Turn right** in Abbots Ripton, staying on B1090 towards Wood Walton.
➤ **Look out:** don't miss the right turn, 2 miles later, staying on B1090 to Wood Walton.
➤ **At the roundabout,** turn right on the old A1, running parallel to the A1(M). Stay on it for 3 miles, crossing three roundabouts, following signs for Glatton.
➤ **Look out:** don't miss the right turn off the old A1 for B660. At the T-junction, turn left towards Glatton.
➤ **At the T-junction,** turn left towards Kimbolton, still on B660.
➤ **Look out:** half a mile outside Old Weston, turn left to stay on B660.
➤ **In Kimbolton,** turn left on B645 and ride through the village. Just as you leave – passing the stately home that's now the school – turn right to resume on B660 to Bedford.

➤ **In Bedford,** join A4280 then A6 and A428 to Northampton.
➤ **At A422 roundabout,** turn left – taking A422 towards Milton Keynes and M1.
➤ **At A509 roundabout,** turn left towards Milton Keynes.
➤ **In Milton Keynes,** cross the many roundabouts following signs for Buckingham and A422, until reaching A5.
➤ **At the major A5 rbt,** turn right to Hinckley.
➤ **At the next rbt,** take the second exit for A422 to Buckingham.
➤ **From Buckingham** take A413 to Aylesbury.
➤ **From Aylesbury,** take A41 to Bicester.

➤ **Look out:** don't miss the left turn on the minor road to Winchendon, by the gatehouse for Waddesdon Manor.
➤ **Go straight on** in Chearsley, to Long Crendon.
➤ **Turn left** in Long Crendon on B4011 to Thame.
➤ **At Thame roundabout,** turn right on A418 to Oxford.
➤ **When A418** meets A40, join the main road to Oxford, where the day's route ends.

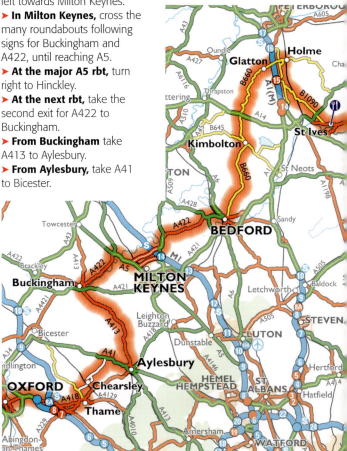

TOUR (42) Hull Relaxed Tour Day 3

DAY 3 MORNING

A FANTASTIC MORNING of riding awaits on the third day of our tour – through the Cotswolds and into the Malvern Hills. The route passes through some of the most beautiful countryside in England, the well-tended farmland dotted with sleepy stone-built villages and shady, fragrant woods. The lunch stop is in the historic town of Ross-on-Wye.

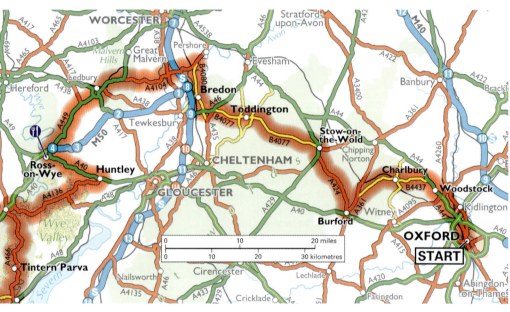

FROM Oxford
TO Ross-on-Wye
DISTANCE 85 miles
RIDING TIME 2 hours

Ross-on-Wye

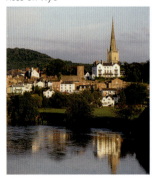

Route Description

➤ **Leave Oxford** on A44 towards Evesham.

➤ **A mile after** passing through Woodstock, turn left on B4437 to Charlbury.

➤ **Go through Charlbury** following signs for the train station, staying on B4437.

➤ **At A361 T-junction,** turn left to Burford.

➤ **At the mini-roundabout,** turn right on the A424 to Stow-on-the-Wold.

➤ **At A429,** turn right to continue into Stow.

➤ **Stow-on-the-Wold** At second set of traffic lights, turn left on A424.

➤ **Look out:** turn left again, immediately, on B4077 to Upper Swell.

➤ **At A46 roundabout,** go straight over to Tewkesbury.

➤ **At the next lights,** turn right on B4079 to Pershore.

➤ **In Bredon,** turn left then right to take B4080 to Pershore.

➤ **At A4104,** turn left to Upton.

➤ **At A38,** turn right then left to stay on the A4104 through Upton-upon-Severn.

➤ **At A449,** turn left to Ledbury.

➤ **Follow A449** around Ledbury and stay on this road to Ross-on-Wye, where the morning's route ends.

DAY 3 AFTERNOON

FROM ENGLAND, into Wales – through the Forest of Dean and the once-disputed border Marches around Monmouth. The afternoon route heads into the hills, with some short stretches of dual carriageway through the valleys to bypass the mining towns that powered the Industrial Revolution. These get us smoothly and quickly to the best riding of the day, flowing into the Beacons and heading for the overnight stop in Brecon.

FROM Ross-on-Wye
TO Brecon
DISTANCE 115 miles
RIDING TIME 3 hours

Route Description

➤ **Leave Ross-on Wye** on A40 towards Gloucester.
➤ **At the traffic lights** in Huntley, turn right on the A4136 to Monmouth.
➤ **At the second roundabout** in Monmouth, turn left to Tintern Parava on A466.
➤ **In Chepstow,** cross the roundabout on A466 then

take the first right: B4235 to Usk.
➤ **At A472,** turn right to Usk. Stay on this road through the village, towards Pontypool.
➤ **Join A4042** towards Newport.
➤ **At the third roundabout,** turn right to resume on A472 to Pontypool.
➤ **Turn right** at the next rbt on the A4043 to Pontypool.
➤ **In Blaenavon,** turn right on B4246 to Abergavenny.
➤ **At the T-junction,** turn left to Govilon.
➤ **At the rbt,** go straight across on A4077 to Crickhowell.

➤ **Crickhowell** – at the traffic lights, carry straight on towards Llangynidr on B4558.
➤ **Look out:** don't miss the badly signed left turn 3½ miles later, for B4560 to Beaufort. If you reach Llangynidr, you've missed the turn.
➤ **In Garnlydan,** join A465 to Merthyr Tydfil.
➤ **Stay on A465** around Merthyr Tydfil, following signs for Neath.
➤ **At A470 roundabout,** turn right and take this road to Brecon, where the day's route ends.

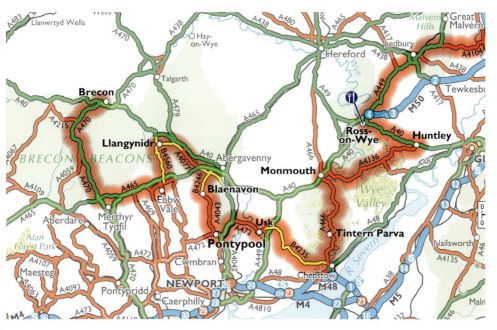

TOUR (42) Hull Relaxed Tour Day 4

DAY 4 MORNING

THE FOURTH day of the tour is deliberately relaxed – either allowing a late start or an early finish, for a bit of sightseeing in historic Warwick at the end of the day. First, though, there's some riding to be done – and the morning has perhaps the finest roads of the trip. From Brecon we head west before turning north on fantastic wide, smooth, flowing roads all the way to the lunch stop in the charming market town of Knighton.

FROM Brecon
TO Knighton
DISTANCE 75 miles
RIDING TIME 1.5 hours

Route Description

➤ **Leave Brecon** on A40 to Llandovery.

➤ **In Llandovery,** just before the level crossing, turn right on A483 to Builth Wells.

➤ **Cross Builth Wells** following signs for Llandrindod Wells (A483). Cross the river, turn right opposite the Royal Welsh Showground, still on A483.

➤ **Look out:** take the first right turn after the showground roundabout, for A481 to New Radnor.

➤ **At A44 T-junction,** turn left to Rhayader.

➤ **In Penybont,** turn right on the A488 to Knighton, where the morning's route ends.

Builth Wells

ROUTE TYPE Tour	**DISTANCE** 75 miles morning	105 miles afternoon

DAY 4 AFTERNOON

FROM WALES, back into England. The afternoon's route winds its way through the Shropshire hills and into Staffordshire, along quiet byways through unspoilt villages. There's a bit of urban riding to cross Kidderminster (a pleasant town for an afternoon coffee) and around Droitwich, before the final push to Stratford-upon-Avon and the day's final destination in Warwick. If you do want to visit Warwick Castle, it may be wise to take the A46 from Alcester straight to Warwick – it's much quicker, though not much of a ride.

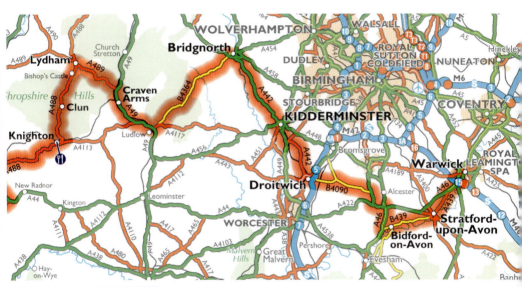

FROM Knighton
TO Warwick
DISTANCE 105 miles
RIDING TIME 2.5 hours

Route Description

➤ **From Knighton,** continue along A488 to Clun.
➤ **In Lydham,** turn right on A489 to Craven Arms.
➤ **At A49 T-junction** turn right to Leominster.
➤ **At Ludlow roundabout,** turn left on A4117 to Kidderminster.
➤ **Look out:** after 1 mile, turn left on B4364 to Bridgnorth.
➤ **Turn right at roundabout** on A458 to Stourbridge.

➤ **At the next roundabout,** turn right on A442 to Kidderminster.
➤ **Cross Kidderminster** following signs for Worcester and M5, taking A449.
➤ **Look out:** at the traffic lights on the way out of Kidderminster, turn left on A442 to Droitwich.
➤ **At roundabout, turn left** on A38 to Bromsgrove.
➤ **At the traffic lights,** turn right on B4090 to Alcester. Turn left at the next set of traffic lights to stay on this road.
➤ **At A441 T-junction,** turn right to Evesham.

➤ **Look out:** don't miss the left turn after 2 miles for A422 to Stratford-upon-Avon.
➤ **At the roundabout,** turn right on A46 to Evesham. At the second roundabout, turn right again to take our main route towards Evesham (or turn left on A46 if you want to shorten the ride).
➤ **At the next roundabout,** turn left on the B439 to Bidford. Stay on this road through Stratford-upon-Avon.
➤ **Leave Stratford** on A439 to Warwick. When this road meets the A46, turn right to continue to Warwick, where the day's ride ends.

TOUR (42) Hull Relaxed Tour Day 5

DAY 5 MORNING

THE FINAL day of this short tour returns to the port of Hull, heading through the heart of England – initially with a stretch of the Fosse Way. Don't worry: there are only a few miles of this Roman road, after which the route concentrates on corners. Using quiet roads across Leicestershire and Rutland, England's smallest county, the route heads to Grantham for lunch.

FROM Warwick
TO Grantham
DISTANCE 85 miles
RIDING TIME 2 hours

Route Description

➤ **Leave Warwick** on A425 towards Banbury.
➤ **Look out:** After crossing the river and one roundabout, take the left turn for Harbury and the Warwick Technology Park.
➤ **At B4455 T-junction** turn left to Leicester.
➤ **At A428,** turn left towards Coventry and then right to continue on B4455.
➤ **In Brinklow,** turn right on B4027 to Lutterworth.
➤ **At A5 rbt,** turn right to Lutterworth on A4303. Cross the motorway and follow A4304 to Market Harborough.
➤ **Market Harborough:** Go straight across town, picking up A427 to Corby.
➤ **Look out:** take the first left after the roundabout for B664 to Uppingham.

➤ **In Medbourne,** turn left to stay on B664 to Uppingham.
➤ **In Uppingham** turn right, then turn left at the traffic lights on the A6003 to Oakham.
➤ **Go straight over** A47 rbt, staying on A6003.
➤ **At Oakham,** go straight over five roundabouts on the A606 to Nottingham.
➤ **In Melton Mowbray,** take the one-way system, following signs for Grantham (A607).
➤ **Take A607** to Grantham, where the morning's route comes to an end.

Market Harborough

| ROUTE TYPE Tour | DISTANCE 85 miles morning | 110 miles afternoon |

DAY 5 AFTERNOON

THE TOUR finishes with a classic afternoon's ride across the rural roads of Lincolnshire. These are some of my favourite roads in England – quiet, scenic and loaded with a fantastic array of corners. If you want to shorten the ride, you can stay on the A15 all the way to the Humber Bridge, but that means missing out on Bardney Bends and the majestic B1203 across the Wolds, which finish the trip off in memorable style.

FROM Grantham
TO Hull
DISTANCE 110 miles
RIDING TIME 3 hours

Route Description

➤ **Leave Grantham** on A52 towards Boston. At the roundabout, turn left to stay on this road.

➤ **At A15 roundabout,** turn left to Sleaford.

➤ **At the main A17 roundabout,** take the second exit to stay on A15 to Lincoln.

➤ **After 11 miles,** turn right on B1178 to Bardney.

➤ **At B1188,** cross the staggered crossroads and continue to Potterhanworth.

➤ **In Potterhanworth,** turn left on B1202 to Bardney.

➤ **At the T-junction,** turn right on B1190 to Bardney.

➤ **When the road turns sharply right** in Bardney, turn left on B1202 to Stainfield and Wragby,

➤ **In Wragby and Market Rasen,** go straight across at the traffic lights. From Rasen, the road becomes B1203.

➤ **At A18 roundabout,** turn left towards Brigg and M180.

➤ **Look out:** don't miss the right turn for B1211 to Ulceby, 2 miles after the dual carriageway stretch of A18 (where A18 turns hard left).

➤ **In Ulceby turn left** on the high street then, after half a mile, turn right on A1077 to Barton-upon-Humber.

➤ **In Barton,** follow signs for the Humber Bridge.

➤ **Join A15** to cross the Humber Bridge and return to Hull, where the tour ends.

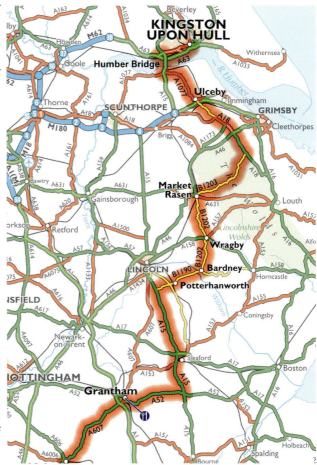

TOUR 43 Hull High-Mile Tour Day 1

DAY 1 MORNING

LIKE THE other Hull tour, this seven-day trip is designed to quickly guide visitors to the UK and Brits in the northern half of the country to the best riding this island has to offer. With longer days and some challenging roads better suited to solo riders than pillion couples, this tour takes in the Highlands and West Coast of Scotland – but it begins by heading across Yorkshire to the glorious Lake District.

FROM Hull
TO Grassington
DISTANCE 115 miles
RIDING TIME 3 hours

Route Description

➤ **Leave Hull** on A1079 to Beverley. Stay on it, following signs for Beverley race course.
➤ **At the Howden roundabout,** take the third exit for A1035 to Bridlington.
➤ **At the next rbt,** turn left on B1248 to Malton.

➤ **In Bainton,** turn right on A614, then, at rbt, carry straight on along B1248 to Malton.
➤ **In Wetwang** turn left on A166 to York.
➤ **At York ringroad,** turn right on A64 to Scarborough, turning right at the next roundabout to stay on this road.
➤ **After 5 miles,** turn left on minor road to Sheriff Hutton.
➤ **At T-junction,** turn right to Terrington.
➤ **In Sheriff Hutton,** go straight across the roundabout.

➤ **At next T-junction,** turn left to Dalby.
➤ **In Hovingham,** turn left on B1257 to Helmsley.
➤ **In Sproxton,** turn left on A170 to Thirsk.
➤ **Cross Thirsk** and take the A61 to Ripon.
➤ **Go through Ripon** town centre and pick up B6265 to Patley Bridge.
➤ **At T-junction,** turn right to stay on B6265. Take this road all the way to Grassington, where the morning route ends.

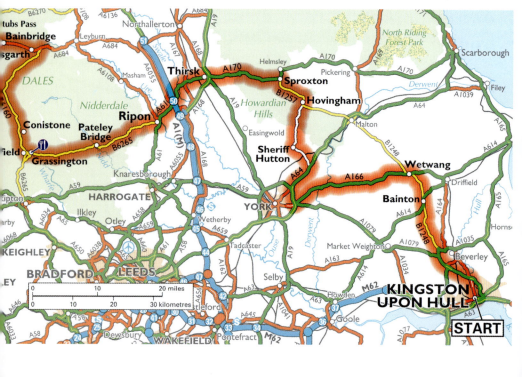

TOUR (43) **Hull High-Mile Tour Day 1**

| **ROUTE TYPE** Tour | **DISTANCE** 115 miles morning | 170 miles afternoon |

DAY 1 AFTERNOON

IF YOU thought the morning ride was good, prepare to recalibrate your expectations. The afternoon route heads through Wharfedale, over Buttertubs Pass and into Cumbria

– challenging roads in spectacular scenery. There's a little functional riding from Kendal to the coast, but from Greenodd onwards the roads are great, building up to the Hardknott and Wrynose passes, before the final run in to the overnight stop in Keswick on the A591.

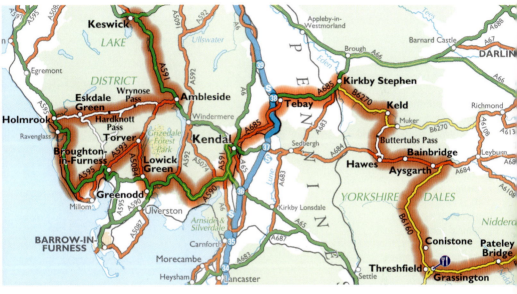

FROM Grassington
TO Keswick
DISTANCE 170 miles
RIDING TIME 3.5 hours

Route Description
➤ **From Grassington,** continue along B6265 to Threshfield.
➤ **In Threshfield,** turn right on B6160 to Conistone.
➤ **At A684,** turn left to Aysgarth.
➤ **Turn left** in Bainbridge to stay on A684 to Hawes.
➤ **In Hawes,** turn right on the minor road to Hardraw.
➤ **Turn left** at T-junction. Take the first right to Simonstone and Muker: Buttertubs Pass.

➤ **Turn left** at the T-junction, taking B6270 to Keld.
➤ **In Nateby,** turn right on B6259 to Kirkby Stephen.
➤ **In Kirkby Stephen,** turn left just before the lights, taking A685 to Kendal.
➤ **Cross Kendal** following signs for Lancaster. At A591, bear left – still towards Lancaster.
➤ **Leave A591** at next junction, taking A590 to Barrow.
➤ **At the Greenodd rbt,** turn right on A5092 to Workington.
➤ **Turn right** in Lowick Green on A5084 to Coniston.
➤ **In Torver,** turn left on A593 to Broughton-in-Furness.
➤ **Turn right** then right again

on A595 to Whitehaven. At T-junction, turn right.
➤ **In Holmrook,** turn right (just before the garage) on the minor road to Wasdale Head.
➤ **Look out:** after long straight, take easily missed right-turn for Eskdale Green. At T-junction, turn right through Eskdale Green.
➤ **Look out:** opposite King George IV pub, turn left to Hardknott Pass.
➤ **Crossing the cattle grid,** turn left in Cockley Beck, towards Wrynose Pass.
➤ **At A593 T-junction,** turn left to Ambleside.
➤ **From Ambleside,** take the A591 to Keswick.

TOUR (43) Hull High-Mile Tour Day 2

DAY 2 MORNING

OUR EXPLORATION of the Lake District continues with three great passes – Honister, Whinlatter and Kirkstone – before taking the majestic Hartside Pass across the Pennines, into England's border country. Our scheduled lunch stop is in picturesque Haltwhistle, but for a peek back in time to when Hardian's Wall marked the edge of the civilized world, it's only a short detour to a Roman fort at Vindolanda or Housesteads.

FROM Keswick
TO Haltwhistle
DISTANCE 115 miles
RIDING TIME 2.5 hours

Route Description

➤ **From Keswick** high street take B5289 to Borrowdale. This is Honister Pass.
➤ **At T-junction,** turn right to stay on this road to Lorton.
➤ **Turn right** in Low Lorton, on the minor road signed for Keswick.
➤ **At the T-junction,** turn right on B5292 to Keswick. This is Whinlatter Pass.
➤ **At A66 T-junction,** turn right to Keswick.
➤ **Cross the Keswick rbt,** then take the next exit from A66 to take A591 back to Ambleside.
➤ **In Ambleside,** turn left to Kirkstone. This is a road called "The Struggle".
➤ **At Kirkstone Pass,** turn left on A592 to Patterdale.

➤ **At A66 roundabout,** turn right towards Penrith.
➤ **Go straight over** M6 rbt. At the next rbt, take the second exit for A686 to Alston. This is Hartside Pass.

➤ **At A69,** turn left to Carlisle. Stay on this road for 8 miles, to reach Haltwhistle, where the morning's route ends.

Kirkstone Pass is easier with an engine

| ROUTE TYPE Tour | DISTANCE 115 miles morning | 160 miles afternoon |

DAY 2 AFTERNOON

LEAVING ENGLAND behind, the afternoon's route powers into the Scottish Borders and takes in some of the finest riding of the entire trip. There's the wild, challenging B709 through Eskdale, the flowing A708 past St Mary's Loch and the epic A701 past the Devil's Beeftub – a gorge where Scottish raiders used to hide cattle stolen from their English neighbours. Our destination is the Scottish capital, Edinburgh.

FROM Haltwhistle
TO Edinburgh
DISTANCE 160 miles
RIDING TIME 3.5 hours

Route Description

➤ **From Haltwhistle,** continue along A69 for 2 miles. Turn right on B630 to Greenhead.

➤ **Go straight across** the staggered crossroads, taking B6318 to Gilsland.

➤ **Turn right in Gilsland,** staying on B6318 to Walton.

➤ **Look out:** don't miss the left turn after crossing the river, staying on B6318 to Roadhead.

➤ **After 6 miles,** dropping down a hill on a long straight, there's a confusing junction: turn right to stay on B6318.

➤ **In Harelaw,** turn left on B6357 to Canonbie.

➤ **In Canonbie,** turn right on A7 to Hawick.

➤ **In Langholm,** turn left on B709 to Eskdalemuir. Continue on B709, then B7009, to Selkirk.

➤ **In Selkirk,** turn left on A707 to Peebles, go past the rugby club, then turn left on A708 to Moffat.

➤ **In Moffat,** turn right on A701 to Edinburgh.

➤ **Turn left** in Leadburn to take A701 to Edinburgh. Stay on this road all the way to the city, where the day's route ends.

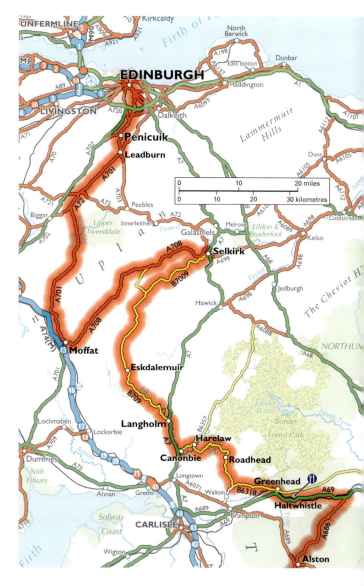

TOUR (43) Hull High-Mile Tour Day 3

DAY 3 MORNING

YOU CAN shorten this third day of the tour if you want some sightseeing time in Edinburgh (see afternoon instructions). From Scotland's capital, the third day of our tour heads to Scotland's favourite seaside resort, the lovely town of Oban. Crossing the Firth of Forth and heading away from the city belt, we pass Scotland's premier motor-racing circuit, Knockhill. We pass two of Scotland's best-loved lochs as well – Loch Earn and Loch Lomond – on the way to our lunch stop beside the scenic sea loch, Loch Fyne.

FROM Edinburgh
TO Inveraray
DISTANCE 120 miles
RIDING TIME 2.5 hours

Route Description

➤ **Leave Edinburgh** and, whichever road you take, look for signs for the Forth Road Bridge: you need to take A90 across the bridge, towards Perth (M90).

➤ **Leave M90** at Junction 2, taking A823(M) into Dunfermline.
➤ **Cross Dunfermline** following signs for A823 to Crieff.
➤ **At A977,** turn right. After 1 mile, turn left to continue on A823.
➤ **At A91,** turn right then carry straight on as the road forks to continue on A823 to Crieff.
➤ **At A822 junction,** turn right to Crieff.

➤ **In Crieff** turn left on A85 to Crianlarich.
➤ **At the T-junction** in Lochearnhead, turn right to stay on A85.
➤ **In Crianlarich,** go under the railway bridge and turn left on A82 to Glasgow. Turn left at the roundabout.
➤ **In Tarbet,** turn right on A83 to Campbeltown. Stay on this road all the way to Inveraray, where the morning route ends.

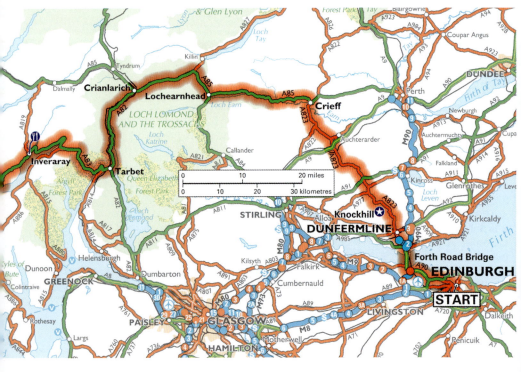

| ROUTE TYPE Tour | DISTANCE 120 miles morning | 160 miles afternoon |

DAY 3 AFTERNOON

THE AFTERNOON route features some of the most scenic roads in Scotland as we head out to Campbeltown on the Kintyre Peninsula. However, if you did want to spend the morning exploring the many delights offered by the elegant city of Edinburgh, you could leave this loop out, saving about 2½ hours, proceeding straight to Oban from Lochgilphead (though you'd need to adjust your lunch stop accordingly).

Campbeltown

FROM Inveraray
TO Oban
DISTANCE 160 miles
RIDING TIME 3.5 hours

Route Description

➤ **From Inveraray,** carry on along A83 towards Campbeltown.

➤ **At the second mini-roundabout** in Lochgilphead, turn left on A83 to continue to Campbeltown. If you've taken time out to explore Edinburgh, turn right to Oban on A816.

➤ **For the full route,** ride to Campbeltown. Once you've admired its sights (and maybe had an ice cream) leave on B842 to Carradale. This is a narrow and, in places, imperfectly surfaced road but has spectacular views.

➤ **Turning inland,** B842 becomes B8001. Stick with it until it meets A83 again.

➤ **Turn right** on A83 to Glasgow.

➤ **In Lochgilphead,** go straight over the mini-roundabout, taking A816 to Oban, where the day's route ends.

TOUR (43) Hull High-Mile Tour Day 4

DAY 4 MORNING

THIS IS where the tour gets serious. There's been some great riding so far – plenty of brilliant roads in beautiful landscapes – but from this point onwards, the Scottish landscape goes into overdrive. The morning route heads inland to Tyndrum, up over wild Rannoch Moor and down through the utterly mindblowing Glen Coe. Which seems like an amazing ride, until you turn onto the A87. The scheduled lunch stop is at the Cluanie Inn, but if you want to eat by Scotland's most romantic, famous castle, hang on for a late lunch at the Eilean Donan visitors' centre.

FROM Oban
TO Cluanie Inn
DISTANCE 130 miles
RIDING TIME 2.5 hours

Route Description

➤ **Leave Oban** on A85 to Crianlarich.
➤ **At Tyndrum,** turn left on A82 to Fort William. Go straight over the Ballachulish roundabout, staying on A82.
➤ **Cross Fort William,** staying on A82 to Inverness.
➤ **In Invergarry,** turn left immediately after the bridge on A87 to Kyle of Lochalsh.
➤ **At the T-junction,** turn left on A87, still to Kyle of Lochalsh. Stay on this road to the Cluanie Inn for lunch.

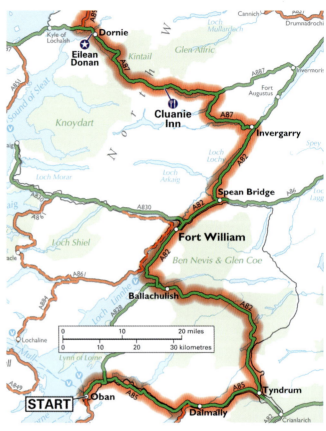

There can be only one Eilean Donan Castle

| ROUTE TYPE Tour | DISTANCE 130 miles morning | 170 miles afternoon |

DAY 4 AFTERNOON

WHETHER YOU stopped for lunch at the Cluanie Inn or at Eilean Donan castle, there's only a little more of the fabulous A87 to be ridden before heading out to the real wilds on the Wester Ross Coastal Trail. The most famous road on the afternoon route is the Bealach Na Ba, the Pass of the Cattle, leading to Applecross. It's narrow, imperfectly surfaced, challenging and utterly glorious – though the coast road round to Sheildaig is just as spectacular. The route hugs the coast through Gairloch, joining the main A835 in the Corrieshalloch Gorge, for the final run into the overnight stop in Ullapool.

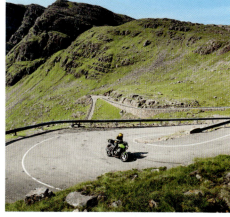

The Pass of the Cattle to Applecross

FROM Cluanie Inn
TO Ullapool
DISTANCE 170 miles
RIDING TIME 3.5 hours

Route Description

➤ **From Cluanie Inn,** continue along A87 towards Kyle of Lochalsh.

➤ **3 miles after** the bridge at Dornie, turn right on A890 to Lochcarron.

➤ **At the T-junction** after Strathcarron, turn left on A896 to Lochcarron.

➤ **After 9 miles,** turn left on the road to Applecross, Bealach Na Ba.

➤ **In Applecross,** turn right to Shieldaig.

➤ **After 24 miles,** turn left at the T-junction, rejoining A896 to Shieldaig. Stay on this road all the way to Kinlochewe.

➤ **In Kinlochewe,** turn left on A832 to Gairloch.

➤ **At A835,** turn left to Ullapool, where the day's route ends.

TOUR (43) Hull High-Mile Tour Day 5

DAY 5 MORNING

FROM ULLAPOOL the tour heads north, and though you may struggle to believe it's possible, the roads get even better. They also get even quieter, especially after passing Loch Assynt and looping out towards Lochinver, across one of the most untamed landscape in Britain. Our lunch stop is Durness, in the farthest northwest corner of Britain – relatively early, but after Durness there's nowhere else to eat for a very long time. The Cocoa Mountain Café is recommended: good sandwiches and our nomination for Europe's best hot chocolate.

Durness

FROM Ullapool
TO Durness
DISTANCE 100 miles
RIDING TIME 2 hours

Route Description
➤ **Leave Ullapool** on A835 to Achiltibuie.
➤ **After 17 miles,** turn left on A837 to Lochinver.
➤ **After 18 miles** turn right on B869 to Achmelvich.
➤ **At A894 T-junction,** turn left to Kylesku.
➤ **Stay on this road** as it becomes A838, taking it all the way to Durness.

ROUTE TYPE Tour	DISTANCE 100 miles morning	180 miles afternoon

DAY 5 AFTERNOON

THE AFTERNOON'S route runs along the north coast of Scotland. We turn south in Thurso, rather than continuing all the way to John O'Groats in the far northeast, simply because we're taking the best roads rather than ticking off tourist destinations. The afternoon run is pretty long, so you could save a little time by staying on the A9 all the way from Thurso to Inverness. However, there's little to recommend the stretch of the A9 south of the Dornoch Firth aside from the Glenmorangie distillery, so we loop inland to Bonar Bridge and take the more entertaining B9176 instead, before rejoining the A9 to reach our overnight stop in the capital of the Highlands.

FROM Durness
TO Inverness
DISTANCE 180 mils
RIDING TIME 3.5 hours

Route Description

➤ **From Durness,** take A838 to Tongue.

➤ **Stay on the road** through Tongue as it becomes A836 to Thurso.

➤ **In Thurso,** turn left at the traffic lights on A9 to Inverness.

➤ **Look out:** after 6 miles, turn right to stay on A9 to Inverness.

➤ **At the T-junction** in Latheron, turn right on A9.

➤ **After 46 miles,** turn right on the A949 to Bonar Bridge.

➤ **In Bonar Bridge,** follow the road round (across the bridge) as it becomes A836 to Ardgay.

➤ **After 4 miles** turn right on B9176 to Ardross.

➤ **Rejoining A9,** turn right and continue to Inverness, where the day's route ends.

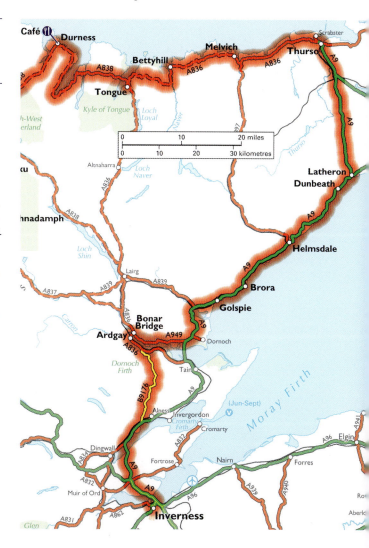

TOUR (43) Hull High-Mile Tour Day 6

DAY 6 MORNING

FROM THE capital of the Highlands, we head along the coast before diving into the heart of the Speyside whisky area and over the Cairngorms. You don't need to go on a tour of a distillery to feel intoxicated up here – this is riding that can go to your head. Best keep some decorum, though, as the route passes close to the Queen's Scottish residence, Balmoral Castle, just before the lunch stop at Braemar.

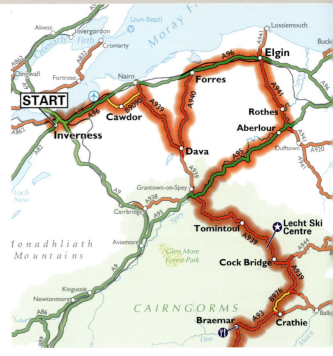

FROM Inverness
TO Braemar
DISTANCE 135 miles
RIDING TIME 3 hours

Route Description

➤ **Leave Inverness** on A96 towards Aberdeen.
➤ **Look out:** don't miss the right turn, 2 miles after Inverness Airport, for B9090 to Cawdor. Keep going straight as this road becomes B9101.
➤ **At A939 T-junction,** turn right to Grantown-on-Spey.

➤ **At the junction** by the vintage AA box, turn left on A940 to Forres.
➤ **In Forres,** rejoin A96 towards Aberdeen.
➤ **At the second roundabout** in Elgin, turn right on A941 to Perth. When it crosses the River Spey, this road becomes A95.

➤ **After 24 miles,** turn left on A939 to Tomintoul. If you reach the roundabout at Grantown on Spey, you've missed the turning by about a mile.
➤ **In Tomintoul,** turn left to stay on A939.
➤ **Look out:** don't miss the right turn half a mile outside the Tomintoul to stay on A939 to Cock Bridge.
➤ **5 miles after** the Lecht Ski Centre, turn right to stay on the A939 to Braemar.
➤ **Turn right** at Gairnshiel Lodge (just after the steep bridge) on the B976 to Crathie.
➤ **At A93,** turn right to go into Braemar for lunch.

Snow poles on the A939 to the Lecht

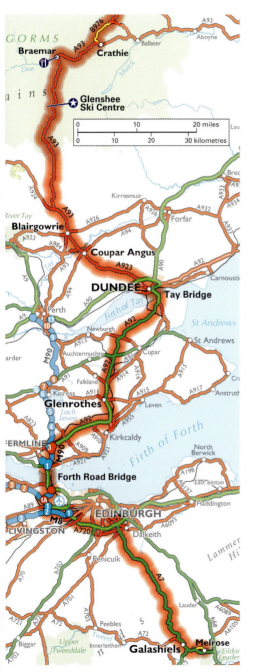

DAY 6 AFTERNOON

THERE'S MORE staggering riding through Scotland's ski country after lunch, heading down through the impressive Glenshee to Blairgowrie. From there the route cuts through relatively well-settled countryside to Dundee and across Angus to reach the Forth Road Bridge again – you can save time by heading to Perth and taking the M90 south, but that's a terribly dull ride. After the necessary evil of the Edinburgh Ring Road, you're rewarded with the ride down the scenic, flowing A7 to our overnight stop in the charming border town of Melrose.

FROM Braemar
TO Melrose
DISTANCE 155 miles
RIDING TIME 3 hours

Route Description

➤ **From Braemar,** continue heading south on A93 to Bairgowrie.

➤ **In Bairgowrie,** turn right through the town centre to pick up A923 to Dundee.

➤ **Take care** in Coupar Angus: cross one rbt, turn right at the next one and then turn left at the traffic lights to stay on the A923 to Dundee.

➤ **Cross Dundee** following signs first for Arbroath and then for the Tay Bridge until you join A92, crossing the Tay Bridge.

➤ **Stay on A92** through Glenrothes and all the way to M90.

➤ **Join M90** to cross the Forth Road Bridge and join M9 then M8 towards Edinburgh.

➤ **At Junction 1 of M8,** turn right on A720 City Bypass South.

➤ **After just over 9 miles** on the Edinburgh city bypass, take the fifth exit at the roundabout for A7 to Galashiels.

➤ **Cross Galashiels** on A7. Go straight over five roundabouts, taking A6091 to Melrose.

➤ **Cross another roundabout** on A6091.

➤ **At next rbt,** go straight over on B6374 to enter Melrose, where the day's route ends.

TOUR (43) Hull High-Mile Tour Day 7

DAY 7 MORNING

THE FINAL day of the trip starts with one of the great British biking roads: the A68 that joins England and Scotland – famed for its spectacular whoops and crests as it rises and falls across the moors. We leave this road before it can get busy, taking the even quieter and more scenic B6278 through Stanhope, heading to Yorkshire and our eventual lunch stop at Leyburn in the Dales.

FROM Melrose
TO Leyburn
DISTANCE 120 miles
RIDING TIME 3 hours

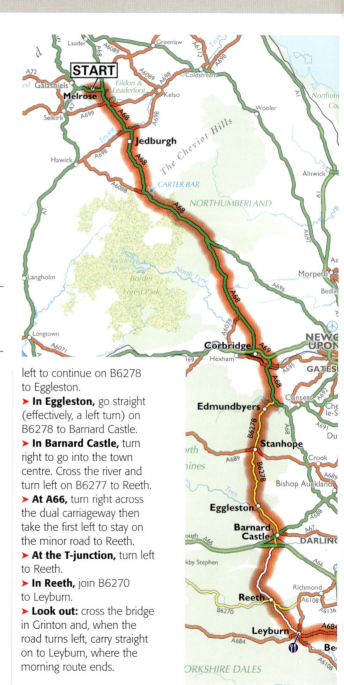

Route Description

➤ **Leave Melrose** on A6091 towards Edinburgh.
➤ **At A68 roundabout,** turn right to Jedburgh.
➤ **Look out:** don't miss the right turn after 34 miles (13 miles from the border at Carter Bar) to stay on A68 to Corbridge.
➤ **At Corbridge,** turn left on A69 towards Newcastle.
➤ **At the roundabout,** turn right on A68 signed to Darlington and the South. Cross the next roundabout, staying on A68
➤ **Look out:** don't miss the right turn 7 miles later for B6278 to Edmundbyers.
➤ **In Stanhope,** turn right on A689 to Alston. After a few hundred metres turn

left to continue on B6278 to Eggleston.
➤ **In Eggleston,** go straight (effectively, a left turn) on B6278 to Barnard Castle.
➤ **In Barnard Castle,** turn right to go into the town centre. Cross the river and turn left on B6277 to Reeth.
➤ **At A66,** turn right across the dual carriageway then take the first left to stay on the minor road to Reeth.
➤ **At the T-junction,** turn left to Reeth.
➤ **In Reeth,** join B6270 to Leyburn.
➤ **Look out:** cross the bridge in Grinton and, when the road turns left, carry straight on to Leyburn, where the morning route ends.

| ROUTE TYPE Tour | DISTANCE 120 miles morning | 160 miles afternoon |

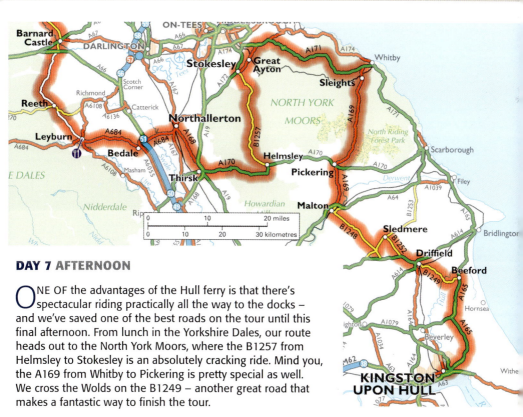

DAY 7 AFTERNOON

ONE OF the advantages of the Hull ferry is that there's spectacular riding practically all the way to the docks – and we've saved one of the best roads on the tour until this final afternoon. From lunch in the Yorkshire Dales, our route heads out to the North York Moors, where the B1257 from Helmsley to Stokesley is an absolutely cracking ride. Mind you, the A169 from Whitby to Pickering is pretty special as well. We cross the Wolds on the B1249 – another great road that makes a fantastic way to finish the tour.

FROM Leyburn
TO Hull
DISTANCE 160 miles
RIDING TIME 3.5 hours

Route Description
➤ **Leave Leyburn** on A684 towards Bedale.
➤ **Look out:** don't miss the left turn on Bedale High Street to stay on A684 to Northallerton (look for signs to A1).
➤ **From Northallerton,** take the A168 to Thirsk.
➤ **At the second roundabout** in Thirsk town centre, turn left on A170 to Scarborough.

➤ **In Helmsley** market square, turn left then right to take B1257 to Stokesley.
➤ **In Stokesley,** turn right at the roundabout, taking A173 towards Great Ayton.
➤ **At A171 roundabout,** turn right to Whitby.
➤ **After 21 miles,** turn right at the rbt on A169 to Sleights.
➤ **Cross Pickering,** staying on A169 to Malton.
➤ **In Malton** turn left at the lights. Cross the railway and, at the second mini-roundabout, turn right on B1248 to Driffield.
➤ **At Fimber roundabout,** turn left on B1251 to Bridlington.

Carry straight on in Sledmere as the road becomes B1252.
➤ **At A166 T-junction,** turn left on A166 to Bridlington.
➤ **Turn left** at roundabout on A614 to Bridlington.
➤ **At the next roundabout,** turn right on B1249 to Driffield town centre. Stay on B1249 towards Hornsea.
➤ **In Beeford,** turn right on A165 to return to Hull, where the tour finishes.

TOUR (44) Maxxis Diamond Ride Day 1

DAY 1 MORNING

TYRE COMPANY Maxxis invited RiDE magazine to set up a challenge for their readers: if they could do a high-mile four-day tour, collecting selfies with landmarks as checkpoints to prove they'd completed it, they'd win a set of the Maxxis Diamond tyres.

While a good number of hardy souls took on the Challenge, we also set up this more laid-back eight-day version of the tour. It uses all the same roads, passes all the landmarks, delivers all the same thrills – but can be enjoyed at a relaxed pace. It starts with a gentle canter through the Peak District.

Buxton's Victorian splendour

FROM Leicester Forest East Services
TO Glossop
VIA Wirksworth and Buxton
DISTANCE 85 miles
RIDING TIME 2 hours

Route Description

➤ **Head north on M1** to Junction 25, taking A52 to Derby.
➤ **From Derby's** Pentagon roundabout, take A61 towards Chesterfield.
➤ **Cross three roundabouts.** At the fourth, turn left on A38, the Derby ringroad.
➤ **Take the first sliproad** up to the roundabout and turn right on A6 to Matlock.
➤ **Look out:** after 2 miles, turn left at the lights on B5023 to Wirksworth.
➤ **In Wirksworth,** keep going straight on B5036 to Cromford.
➤ **At the lights** in Cromford, turn left on A5012 to Newhaven.
➤ **At the Newhaven** T-junction, turn right on A515 to Buxton.

➤ **Cross Buxton** town centre to take A5004 to Whaley Bridge.
➤ **At the lights** in Whaley Bridge, turn right on B5470 to Chapel-en-le-Frith.

➤ **In Chapel-en-le-Frith** town centre, turn left on A624 to Glossop, where the morning's route ends.

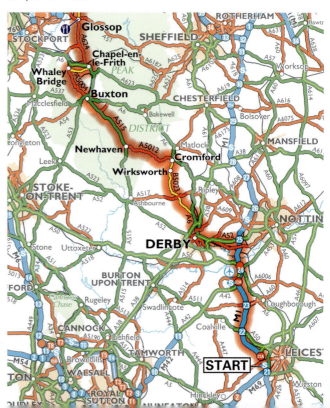

| **ROUTE TYPE** Tour | **DISTANCE** 85 miles morning | 105 miles afternoon |

DAY 1 AFTERNOON

A SUPERB AFTERNOON'S riding takes us from the Peaks into the Yorkshire Dales. After crossing Holme Moss, the route zigzags across the moors to dodge the urban sprawl of Huddersfield, Halifax and Bradford. From Settle, it heads into the wilds of the Yorkshire Dales National Park, to the lovely market town of Hawes.

FROM Glossop
TO Hawes
VIA Holmfirth, Keighley and Settle
DISTANCE 105 miles
RIDING TIME 3.5 hours

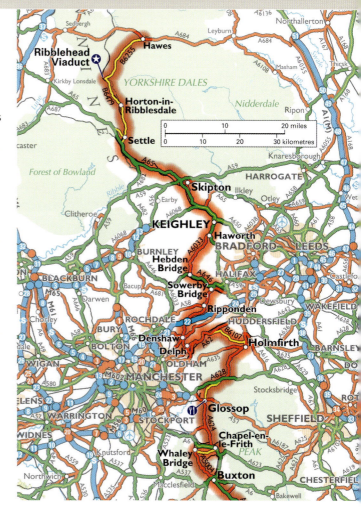

Route Description

➤ **Leave Glossop** on B6105 (passing the station).

➤ **Turn right** on A628 towards Barnsley.

➤ **After half a mile** turn left on A6024 to Holmfirth.

➤ **Go through Holmfirth** town centre, then turn left on B6107 to Netherthong (if you reach the hospital, you've missed the turning).

➤ **When the road** reaches a crossroads, go straight across (ignore the sign telling you to turn right for Meltham). Carry straight on through Meltham centre, to continue on B6107 to Marsden.

➤ **At A62 juction** turn left towards Manchester.

➤ **Look out:** take the easily missed right turn in Delph for A6052 to Denshaw.

➤ **In Denshaw,** turn left then right on A672 to Halifax.

➤ **Carry straight on** at the traffic lights in Ripponden, as the road becomes A58.

➤ **From Sowerby Bridge,** take A646 to Burnley.

➤ **In Hebden Bridge,** turn right on A6033 to Keighley.

➤ **In Haworth,** turn left on A629 to Keighley. Stay on A629 all the way to Skipton.

➤ **Don't go** into Skipton town centre: follow signs for A65 to Kendal and Settle.

➤ **At the roundabout** turn right on B6480 into Settle.

➤ **Go through Settle** town centre and take B6479 to Horton-in-Ribblesdale.

➤ **At the Ribblehead** T-junction, turn right on B6255 to Hawes, where the day's ride ends.

TOUR (44) Maxxis Diamond Ride Day 2

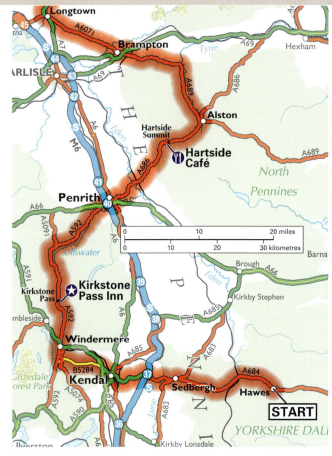

DAY 2 MORNING

A SIMPLE BUT simply brilliant ride for the morning, from the Yorkshire Dales into the Cumbrian Lake Distric. If you want to take a little time to explore this popular tourist area, follow the signs from Kendal to take the ferry across Windermere to Hawkshead village. It's simple to get back on route from there by following the signs to Ambleside and then to Kirkstone Pass. After that, the route heads up the lovely Hartside Pass to our lunch stop at the bike-friendly Hartside Café. One note: it doesn't accept credit cards, so take cash to pay for lunch.

FROM Hawes
TO Hartside Pass
DISTANCE 75 miles
RIDING TIME 2.5 hours

Route Description

➤ **Leave Hawes** on A684 to Sedbergh. Stay on this road all the way to Kendal.
➤ **Cross Kendal** following signs for Windermere (A591).

➤ **At the oval** A591 roundabout, go straight across on B5284 – signed for Hawkshead via Ferry.

➤ **At A5074** T-junction, turn right towards Windermere.
➤ **Cross the town of Windermere** following signs for Ullswater (A592).
➤ **Stay on** A592 over Kirkstone Pass and around Ullswater.
➤ **At A66** roundabout, turn right towards Penrith.
➤ **Go straight over** M6 roundabout. At the next roundabout, take the second exit for A686 to Alston. Stay on this road to the café at the summit of Hartside Pass.

Kirkstone Pass

TOUR (44) Maxxis Diamond Ride Day 2

| ROUTE TYPE Tour | DISTANCE 75 miles morning | 105 miles afternoon |

DAY 2 AFTERNOON

A SLIGHTLY LONGER ride on more challenging roads, heading from England into the Scottish Borders. There are fewer sights to stop and see on the afternoon route, cutting through wild country – unless you wish to ride a short way off the route to visit the Tibetan Tea Rooms at the Samye Ling Monastery in Eskdale. Our overnight is in the toffee capital of the borders, Moffat, where we stay in the bike-friendly Buccleuch Arms.

FROM Hartside Pass
TO Moffat
DISTANCE 105 miles
RIDING TIME 3 hours

Route Description
➤ **From the Hartside Café,** continue along A686 towards Alston.
➤ **After 5½ miles,** turn left by the war memorial on A689 to Brampton – if reach Alston, you've missed the turn.
➤ **Go straight over** the staggered crossroads with A69, into Brampton. Turn left (going straight, effectively) at the green. Half a mile later, turn right on A6071 to Longtown.
➤ **In Longtown,** turn right on A7 towards Galashiels.
➤ **In Langholm,** turn left (to cross a bridge) on B709 to Eskdalemuir.
➤ **After 13 miles,** after crossing the bridge in Eskdalemuir, turn left by the church on B723 to Lockerbie.
➤ **Look out:** don't miss the left turn to stay on B723 to Lockerbie, about 3 miles after Boreland.

➤ **At the lights** by the church in Lockerbie town centre, turn right on A709 to Lochmaben.
➤ **Turn right** at A75 roundabout, towards Stranraer.
➤ **At the next roundabout,** turn right on A701, signed for A74(M) and Glasgow.
➤ **At A74(M)** roundabout, turn right to take A701 into Moffat, where the day's route ends.

TOUR (44) Maxxis Diamond Ride Day 3

DAY 3 MORNING

THIS MORNING'S ride starts with the epic A701, passing the Devil's Beeftub. From there, it must be said, the emphasis is on pleasant but functional riding to get past Glasgow. If you want to hurry to the lunch stop, it is possible to head from Carluke to Cumbernauld by motorway – heading for the M74, to join the M73/M80 – but why waste time on motorways when there are scenic roads to be ridden?

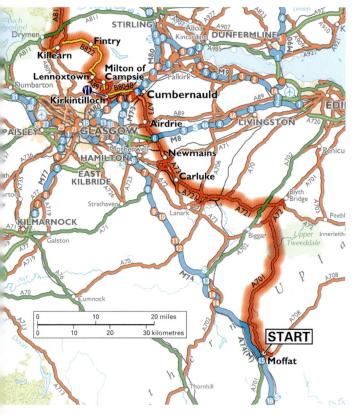

Duke's Pass (afternoon section)

FROM Moffat
TO Kirkintilloch
DISTANCE 70 miles
RIDING TIME 2 hours

Route Description

▶ **Leave Moffat** on A701 towards Edinburgh. This road becomes A72.

▶ **Look out:** don't miss the left turn for A721 to Glasgow, about 28 miles after leaving Moffat.

▶ **Go straight across** the staggered crossroads with A702, staying on A721 to Glasgow.

▶ **In Carluke,** join A73 to Glasgow. Stay on A73 all the way through Newmains and Airdrie to Cumbernauld.

▶ **When A73** meets M80 at Cumbernauld, take B8048 to Kirkintilloch, where the morning route ends.

TOUR (44) **Maxxis Diamond Ride Day 3**

| **ROUTE TYPE** Tour | **DISTANCE** 70 miles morning | 110 miles afternoon |

DAY 3 AFTERNOON

WITH THE city belt behind us, the afternoon's ride heads for the hills. It begins with the majestic Crow Road, then the tight and challenging Duke's Pass in the Trossachs – for a good coffee stop, take the short detour to Loch Katrine at the far side of the pass. The route then carries on along the sublime A84 and A85 before looping down to our overnight stop in Inveraray.

FROM Kirkintilloch
TO Inveraray
DISTANCE 110 miles
RIDING TIME 3 hours

Route Description

➤ **Leave Kirkintilloch** on A803 to Kilsyth.
➤ **Look out:** don't miss the left turn for B757 to Milton of Campsie, about a mile and a half outside Kirkintilloch. Turn left when this road meets A891 to Lennoxtown.
➤ **Turn right** in Lennoxtown, on B822 to Fintry.
➤ **Carry straight on** in Fintry as the road becomes B818 (DON'T take the turn for B822).
➤ **At A875 junction,** turn left to Killearn.
➤ **In Killearn,** turn right by the church on B834 to Drymen.
➤ **At the roundabout,** turn right on A81 to Aberfoyle.
➤ **At the Rob Roy roundabout,** turn left on A821 to Aberfoyle.

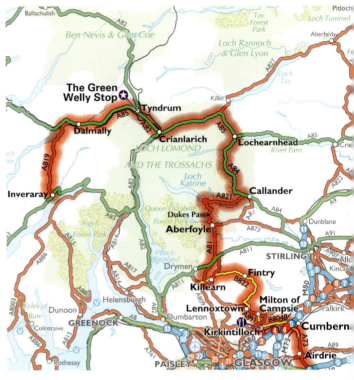

➤ **Look out:** follow the road round to the right at the end of Aberfoyle high street, staying on A821 to Callander.
➤ **At A84 T-junction,** turn left towards Crianlarich. Stay on this road as it becomes A85.

➤ **From Crianlarich,** turn right on A82 to Tyndrum.
➤ **In Tyndrum,** turn left on A85 to Oban.
➤ **Look out:** don't miss the left turn 13 miles later, for A819 to Inveraray, where the day's route ends.

The view over Inveraray and Loch Fyne

TOUR (44) Maxxis Diamond Ride Day 4

DAY 4 MORNING

THE DAY begins with one of our favourite rides in Scotland, along the bucolic shores of peaceful Loch Fyne. On a sunny day, it's as close to heaven as you can get on a tarmac road. Mind you, the ride from Lochgilphead to Oban gives it a run for its money in the unspoilt-scenery stakes. The lunch stop is the famous Green Welly Stop in Tyndrum. This is a real biking institution and you're sure to meet other touring riders here.

FROM Inveraray
TO Tyndrum
DISTANCE 95 miles
RIDING TIME 2.5 hours

Route Description

➤ **Leave Inveraray** on A83 to Campbeltown.

➤ **At the third roundabout** in Lochgilphead, turn right on A816 to Oban.

➤ **Ride through Oban,** joining A85 to Crianlarich.

➤ **At A82 T-junction,** turn right into Tyndrum and get some lunch.

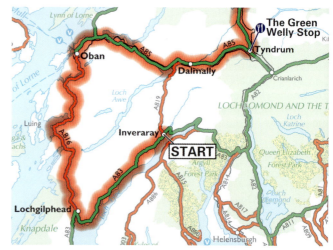

The A87 by Loch Garry

| ROUTE TYPE Tour | DISTANCE 95 miles morning | 130 miles afternoon |

DAY 4 AFTERNOON

A BIG AFTERNOON, in every sense – big scenery, big miles, big satisfaction… Every mile of the afternoon route could be the highlight of any other ride-out. From Tyndrum we cross Rannoch Moor and head through magnificent Glen Coe. Passing through Fort William, at the foot of Ben Nevis, we take the Road to the Isles, the majestic A87 – possibly Scotland's best road. It also features Scotland's most-photographed castle, the Eilean Donan.

On the A87 – possibly the best road in Scotland

FROM Tyndrum
TO Strathcarron
DISTANCE 130 miles
RIDING TIME 3 hours

Route Description

➤ **From Tyndrum,** take A82 to Fort William. Stay on this road, passing the Commando Memorial after Spean Bridge, to Invergarry.

➤ **In Invergarry,** turn left on A87 to Kyle of Lochalsh.

➤ **At the T-junction,** turn left on A87, still to Kyle of Lochalsh.

➤ **Look out:** don't miss the right turn for A890 to Lochcarron, about 3 miles after Eilean Donan castle.

➤ **Stay on this road** to Strathcarron, where the day's route ends.

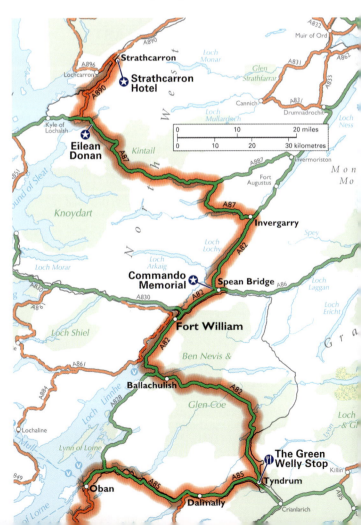

TOUR (44) Maxxis Diamond Ride Day 5

DAY 5 MORNING

RIDERS OF touring bikes may feel that the A87 is Scotland's finest roads, but many adventure-bike owners would argue that it's the Pass of the Cattle, the Bealach Na Ba, leading to Applecross. Our morning ride starts with this fabulous but demanding road, with its crop of near-Alpine hairpins. Fans of wider, smoother, sweeping roads may prefer the A832 from Kinlochewe to Garve, which leads to our lunch stop.

FROM Strathcarron
TO Tarvie Services
DISTANCE 90 miles
RIDING TIME 3 hours

Route Description

➤ **Leave Strathcarron** on A890 towards Gairloch.
➤ **At the T-junction,** turn left on A896 to Lochcarron. There is a filling station in Lochcarron: we recommend using it.
➤ **After 9 miles,** turn left on the road to Applecross, Bealach Na Ba. This is the famous – and challenging – Pass of the Cattle.
➤ **In Applecross,** turn right to Shieldaig. For a good coffee, we'd stop at the Applecross Walled Garden.

➤ **Stay on this road** for 24 miles, turn left at the T-junction rejoining A896 to Shieldaig. Stay on A896 to Kinlochewe.
➤ **If you didn't fill up** with fuel in Lochcarron, turn left to fill up in Kinlochewe. Otherwise, turn right on A832 to Achnasheen.

➤ **Go straight over** the roundabout in Achnasheen, taking A832 to Ullapool.
➤ **At A835 T-junction,** turn right towards Inverness. Our lunch stop is at the Tarvie Services, 3 miles past Garve.

Kessock Bridge on the A9

| ROUTE TYPE Tour | DISTANCE 90 miles morning | 110 miles afternoon |

DAY 5 AFTERNOON

THE AFTERNOON'S ride takes us from Scotland's wild West Coast into the Cairngorms. There's a little functional riding to be done, getting past Inverness, before the climb into the mountains. If you're a fan of whisky, the route passes through Grantown-on-Spey – careful planning may allow you to add a detour for a distillery visit. Just don't take a tipple before getting back on the bike.

FROM Tarvie Services
TO Braemar
DISTANCE 110 miles
RIDING TIME 3 hours

Route Description

➤ **Continue along** A835 towards Inverness.

➤ **At the Tore roundabout,** turn right on A9 to Inverness. (For fuel, there's a service station on the other side of this roundabout on A832.)

➤ **Cross the Beauly Firth** on the Kessock Bridge, go straight across the roundabout, then take the sliproad to join A96 to Aberdeen.

➤ **Look out:** don't miss the right turn, 2 miles after Inverness

Airport, for B9090 to Cawdor. Keep going straight as this road becomes B9101.

➤ **At A939 T-junction,** turn right to Grantown-on-Spey. At the T-junction in Dava, turn right (effectively straight on) to stay on this road.

➤ **At the traffic lights** in Grantown, turn left to Tomintoul (A939).

➤ **Go straight across** the roundabout on A95 to Keith.

➤ **After 1 mile** turn right on A939 to Tomintoul.

➤ **Look out:** turn left in Tomintoul, then – about half a mile outside the village – turn right to stay on A939 to Cock Bridge. This road goes past the Lecht Ski Centre.

➤ **Look out:** take the easily missed right turn, 5 miles after the Lecht, to stay on A939 to Braemar.

➤ **At A93 T-junction,** turn right to Braemar, where the day's route finishes.

TOUR (44) Maxxis Diamond Ride Day 6

DAY 6 MORNING

A BEAUTIFUL MORNING'S ride – especially if you're lucky with the weather. When the sun is high in the sky, there are few places more beautiful than Glenshee. The morning route runs down through the ski area, before heading east to Pitlochry and Aberfeldy. If you wanted to extend the ride by 30 miles, it's very pleasant to carry on along the A827 from Aberfeldy, riding beside Loch Tay, and then loop back along the shores of Loch Earn on the A85 to reach the lunch stop in Crieff.

FROM Braemar
TO Crieff
DISTANCE 85 miles
RIDING TIME 2.5 hours

Route Description

➤ **From Braemar,** head south on A93 to Spittal of Glenshee and Blairgowrie.

➤ **At Bridge of Cally,** turn right on A924 to Pitlochry.

➤ **Turn left** in Pitlochry town centre and follow signs for Perth.

➤ **Join A9** to Perth.

➤ **After 3 miles,** take the exit for Ballinluig, joining A827 to Aberfeldy.

➤ **At the traffic lights** in Aberfeldy, turn left on A826 to The Birks and Crieff.

➤ **At A822 T-junction,** turn right to Crieff.

➤ **Turn right** at A85 T-junction to go into Crieff, where the morning's route ends.

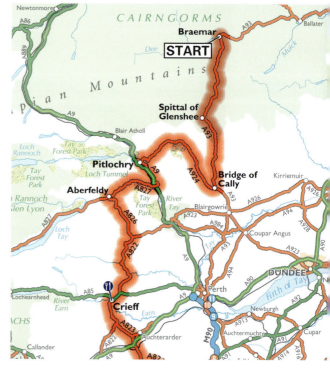

The Queen's View near Pitlochry
Opposite: The Forth Rail Bridge can be seen as you cross the road bridge.

TOUR 44 Maxxis Diamond Ride Day 6

ROUTE TYPE Tour	DISTANCE 85 miles morning	90 miles afternoon

DAY 6 AFTERNOON

AFTER THE quiet roads across rural Fife that start the afternoon's ride, the motorway across the Forth Road Bridge and the multi-lane Edinburgh ring-road may be a bit of a shock to the system. They're a necessary evil because, even if they're congested (as they sometimes are), they're still better than battling through busy suburbs. Besides, it is worth it as they lead to the swooping A7 to Melrose – though watch your speed, as there are plenty of cameras on this road.

FROM Crieff
TO Melrose
DISTANCE 90 miles
RIDING TIME 2.5 hours

Route Description

➤ **Leave Crieff** on A822 to Stirling.
➤ **Look out:** after about 10 miles, turn left on A823 to Dunfermline. The junction's on a tight right-hand bend, just after a tight left-hander.
➤ **Turn right** when the road meets A91, then turn left to carry on along A823.
➤ **At A977 T-junction,** turn right to the Kincardine Bridge.
➤ **In Powmill,** turn left to rejoin A823 to Dunfermline.
➤ **Cross Dunfermline** following signs for the Forth Road Bridge and M90.
➤ **Take A823(M)** to M90, following signs for Edinburgh. Cross the Forth Road Bridge and follow signs for Edinburgh and the Edinburgh ring road.
➤ **Take the A720** Edinburgh ring road to Dalkeith.
➤ **Pick up the A7** and follow it all the way to Galashiels.
➤ **Leaving Galashiels,** go straight over the roundabout on the A6091 towards Jedburgh, Tweedbank and the hospital. Stay on this road to Melrose, where the day's route ends.

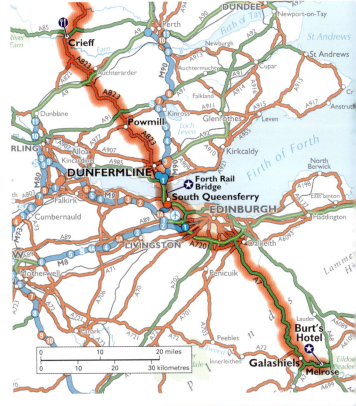

TOUR (44) Maxxis Diamond Ride Day 7

DAY 7 MORNING

IT'S NATURAL to feel a little sad when leaving Scotland, after so much brilliant riding, but we're going out on a high. The A68 is an iconic biking road – especially the final Scottish stretch leading up to Carter Bar. Crossing into England, this majestic rollercoaster of a road continues to delight, whooping its way to Hadrian's Wall country and our lunch stop in Corbridge – though if you want to extend the ride, a detour through Bellingham to Kielder Water is outstandingly scenic.

FROM Melrose
TO Corbridge
DISTANCE 60 miles
RIDING TIME 1.5 hours

Route Description

➤ **From Melrose,** take A6091 towards Jedburgh.
➤ **At A68** roundabout, turn right towards Jedburgh.
➤ **Look out:** don't miss the right turn, 13 miles after the Carter Bar border, to stay on A68 to Corbridge.
➤ **Stay on this road,** all the way to Corbridge for lunch.

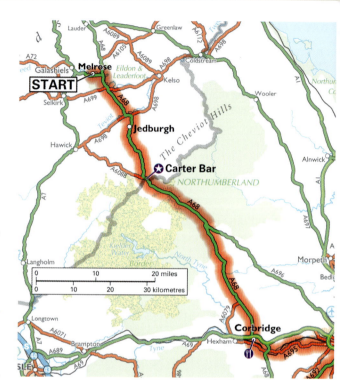

The A68 at Carter Bar

TOUR 44 Maxxis Diamond Ride Day 7

ROUTE TYPE Tour	DISTANCE 60 miles morning	110 miles afternoon

DAY 7 AFTERNOON

THE AFTERNOON route heads towards Newcastle before swinging out across the quiet moorland on the wild and scenic road to Barnard Castle. This area is as magnificent a wilderness as the wilder shores of Scotland visited earlier in the tour – all the more surprising for being so close to a major conurbation. Our overnight stop is planned for the bike-friendly Buck Inn in Chop Gate on the edge of the North York Moors, but if that's full you could equally well stop in nearby Stokesley.

FROM Corbridge
TO Chop Gate
DISTANCE 115 miles
RIDING TIME 3.5 hours

Route Description

➤ **From Corbridge,** take A695 to Newcastle.
➤ **Follow signs** to join A1 to Morpeth and the South.
➤ **Stay on A1 for 3 miles,** taking the fourth exit for A692 to Consett. Follow this road all the way to Castlesides.
➤ **In Castlesides,** cross A68 and take the minor road signed to Stanhope.

➤ **At B6278 T-junction,** turn left to Stanhope.
➤ **Turn right** then left in Stanhope, continuing on B6278 to Barnard Castle.
➤ **From Barnard Castle** take the A67 to Darlington.
➤ **Don't go into Darlington** town centre: at the garden centre roundabout turn right following signs for Teeside (A66). At the third roundabout on A66, turn right to continue on A67 to Yarm.
➤ **Go through Yarm** then turn left at roundabout by petrol station to take A1044 (signed Teeside Industrial Estate).

➤ **Stay on A1044** to A174 – but don't join main road. Take third exit on roundabout, to Hemlington.
➤ **At B1365 roundabout,** turn right to Stokesley.
➤ **In Stokesley** cross two roundabouts to pick up B1257 to Helmsley.
➤ **Stay on this road** to Chop Gate, where the ride ends.

TOUR ④④ Maxxis Diamond Ride Day 8

DAY 8 MORNING

THE MORNING of the final day starts with an absolutely brilliant road – the B1257 from Stokesley to Helmsley. The quality of the riding doesn't slacken as the route moves to Humberside, swooping across the moors to the selfie checkpoint at Sledmere – if you have time, the stately home is well worth a visit. After crossing the Humber Bridge, we double back into historic Barton-upon-Humber for lunch.

FROM Chop Gate
TO Barton-upon-Humber
DISTANCE 75 miles
RIDING TIME 2 hours

Route Description

➤ **Continue along** B1257 to Helmsley.
➤ **In Helmsley,** turn right on A170 to Thirsk.
➤ **After 1 mile** turn left on B1257 to Malton.
➤ **From Malton,** take B1248 to Driffield.

➤ **At the Fimber rbt,** turn left on B1251 to Bridlington.
➤ **In Sledmere,** this road becomes B1252. Stay on it to Garton-on-the-Wolds.
➤ **At A166** turn right to York.
➤ **In Wetwang,** turn left on B1248 to Beverley.
➤ **Go straight over** the roundabout on A614.
➤ **Look out:** don't miss the left turn in Bainton, to stay on B1248 to Beverley.
➤ **Turn right** at Cherry Burton rbt, on A1035 to York and Hull.

➤ **Take the third exit** at the next roundabout, on the minor road to Walkington. Carry on straight at the lights in Walkington.
➤ **Turn right** on A164 to Hull. Follow the signs to cross the Humber Bridge (no toll for motorcycles).
➤ **On the south bank,** take the first exit from A15 for Barton-upon-Humber where the morning route ends.

The Humber Bridge

TOUR (44) **Maxxis Diamond Ride Day 8**

| **ROUTE TYPE** Tour | **DISTANCE** 75 miles morning | 125 miles afternoon |

DAY 8 AFTERNOON

THE DIAMOND Ride loops back to its point of origin at the Leicester Forest East services on the M1, but you can adapt it to get you home at any point. It'd be a shame to miss some of the final roads, though, as they're absolutely cracking – especially the initial stretch, which shoots across the Lincolnshire Wolds in a blaze of glory. The final run from Melton Mowbray on the A607 is the perfect way to finish this sublime, rewarding tour.

FROM Barton-upon-Humber
TO Leicester Forest East Services
DISTANCE 125 miles
RIDING TIME 3 hours

Route Description
➤ **Leave Barton** on A1077 to Barrow upon Humber.
➤ **At the T-junction** in Ulceby, turn right on B1211, signed for M180 and airport.
➤ **Turn left** on A18 to airport.
➤ **Look out:** don't miss the right turn, soon after Great Limber, for the minor road to Caistor.
➤ **Carry straight on** (really a right turn) at A1173 T-junction to Caistor.
➤ **Go straight across** the staggered crossroads with A46, to take B1225 to Horncastle.
➤ **Go straight over** several crossroads, until reaching A158. Turn left to Horncastle.

➤ **At the second set** of traffic lights in Horncastle, turn right on A153 to Sleaford.
➤ **Look out:** don't miss the left turn just after leaving Horncastle for B1183 to Scrivelsby.
➤ **At A155 T-junction,** turn right to Marham le Fen.
➤ **At the roundabout,** turn left on A153 to Sleaford.
➤ **At mini-rbt** (after steep bridge) turn left to Sleaford.
➤ **Look out:** after half a mile, turn right on B1209 to Leasingham.
➤ **Turn left** on A15 to Sleaford.
➤ **At the roundabout,** turn right on A17.

➤ **After 5 miles** turn left on B6403 to Ancaster.
➤ **At A52 T-junction,** turn right to Grantham.
➤ **At the roundabout,** go straight over on B6403 to Colsterworth.
➤ **Look out:** about 4 miles after railway bridge, turn left to cross A1.
➤ **Turn left** for Colsterworth. In the village, turn right on B676 to Melton Mowbray.
➤ **From Melton Mowbray,** take A607 to Leicester.
➤ **At Syston,** join A46 then follow signs for M1, ending the tour at Leicester Forest East services.

DISTANCE CHART and Journey Times

Journey times

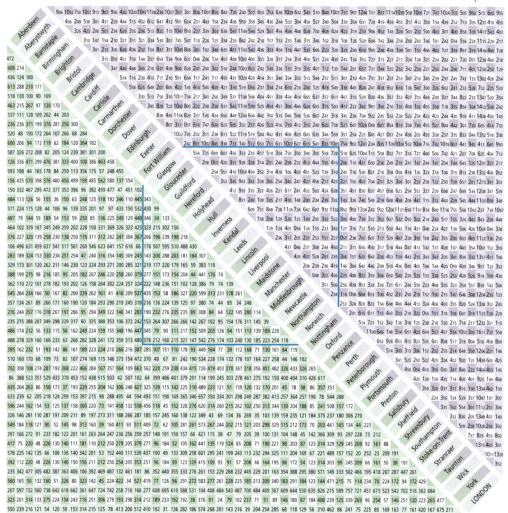

Distances in miles (1 mile equals 1.6093km)

Distances and journey times

The mileage chart shows distances in miles between two towns along AA-recommended routes. Using motorways and other main roads this is normally the fastest route, though not necessarily the shortest. The journey times, shown in hours and minutes, are average off-peak driving times along AA-recommended routes. The times are given as a guide only and do not allow for unforeseen traffic delays, rest breaks or fuel stops. For example, the 378-mile journey between Glasgow and Norwich should take around 7 hours 28 minutes.

MAP LEGEND

M4	Motorway with number	5	Distance in miles between symbols
Toll / T4	Toll motorway with junction	Toll	Road toll
40	Motorway junction with and without number	or V	Vehicle ferry
40	Restricted motorway junction		Fast vehicle ferry or catamaran
Fleet / S	Motorway service area		National boundary
	Motorway under construction		County, administrative boundary
A40	Primary route single/dual carriageway	H	Heliport
26	Primary junction with and without number	BRISTOL	Airport
25	Restricted Primary junction		Viewpoint
S	Primary route service area	SNAEFELL 620	Spot height in metres
A33	Other A road single/dual carriageway		River, lake and coastline
B4224	B road		Ride route
	Unclassified road		Direction of route
	Road under construction/approved		Place of interest
	Narrow Primary, other A or B road with passing places (Scotland)		Lunch stop

As maps of differing scales have been used throughout this book, not all features are present on every map.

PORT PLANS

IF YOU'RE TRAVELLING from Europe, the maps below provide a guide to the layouts of the ports of Dover (for tours 40 and 41) and Hull (for tours 42 and 43).

Dover

Contact: 01304 240400 or visit www.doverport.co.uk
Operators: P&O Ferries www.poferries.com and DFDS Seaways www.dfdsseaways.co.uk
Access: Approximately 70 miles from London, the port is accessible by road from the M20/A20 and the M2/A2, and also by train at Dover Priory.

Hull

Contact: To contact the port directly: 01482 327 171 or visit www.abports.co.uk/our_locations/humber/hull/
Operator: P&O Ferries 0800 130 0030 or visit www.poferries.com
Access: Approximately 60 miles from Leeds, the port is accessible by road from the M62/A63 and the M180/A15/A63; also by train and by bus/coach.

ACKNOWLEDGEMENTS

AA Media would like to thank the following photographers, companies and picture libraries for their assistance in the preparation of this book.
Abbreviations for the picture credits are as follows: (t) top; (b) bottom; (c) centre; (l) left; (r) right; (AA) AA World Travel Library

1 RiDE/Bauer Media; 2/3 RiDE/Bauer Media; 4/5 RiDE/Bauer Media; 6/7 RiDE/Bauer Media; 8 RiDE/Bauer Media; 10 RiDE/Bauer Media; 11 RiDE/Bauer Media; 13 RiDE/Bauer Media; 14l AA/M Moody; 14r Courtesy of Eden Project; 15t James Osmond/Alamy; 15m eye35/Alamy; 15b funkyfood London/Paul Williams/Alamy; 16t Niall Ferguson/Alamy; 16m Skyscan Photolibrary/Alamy; 16b AA/L Noble; 17t AA/J Hunt; 17m Gary Stones/Alamy; 17b eye35.pix/Alamy; 18t AA/S Lewis; 18b Rick Strange/Alamy; 19t Stephen Emerson/Alamy; 19m AA/S Whitehorne; 19b John McKenna / Alamy; 20/21 RiDE/Bauer Media; 22 AA/T Mackie; 23 Ian Dagnall/Alamy; 24 Robin Weaver/Alamy; 26 AA/N Setchfield; 28 Annie Eagle/Alamy; 30 AA/C Jones; 32 AA/M Moody; 35 Brian Hewitt/Alamy; 40 AA/T Mackie; 42/43 RiDE/Bauer Media; 44 David Wall/Alamy; 46 Jack Sullivan/Alamy; 48 Helen Dixon/Alamy; 49 Kevin Freeborn / Alamy; 50 Christopher Nicholson/Alamy; 52 robertharding / Alamy; 54 RiDE/Bauer Media; 56 RiDE/Bauer Media; 58 Clive Burgess/Alamy; 60/61 RiDE/Bauer Media; 65 fotolincs/Alamy; 66 RiDE/Bauer Media; 68 Robert Morris/Alamy; 70 AA/P Bennett; 72 LEE BEEL/Alamy; 76 Wayne HUTCHINSON/Alamy; 82 RiDE/Bauer Media; 83 AA; 84 J. Schwanke/Alamy; 85 CW Images/Alamy; 86/87 RiDE/Bauer Media; 88 RiDE/Bauer Media; 90 Electric Egg/Alamy; 92 AA/M Bauer; 94 AA/M Bauer; 97 RiDE/Bauer Media; 100 Keith Morris / Alamy; 102 RiDE/Bauer Media; 104 CW Images/Alamy; 108/109 RiDE/Bauer Media; 110 D.G.Farquhar/Alamy; 112 AA/P Sharpe; 116 RiDE/Bauer Media; 118 RiDE/Bauer Media; 120 AA/J Smith; 122 Realimage/Alamy; 125 AA/J Beazley; 128 Duncan Shaw/Alamy; 132 AA/J Smith; 134 Angus Forbes/Alamy; 135 imageBROKER/Alamy; 136/137 RiDE/Bauer Media; 138/139 RiDE/Bauer Media; 140 Manor Photography/Alamy; 144 James Davies/Alamy; 145 AA/M Bauer; 146 AA/S Watkins; 150 Bax Walker/Alamy; 156 Scottish Viewpoint/Alamy; 159 Robert Morris/Alamy; 162 Joana Kruse/Alamy; 163 Ian Dagnall/Alamy; 165 Washington Imaging/Alamy; 166 AA/M Birkitt; 168 AA/H Williams; 170 robertharding/Alamy; 172 Elmtree Images/Alamy; 176 JOHN WHEELER/Alamy; 179 Phil Seale/Alamy; 180 AA/S Whitehorne; 181 RiDE/Bauer Media; 182 imageBROKER/Alamy; 184 Matthew Rees/Alamy; 188 AA/P Baker; 190 David Lyons/Alamy; 192 DGB/Alamy; 193 Jon Sparks/Alamy; 194 RiDE/Bauer Media; 195 RiDE/Bauer Media; 196 William Gum/Alamy; 198 AA/J Smith; 199 AA/J Smith; 200 Scott Hortop Travel/Alamy; 202 AA/G Rowatt

Every effort has been made to trace the copyright holders, and we apologise in advance for any unintentional omissions or errors. We would be pleased to apply any corrections in a following edition of this publication.

Find the best routes and we'll search for the best insurance

67% of AA customers pay less than £200 for their bike insurance*

Using our panel of leading insurers, we'll find insurance that's tailored to your individual needs at the best price we can.

Why choose AA Motorcycle Insurance?

- No-claims discount can be transferred from other insurers
- Choose from comprehensive, third party only or third party, fire & theft
- Multi-bike policies available
- Wide range of motorcycles covered including tourers, mopeds, superbikes, scooters

For Motorcycle Insurance
call **0344 335 2932**